The Last Conceptual Revolution

SUNY series in the Philosophy of the Social Sciences
Lenore Langsdorf, editor

and

SUNY series in Speech Communication
Dudley D. Cahn, editor

The Last Conceptual Revolution

*A Critique of Richard Rorty's
Political Philosophy*

Eric M. Gander

STATE UNIVERSITY OF NEW YORK PRESS

Published by
State University of New York Press, Albany

© 1999 State University of New York

For information, address State University of New York Press,
State University Plaza, Albany, N.Y. 12246

Production by Cathleen Collins
Marketing by Anne Valentine

Library of Congress Cataloging-in-Publication Data

Gander, Eric.
    The last conceptual revolution : a critique of Richard Rorty's
political philosophy / Eric M. Gander.
        p.   cm. — (SUNY series in the philosophy of the social
sciences) (SUNY series in speech communication)
    Includes bibliographical references and index.
    ISBN 0-7914-4009-5 (alk. paper). — ISBN 0-7914-4010-9 (pbk. : alk.
paper)
    1. Rorty, Richard—Contributions in political science.
2. Political science—Philosophy. 3. Liberalism—Philosophy.
I. Title. II. Series. III. Series: SUNY series in speech
communication.
JC251.R59G35 1998
320'.01'1—dc21   98-5277
                                                                          CIP

10 9 8 7 6 5 4 3 2 1

To My Father,
First Philosopher

Contents

Preface

The present essay is a reflection on some of the most crucial aspects of a political philosophy that has come to be known as liberalism, as that philosophy has been reinterpreted and "rediscribed" by one of the most provocative thinkers of our time. Richard Rorty may be, as Harold Bloom asserts, "the most interesting philosopher in America today."[1] He is, by his own account, a liberal. He is also, as I hope to show, an insightful—though not always consistent—*philosopher* of liberalism.

The type of study I have attempted is relatively common: a critic approaches the work of another with the intention of illuminating some general idea. There are, of course, various types of "encounters" that may occur between the critic and the "other." A brief sketch of several different types of "critical encounters" will help explain more fully what I am trying to do in the following pages. Of equal importance, it will allow me the opportunity to "position" myself within the "dialogue" that I hope to establish in these pages.

One type of critical encounter occurs when the critic selects, as the object of study, an individual with whose ideas he or she is in substantial agreement, and then proceeds simply to explicate these ideas. I think something like this type of encounter is occurring when Kant's *Critique*

---

1. This accolade appears on the cover of a very provocative volume of criticism on Rorty, entitled *Reading Rorty*, ed. Alan Malachowski (Oxford: Basil Blackwell, 1990).

of Judgment is explicated in Friedrich Schiller's *Letters on the Aesthetic Education of Man*. Perhaps the most serious drawback to this approach is that it runs the risk of simply recounting the original idea, without adding anything of substance. A second type of critical encounter occurs when the critic selects an individual or a group with whose ideas he or she is in substantial *disagreement*, and then proceeds to attack those ideas. Nietzsche's attacks on Christianity come to mind here, as do some of the attacks taking place between contemporary French and German philosophers. Perhaps the most serious drawback to this approach is that, in many cases, the critic so misrepresents the ideas he or she is attacking as to make those ideas unrecognizable to the individual or group alleged to have advanced them. A third type of critical encounter occurs when a critic selects an individual with whose ideas he or she is in substantial disagreement, and then proceeds to argue *for* these ideas. This type of "devil's advocate" approach is rare, owing, I think, to the fact that if it succeeds the critic may feel that he or she has actively done some harm, and if it fails the critic is not left with any *positive* set of ideas that can command his or her assent. Finally, a fourth type of critical encounter occurs when a critic selects an individual with whose ideas he or she is in substantial agreement, and then proceeds to *attack* those ideas. Like the third type of encounter, this approach also suffers from a drawback: if it succeeds, the critic may feel that some harm has been done. But it also has the benefit of allowing the critic to engage in a *positive* act of self-reflection. Exactly to the extent that these attacks *fail*, the critic may have just that much more certainty in his or her beliefs. This type of encounter also chimes well with the liberal view on truth—a view that holds that an *untested* truth is not worth the assent given to it. On this point, one might do well to recall John Stuart Mill's remark, "He who knows only his side of the case knows little of that. His reasons may be good, and no one may have been able to refute them. But if he is equally unable to refute the reasons on the opposite side, if he does not so much as know what they are, he has no ground for preferring either opinion."[2] Following Mill's insight, and in keeping with the liberal tradition, I have therefore chosen to engage in the fourth type of critical encounter.

I write as a liberal—broadly speaking. I find myself in substantial agreement with many of the practical approaches to liberal politics that

---

2. John Stuart Mill, *On Liberty* (New York: Macmillan/Library of Liberal Arts, 1965), 45.

Rorty advocates. But I think that liberalism requires a better explanation *of* itself—and perhaps a better defense *for* itself—than Rorty provides. It is hoped that the pages that follow will help strengthen the cause of liberalism, at least by helping to identify some theoretical problems in the work of one of liberalism's most persuasive defenders.

Having said that, this is perhaps the time and place for me to note that, aside from two graduate classes that I audited in the mid 1980s, and from a brief conversation I had in 1991, I have had no contact with Richard Rorty—except, of course, through his published writings. I make no claim, therefore, that the following essay accurately represents what Rorty thinks. I claim only that it accurately represents what he has written and published. The conjunction between what an individual thinks and what he writes is not always straightforward—especially not for those (like myself and, I think, Rorty) who believe that the meaning of a text is never completely self-evident. All writing must be interpreted, and hence all writing runs the risk of being misinterpreted. I imagine all writers are constantly aware of the danger that their work will find itself subject to misinterpretation (sometimes grievous misinterpretation) by subsequent readers and critics. Here it is not Mill but rather Plato who is on point. "Once a thing is put in writing, it rolls about all over the place, falling into the hands of those who have no concern with it just as easily as under the notice of those who comprehend; it has no notion of whom to address or whom to avoid. And when it is ill-treated or abused as illegitimate, it always needs its father to help it, being quite unable to protect or help itself."[3]

My intention, as I have said, is not to abuse Rorty's writings, but rather, by critiquing them, to use them as a way of advancing the cause of liberalism. Therefore, the tone I have tried to adopt in the following pages is one of constructive criticism.

In the late 1980s I began thinking in earnest about Rorty's work, as I was preparing to write my doctoral dissertation. At that time my thoughts on Rorty were greatly clarified by the members of my dissertation committee: Michael Hyde, David Zarefsky, and Michael Leff. Since then I have benefited from discussing my ideas, about Rorty and about political philosophy in general, with a number of individuals. I have benefited most from my discussions with James Aune, a professor who taught

---

3. Plato *Phaedrus* 275d in *Phaedrus*, trans. W.C. Helmbold and W.G. Rabinowitz (Indianapolis: Bobbs-Merrill Educational Publishing, 1956), 69–70.

me what I didn't know I didn't know. I would also like to acknowledge the contribution of my students over the years, many of whom (unbeknownst to them) had some of the ideas in this book inflicted upon them, and whose criticisms were often quite insightful. Additionally, I am grateful to Lenore Langsdorf for providing extraordinarily insightful editorial comments on several versions of the manuscript. Research for this project was made possible, in part, by a Professional Staff Congress/City University of New York grant. My research was also facilitated by the helpful staff members of the New York Public Library and the Library of the City University of New York. I am grateful to Cambridge University Press for permission to quote from the following copyrighted works by Richard Rorty: *Contingency, Irony, and Solidarity* (1989); *Objectivity, Relativism, and Truth: Philosophical Papers, Volume I* (1991); and *Essays on Heidegger and Others: Philosophical Papers, Volume II* (1991). Finally, I would like to thank my wife Lauralee, the most *imaginative* person I know, who, along with Ren, has filled my life with wonder and love.

Eric M. Gander
New York City
1998

Introduction

The Sense of an Ending

Writing in late November, but still well *before* the year had finished producing all the history it had in store for us, George F. Will, a political columnist who fancies himself something of an Edmund Burke conservative, and whom we might therefore expect to be circumspect in his characterizations, said of 1989 that it had been "the most startling, interesting, promising and consequential year *ever*."[1] Mr. Will was not being hyperbolic, he was being observant. As I write these words, nine years later, it is *still* a bit startling to recall what did happen in 1989: the once mighty and now former Soviet Union withdrew in defeat from Afghanistan, a Third World nation; a Gdansk shipyard worker with a vocational education in "agricultural mechanization" helped Poland become the first Eastern European nation to hold free elections since the end of the Second World War; the symbol and substance of a closed society—the Berlin Wall—literally became history on November 9; and, in the month and a half following that, something of a liberal–democratic domino effect ensued, wherein Eastern bloc countries threw off their totalitarian governments in what was (with the exception of Romania) a remarkably nonviolent series of democratic revolutions.

---

1. George F. Will, "Europe's Second Reformation," *Newsweek* (November 20, 1989): 90, emphasis in original.

1

Within this swirl of history, I have come across two quotations that invite closer analysis. Both quotations were published in 1989, and both have about them a thoroughly American—which is to say, optimistic—ring. What makes them so interesting is that they represent a convergence *of sorts* between what might appear a very unlikely pair: a relatively young, neoconservative bureaucrat, who transitioned easily from the Rand Corporation to George Bush's State Department, and an older, analytic philosopher turned provocative political theorist, who once referred to himself as a "postmodern bourgeois liberal." Each has something to say about the state of liberal democracy.

> What we may be witnessing is not just the end of the Cold War, or the passing of a particular period of postwar history, but the end of history as such; that is, the end point of mankind's ideological evolution and the universalization of Western liberal democracy as the final form of human government.

> I think that contemporary liberal society already contains the institutions for its own improvement. . . . Indeed, my hunch is that Western social and political thought may have had the last *conceptual* revolution it needs.

The first quotation is from Francis Fukuyama's article "The End of History?" published in the neoconservative journal *The National Interest*.[2] At the time of the article's appearance, Fukuyama was the deputy director of the State Department's policy planning staff. That makes him a bureaucrat. Whether he is neoconservative may be open to question. What is not open to question is the significant impact that Fukuyama's short, sixteen-page article has had in public policy circles. James Atlas, senior editor for the *New York Times*, noted that within days of its appearance "The End of History?" became "the hottest topic around."[3] Translations were immediately scheduled to appear in various languages, including Japanese and Iclendic. Number Ten Downing Street called for a copy of the article. A newsdealer in Washington, D.C., was reported to have remarked that the issue of *The National Interest* containing Fukuyama's article was "outselling everything, even

2. Francis Fukuyama, "The End of History?" *The National Interest* (summer 1989): 4.
3. James Atlas, "What is Fukuyama Saying?" *New York Times Magazine*, October 22, 1989.

the pornography." A little more than a month after the article's appearance, Peter Tarnoff, president of the Council on Foreign Relations, seemed to suggest that Fukuyama's thesis might be "laying the foundation for a Bush doctrine."[4] By the end of January 1990, House Majority Leader Thomas Foley, delivering the Democratic reply to President Bush's State of the Union message, felt it necessary to express what appears to be a firm *rejection* of Fukuyama's thesis. Commenting on the events of 1989, Foley said, "We are perhaps near the end of a great struggle, *but we are certainly not at the end of history.*" A year and a half later, President Bush, speaking at the opening of the 46th session of the United Nation's General Assembly, seemed also to be rejecting the end of history thesis when he argued that the end of the cold war has caused "the *resumption* of history."[5] Clearly, Fukuyama's article got noticed. So much so, in fact, that by early 1992, when Fukuyama's book *The End of History and the Last Man* hit the bookstores, it caused quite a sensation—appearing, as it did, just *weeks* after the Soviet Union had come to an end (not, as everyone had expected, at the point of a gun, but at the point of Mikhail Gorbachev's pen). Commenting on Fukuyama's book, Eduard Shevardnzdze, the former foreign minister of the former Soviet Union, opined that it amounted to "an attempt to arm Western political thought with new fundamental theoretical arguments to reinforce its practical actions. Moreover, it is not an unsuccessful attempt. . . ."[6]

The second quotation I have mentioned is from Richard Rorty's book *Contingency, Irony, and Solidarity.*[7] Before his recent move to Stanford University, Rorty was University Professor of Humanities at the University of Virginia—a position he assumed in the early 1980s after leaving Princeton's philosophy department. That department has been characterized as "one of the citadels of analytic philosophy."[8] Rorty himself is thoroughly schooled in the tradition of analytic philosophy. But well

4. Quoted in James Atlas, "What is Fukuyama Saying?"
5. George Bush, "Speech Before the United Nations General Assembly, September 23, 1991" in *Vital Speeches of the Day*, October 15, 1991, p. 2.
6. This remark appears on the book jacket of Fukuyama's book. See Francis Fukuyama, *The End of History and the Last Man* (New York: The Free Press, 1992).
7. Richard Rorty, *Contingency, Irony, and Solidarity* (Cambridge: University Press, 1989), 63, emphasis in original.
8. See Thomas McCarthy, "Private Irony and Public Decency: Richard Rorty's New Pragmatism," *Critical Inquiry* 16 (winter 1990): 357.

before he left Princeton, he began writing about the uselessness of asking the kinds of questions analytic philosophers have traditionally asked and the need for his colleagues in philosophy departments to turn their attention toward broader questions. That suggestion—and the numerous responses to it—coupled with Rorty's own writings on literature, philosophy, and social criticism, has made him one of the most interesting figures both inside and outside of the academy. In 1983, Rorty somewhat offhandedly referred to himself as a "postmodern bourgeois liberal"—a phrase that left many of Rorty's colleagues and critics with questions about his political philosophy and his approach to social criticism.[9] *Contingency, Irony, and Solidarity* is an attempt to address some of these questions. It is Rorty's most comprehensive statement yet on the relationship between philosophy, political theory and practice, and contemporary, post–industrial, liberal–democratic societies. Writing in April 1989, Jenny Teichman, a Cambridge philosopher, predicted that "*Contingency, Irony, and Solidarity* will have many readers."[10] Judging from all the *talk* about Rorty in recent years, she appears to have been correct. Indeed, the appearance in 1991 of the long-awaited two-volume collection of Rorty's writings throughout the 1980s led Anthony Gottlieb to remark, "Of American philosophers, Mr. Rorty is probably the most talked about outside of philosophy departments."[11] If this is so, a good deal of the credit goes to Rorty himself, who has attempted to reach a wider public by writing not only in academic journals but also in publications like *Dissent, The New Republic, The London Review of Books*, the op–ed page of the *New York Times* and the *New York Times Magazine*.[12]

So why have I now juxtaposed these two quotations and the authors who composed them? My primary purpose in doing so is to underscore

---

9. See Richard Rorty, "Postmodern Bourgeois Liberalism," in *Objectivity, Relativism, and Truth: Philosophical Papers, Volume II* (Cambridge: University Press, 1991): 197–202.

10. Jenny Teichman, "Don't Be Cruel or Reasonable," *New York Times Book Review*, April 23, 1989.

11. Anthony Gottlieb, "The Most Talked-About Philosopher" in the *New York Times Book Review*, June 2, 1991, p. 30. Rorty's two volumes of Philosophical Papers are published by Cambridge University Press as *Objectivity, Relativism, and Truth* and *Essays on Heidegger and Others*.

12. For interesting examples of Rorty's work in these last two publications see Richard Rorty, "The Unpatriotic Academy," the *New York Times*, February 13, 1994, section 4, p. 15 and "Fraternity Reigns: The case for a society based not on rights but on unselfishness," the *New York Times Magazine*, September 29, 1996, 155–158.

the provocative *political* implications of Rorty's recent writings. Oddly, for all the talk about Rorty over the last several years, only a few sustained, book-length treatments of his work have appeared.[13] Despite this, there is a curious way in which Rorty seems to have become everybody's political "foil," both inside and outside of the academy. Unfortunately, few commentators have really *developed* their political criticisms of Rorty. This has led to a situation in which the political elements of Rorty's philosophy have been loosely characterized in vastly different ways by groups with vastly different political agendas. A sampling of some of the more politically oriented criticisms of Rorty's work will help illustrate what I mean.

Among members of what one might call the "academic Left," the principal political criticism of Rorty seems to be that his work is insufficiently radical. Richard Bernstein, for example, notes that "despite occasional protests to the contrary, it begins to look as if Rorty's defense of liberalism is little more than an *apologia* for the status quo—the very type of liberalism that Dewey judged to be 'irrelevant and doomed.'"[14] Thomas McCarthy puts the point very succinctly when he argues that one of Rorty's "rules for action" appears to be, "Don't engage in radical criticisms of *our* culture and society."[15] Frank Lentricchia asserts that Rorty has simply sold out to the bourgeoisie. Lentricchia, who says that he "come[s] down on the side of those who believe that our society is mainly unreasonable,"[16] argues that Rorty's

---

13. For book-length treatments of Rorty's recent work, see Norman Geras, *Solidarity in the Conversation of Humankind: The Ungroundable Liberalism of Richard Rorty* (London: Verso Books, 1995); David Hall, *Richard Rorty: Prophet and Poet of the New Pragmatism* (Albany: State University of New York Press, 1994); Konstantin Kolenda, *Rorty's Humanistic Pragmatism: Philosophy Democratized* (Tampa: University of South Florida Press, 1990); Ronald Alexander Kuipers, *Solidarity and the Stranger: Themes in the Social Philosophy of Richard Rorty* (Bethesda, Maryland: University Press of America, 1997); Kai Nielsen, *After the Demise of the Tradition: Rorty, Critical Theory, and the Fate of Philosophy* (Boulder, Colo.: Westview Press, 1991); and D. Vaden House, *Without God or His Doubles: Realism, Relativism, and Rorty* (New York: E. J. Brill, 1994).
14. Richard Bernstein, "One Step Forward, Two Steps Backward: Richard Rorty on Liberal Democracy and Philosophy," *Political Theory* 15 (November 1987): 541.
15. Thomas McCarthy, "Ironist Theory as a Vocation: A Response to Rorty's Reply," *Critical Inquiry* 16 (spring 1990): 648, emphasis in original.
16. Frank Lentricchia, *Criticism and Social Change* (Chicago: University of Chicago Press, 1983), 2.

key value terms are hedonic; they refer to the possible pleasures of autonomous subjects—maybe that is why he says that
"bourgeois capitalist society" is the "best polity actualized so
far." The pleasures of imagination, of creativity and original-
ity, are the poetic pleasures of a private subject; it is not clear
that they require community. Late capitalist economy, at any
rate, seems to be in the business of generating the commodity
no longer for its use and exchange values (as classical Marxism would have it) but mainly (as Guy Debord has argued) for
its imagistic and spectacular value. Its purpose is to appropriate Romantic literary values such as Rorty's for its own economic perpetuation. One sort of Marxist response to Rorty
would be that his values of ungrounded cultural conversation
have been decisively co-opted by late capitalist economy. It,
too, wants to send things in new directions without reaching
any goals, since the classic goals of the commodity are no
longer of the essence for proper maintenance of the economic
structure: the Romantic yearning for the new is now transformed into an energetic consumerism.[17]

All of this allows Lentricchia to conclude, derisively, that "Rorty's vision
of culture is the leisured vision of liberalism: the free pursuit of personal
growth anchored in material security. . . ."[18] Even Cornell West, one of
Rorty's most sympathetic critics on the Left, argues that while Rorty's
philosophical thoughts are pregnant with numerous (more or less) radical possibilities and potentialities, in the end that philosophy "refuses to
give birth to the offspring it conceives. . . ." In an essay entitled "The Politics of American Neo-Pragmatism," West concludes,

> Rorty's neo-pragmatism ingeniously echoes the strident anti-
> humanist critiques—such as those of Martin Heidegger,
> Jacques Derrida, and Michel Foucault—of a moribund bour-
> geois humanism. Yet his brand of neo-pragmatism domesti-
> cates these critiques in a smooth and witty Attic prose and,
> more importantly, dilutes them by refusing to push his own
> project toward cultural and political criticism of the civiliza-
> tion he (and, in varying degrees, we) cherishes.[19]

---

17. Ibid., 18.
18. Ibid., 19.
19. Cornell West, "The Politics of American Neo-Pragmatism," in *Post–Analytic Philos-*

So much for the Left. Among academics (anywhere on the political spectrum) who are alive to the tradition of rhetoric and whose job it is to teach the arts of advocacy (and not just criticism), Rorty's work seems to fare no better. John Lyne, a self-professed "Rorty fan," nonetheless finds it frustrating that nowhere in his work does Rorty provide a serious engagement with political texts or political arguments. Lyne notes that Rorty has simply opted out of the real world of practical political discourse and progressive social change—the world of "rhetoric" understood in the best, *traditional* sense of that term—by "tak[ing] the status of a conscientious objector. He has become an expatriate in an island world, leaving arguments behind to explore vocabularies and feed on the fruits of the poetic imagination."[20] James Aune also finds fault with Rorty's impoverished understanding of rhetoric and his corresponding overemphasis on the realm of imaginative literature. Noting that Rorty's own liberal hero, John Dewey, was very concerned with improving the "methods and conditions of debate, discussion, and persuasion" *in the public realm*, Aune finds it troubling that

> Rorty's only real program is a technocratic Mondale liberalism combined with an academic project that involves extending even further the paralyzing grip of the English department on liberal education. Students who once learned the arts of citizenship by speaking and debating public issues will now only learn the passive pleasures of liberal irony from Nabokov.[21]

The criticisms that I have just recounted, including the last two, strongly imply that Rorty's philosophical ideas are, at worst, not very dangerous to the political status quo, and, at best, very congenial to it. One would think that this would be taken as good news by political conservatives both inside and outside of the academy. Indeed, one might suspect that Rorty could find some friends among the cultural and academic "Right" in America. But this has been far from the case. Dinesh D'Souza, whose 1991 book *Illiberal Education* advanced the claim that feminists and radicals have all but taken over the best American universities, argues that Rorty and other "postmodernists" are largely responsible for this development. Writing in no less a conservative institution than the *Wall*

ophy, eds. John Rajchman and Cornell West (New York: Columbia University Press, 1985), 267.

20. John Lyne, "The Culture of Inquiry," *Quarterly Journal of Speech* 76 (1990): 196.

21. James Arnt Aune, *Rhetoric & Marxism* (Boulder, Colo.: Westview Press, 1994), 132.

Street Journal, D'Souza asserts that Rorty "radically calls into question the notions of truth and merit," thus providing "ammunition for an assault on the traditional standards of the liberal arts. . . ." The consequences of all of this, according to D'Souza, "are not simply a debasement of the Western tradition but in many cases the promulgation of mediocrity and ignorance."[22] Yet another conservative critique of the consequences of Rorty's philosophical relativism is provided by Harvard Professor Harvey Mansfield, who in the late 1980s was appointed by President Bush to the National Council for the Humanities. In an exchange with Rorty on the merits of Allan Bloom's book *The Closing of the American Mind*, Mansfield flatly accuses Rorty of having "given up on America."[23] Mansfield fills out this criticism by noting that "Rorty's historicism leads to a thoroughly *politicized* view of the university. Since every position is in the politics of one's times, one may as well accept the inevitable and charge ahead toward the political solution of one's liking."[24] But outside of the academy, the situation may be even more dire. Mansfield continues,

> Besides politicizing the university, Rorty's historicism makes for bad democrats and irresponsible citizens. Good democrats think democracy can be good, and when they see it is not, they take responsibility for reforming it. Their responsibility is based on their holding democracy to the standard of good government. To do this, they must think that good government as a standard is above democracy; it is what democracy aims at, for example, the ends stated in the preamble to the Constitution. . . .
>
> Rorty's democrat is altogether different. He believes he cannot know what the good is, hence cannot know whether democracy is good or not. Instead of holding democracy to a higher standard outside itself, thus dividing his loyalties, he saves all his love for democracy. The only way he can tell whether democracy works is by judging whether it is becoming more democratic. Instead of a picture of a mixed regime, he carries in his mind a picture of perfect democracy, a

---

22. Dinesh D'Souza, "Pied Pipers of Relativism Reverse Course," the *Wall Street Journal*, July 27, 1993, p. A18.
23. Harvey C. Mansfield Jr., "Democracy and the Great Books," *The New Republic*, April 4, 1988, p. 36.
24. Ibid., 34, emphasis added.

regime whose goal is, in Rorty's words, "to maximize freedom and equality." This is the criterion of democrats who want no criterion. . . .

In consequence, Rorty, for all his "honesty," flatters the people and invites the intervention of extremists who are interested in maximizing but don't care about freedom and equality.[25]

If the aforementioned criticisms tell us anything, they seem to suggest that Rorty has yet to find a sympathetic audience for his political philosophy. One needs to ask, what precisely is going on here? How is it that Rorty seems to be equally out of favor with the intellectual Right *and* Left? The answer I think lies in the complex (and, admittedly, often contradictory) nature of Rorty's political philosophy. Simply put, Rorty has been unable, over the course of the last decade or so, to make a persuasive case that we citizens of late twentieth century, advanced industrial societies should now try to think of ourselves as (in Rorty's words) "liberal ironists." But the persuasiveness of Rorty's entire political philosophy stands or falls on the issue of whether we can — or whether we wish to — see liberal ironists as good citizens of a political community. Rorty's critics simply do not see the liberal ironist (or Rorty himself) as such a good citizen.

In the chapters that follow, I try to explain exactly why this is so by sketching and critiquing the portrait of a liberal ironist. As a way of *orienting* the discussion that is to come, I want now to provide a brief outline of some of the central elements of liberal political philosophy. This outline will help get my critique of the liberal ironist started. It is important to emphasize that my intention in the next few pages is *not* to provide an in-depth analysis of liberal political philosophy. Such an analysis would be both unnecessary and perhaps out of place, given the treatment Rorty himself gives to liberal political philosophers throughout *Contingency, Irony, and Solidarity*. That treatment, to put it mildly, is not very rigorous. Consider, for example, the case of John Dewey—Rorty's philosopher–hero, and surely a central figure in both the liberal and the pragmatic philosophical traditions. If one examines *Contingency, Irony, and Solidarity* closely, one finds that the word "Dewey" or "Deweyan" is used (I am tempted to say "dropped") exactly sixteen times. On only two

---

25. Ibid., 35–36.

occasions are specific texts by Dewey quoted. We get one sentence from *Reconstruction in Philosophy* and three rather awkwardly arranged sentences from *Art as Experience*. In neither case is the quoted material subjected to any type of analysis or critique. That is the sum and substance of Rorty's treatment of John Dewey in *Contingency, Irony, and Solidarity*. A *casual* reader of Harold Bloom might think Rorty suffers from a certain "anxiety of influence" with respect to Dewey. But that is not really it either. Rorty calls himself a liberal and a pragmatist, and he drops Dewey's name a fair amount. The problem is that Rorty just does not seem too interested in Dewey's *actual writings*—and where there is no real interest, there can be no anxiety. Numerous critics of Rorty make exactly this point. For example, James Gouinlock writes, "One can only guess how Rorty would take a given passage [from Dewey] for he rarely cites specific texts. His references to pragmatism are typically offhand, rather than carefully documented."[26] The same is true, I would argue, for much of Rorty's treatment of other liberal philosophers like Thomas Jefferson, John Stuart Mill, and even John Rawls (whose name Rorty invokes fairly often). In one sense, then, Rorty's liberalism may be largely his own creation. Still, Rorty is more recognizably liberal than he is anything else. Hence a good place to begin an understanding of Rorty is, as I said, with a brief outline of some of the central elements of liberal political philosophy. I realize, of course, that "liberalism" is a broad term and that there are important and significant differences between the liberalism of Immanuel Kant and that of, say, John Stuart Mill, just as there are important and significant differences between the liberalism of these two theorists and the liberalism of John Dewey. If one adds to the discussion the versions of liberalism espoused by philosophers as different as John Rawls and Robert Nozick, it begins to look as though any definition of the term will be little more than an arbitrary selection of positions held by one's favorite philosophers. Perhaps this is ultimately so—for every political philosophy. But for now I will follow Ronald Dworkin in assuming that there are some core ideas connected with liberalism. Those are the ideas I wish to sketch.

To start with, liberalism, like any political philosophy, concerns itself with the relationship between the individual and society. To its critics, lib-

---

26. James Gouinlock, "What is the Legacy of Instrumentalism? Rorty's Interpretation of Dewey," in *Rorty & Pragmatism*, ed. Herman J. Saatkamp Jr. (Nashville: Vanderbilt University Press, 1995), 74.

eralism has little of *substance* to say about this relationship, because it has little of substance to say about anything. Ronald Beiner, in his aptly titled book *What's the Matter With Liberalism*, raises just this point. He argues that there is no "matter" to liberalism; there is no substance at its core. Liberalism, on Beiner's account, fails to matter precisely because it fails to engage the really important questions, like what constitutes the good life for the individual, and what constitutes the good society for us all.[27]

But liberals of all types (whether followers of Kant or Mill, Rawls or Nozick) will have essentially the same response to Beiner. Liberals must insist that substantive questions like what constitutes the good life are properly answered by the individual himself or herself, not by the collective. A society that dictates to its citizens what constitutes the good life cannot therefore be liberal. In a liberal society, all collective decisions — which is to say, all political decisions — must remain neutral to competing claims of what constitutes the good life. Ronald Dworkin puts this point succinctly when he argues that liberalism takes, as its "constitutive political morality," the idea that "political decisions must be, as far as is possible, independent of any particular conception of the good life, or of what gives value to life."[28] Michael Sandel, one of liberalism's best contemporary *critics*, makes essentially this point when he argues that the "core thesis" of liberalism can be put as follows:

> [S]ociety, being composed of a plurality of persons, each with his own aims, interests, and conceptions of the good, is best arranged when it is governed by principles that do not *themselves* presuppose any particular conception of the good. . . .[29]

Both of these views chime very well with John Stuart Mill's famous statement in *On Liberty*, that "Over himself, over his own body and mind, the individual is sovereign."[30]

From this it should be clear that the "individual" is the starting point for liberal political theory — although society is, of course, still rel-

---

27. See Ronald Beiner, *What's the Matter With Liberalism* (Berkeley: University of California Press, 1992).
28. Ronald Dworkin, "Liberalism," in *Public and Private Morality*, ed. Stuart Hampshire (Cambridge: University Press, 1978), 127.
29. Michael J. Sandel, *Liberalism and the Limits of Justice* (Cambridge: University Press, 1982), 1, emphasis in original.
30. John Stuart Mill, *On Liberty*, ed. Currin V. Shields (New York: Macmillan Publishing Company, 1956), 13.

evant, for no man is an island. Still, on the liberal view, for an entity to be an "individual," it is necessary and sufficient that the entity have the capacity, and be guaranteed the ability, to make moral and ethical choices regarding the ultimate questions of life. Hence liberal societies protect the individual by securing free choice as a matter of right and principle. This is justice.

It is not, however, a license for completely unregulated behavior. Precisely because society must remain neutral to each individual's conception of the good, society must see every individual as being essentially equal. This means, as John Rawls explains, that the first principle of justice in a liberal society must be that "each person is to have an equal right to the most extensive basic liberty *compatible with a similar liberty for others.*"[31] In other words, a liberal society must remain neutral to any individual's personal conception of the good, allowing him the right to choose any action (even action seen as worthless or evil by society), until such action interferes with the rightful action of another. Again, this position chimes very well with the "one very simple principle" that Mill sets forth in *On Liberty*—the principle that "govern[s] absolutely the dealings of society with the individual in the way of compulsion and control. . . ." As Mill explains,

> That principle is that the sole end for which mankind are warranted, individually or collectively, in interfering with the liberty of action of any of their number is self-protection. That the only purpose for which power can be rightfully exercised over any member of a civilized community, against his will, is to prevent harm to others. His own good, either physical or moral, is not a sufficient warrant.[32]

This does not mean—*pace* liberalism's communitarian critics— that a liberal individual is necessarily *unconcerned* with the good. An individual can be good because of the free choices he or she makes. But, in liberalism's view, an individual who is made good by the forced dictates of another cannot truly be called good, because such an individual cannot truly be called a *person* in any meaningful sense of the term.

Liberalism holds that personhood *is* the ability to make choices among available options (those that do not violate the rights of others).

---

31. John Rawls, A *Theory of Justice* (Cambridge: Harvard University Press, 1971), 60, emphasis added.
32. Mill, *On Liberty*, 13.

Crucially, these choices cannot be forced, for then they would not truly be choices. But they can be influenced by *persuasion*. Determining how and where to draw the line between persuasion and force becomes, for liberalism, the preeminent concern. If that line cannot be drawn, or if it does not exist, then liberalism may properly be said not to exist.

But here we need to be extremely careful. The precise relationship between liberalism and persuasion has, I would argue, not received the kind of theoretical attention it deserves. In the pages that follow, I try to examine this relationship in some detail. For now, let me simply point out a tension between liberalism and persuasion—a tension that tells us much about liberal political philosophy. On the one hand, liberalism has been, and continues to be, zealously concerned with protecting the right to freedom of speech and expression. Such concern is evident in the work of liberal thinkers dating from at least as far back as the seventeenth century. John Milton's political pamphlet entitled *Areopagitica* is a perfect example. Written in 1644, and published illegally (since it had not been submitted beforehand to the censors), Milton's work makes a bold and persuasive argument against the very law—and, by extension, the type of government—that prohibited its own publication. Milton articulated a core principle of liberalism: regimes that do not guarantee freedom of speech to their citizens, and certainly regimes that practice outright censorship (Plato's *Republic* comes to mind here) cannot be considered liberal.

Yet, *on the other hand*, it is not quite clear *why* political speech matters so much to liberalism. If the individual is the ultimate arbiter of moral and ethical questions—indeed, if these questions are not even properly within the realm of the political—then surely the scope of politics is drastically limited. For liberals, politics is not what it was for the ancients. The very substance of classical political oratory—discussions of civic virtue, of the good life, of what constitutes the proper ends of man—must be irrelevant to liberal politics. It is no surprise then that liberal political rhetoric often seems—to be frank—more banal than its classical counterpart.

More than a few liberals have worried about what this might mean for liberal politics in general. John Dewey, for example, was concerned about the tendency of liberalism to reduce the statesman to the status of what we would today call a mere "technocrat"—a manager of political details. He also was quite concerned about the tendency of liberalism to reduce the public to (at best) the status of mere spectators—citizens in name only, completely unable to understand what the technocrats were saying or doing. In his much neglected little book *The Public and Its Problems*, Dewey sought to rehabilitate liberal politics, and especially our concept of the "Public," by exploring ways in which public discourse could be improved. That exploration was carried out entirely from a liberal perspective. Dewey had no desire to revive the classical conceptions of rhetoric or political oratory. His audience and his concerns were wholly of the twentieth century. He wanted most to help bring about a liberal political condition in which "secrecy, prejudice, bias, misrepresentation, and propaganda as well as sheer ignorance are replaced by inquiry and publicity. . . ."[33] Writing in the early part of the century, Dewey displayed a characteristically American optimism that this condition could be brought into being. Its actualization would represent the first step in bringing about a truly "articulate" Public. But for the potential of the Public to be fully realized, Dewey concluded that,

> The highest and most difficult kind of inquiry and a subtle, delicate, vivid and responsive art of communication must take possession of the physical machinery of transmission and circulation and breathe life into it. When the machine age has thus perfected its machinery it will be a means of life and not its despotic master. Democracy will come into its own, for democracy is a name for a life of free and enriching communion. It had its seer in Walt Whitman. It will have its consummation when free social inquiry is indissolubly wedded to the art of full and moving communication.[34]

Aside from representing one of the few poetical moments in Dewey's writing, this passage helps us see more clearly the nature of the relationship between liberalism and persuasion. Despite its emphasis on the individual, liberalism cannot, of course, escape politics. By this I mean simply that liberalism cannot escape addressing questions concerning the relationship among individuals. As Dewey notes at the beginning of *The Public and Its Problems*, a "public" is brought into being as soon as the consequences of individual or collective action are serious enough to affect others not directly involved in the action. Harmonizing these actions and their consequences, in a way that maximizes individual

---

33. John Dewey, *The Public and Its Problems* (Athens, Ohio: Swallow Press, 1980), 209.
34. Ibid., 184.

freedom, without imposing on anyone a collectively sanctioned view of the "good," is, to liberals, the only legitimate concern of politics. Yet this is indeed a large and important concern.

Liberals believe that such a harmony is *ultimately* possible *through persuasion alone*. This is the essence of liberal democracy. Liberalism holds that as democratic discussion proceeds, humankind approaches higher levels of social harmony. Liberalism's "faith" (as I call it) in the ability of persuasion alone to bring this about is grounded on the liberal belief that humans are inherently rational, and on the belief that (what I also call) the *unforced* force of reason is (ultimately) the most powerful voice in the discussion. To be sure, this is a monumental faith upon which to build a political philosophy. But it is a faith that liberalism cannot do without. Deprived of that faith, liberalism would not be able to draw any *consistent and principled* distinction between persuasion and force—the very distinction, it will be remembered, upon which liberalism was said to rest. But when the distinction between persuasion and forces goes, so too does liberalism's only reason to resist censorship. After all, if all action is merely a species of force, then questions concerning what to do about speech or expression that we do not like become matters of simple calculation regarding the efficiency of using one type of force (censorship) versus another type of force (persuasion). Again, without the ability to distinguish between persuasion and force, there would be no way for liberals to reject censorship *before* the aforementioned calculation was performed.

I conclude therefore that liberal democracy stands or falls on its ability to articulate a consistent and principled distinction between persuasion and force. Rorty would flatly reject this conclusion. Yet he would reject it *only* because it includes the words "consistent" and "principled." Earlier I noted that Rorty's political philosophy is complex and often contradictory. But if there is one point on which Rorty has never wavered—at least not in the last two decades—it is that liberalism needs no "foundation" upon which to rest, no "principles" to back it up. Rorty's liberal ironist would try his best to substitute persuasion for force, but if he were asked to articulate a principle that justified (indeed, even that guided) his actions in this regard, he might well respond, "Sorry, I don't do principles." The insouciant tone of this response captures perfectly the perspective Rorty wants us to adopt with respect to all types of questions that demand of us any sort of justification for our actions. In the end, Rorty believes that we no longer need political *theory*, we simply need to get on with the business of extending liberal *practices*.

Of course, Rorty thinks these practices are fairly sound. Indeed, he firmly embraces almost every practical aspect of the liberal view I just sketched. He agrees—I am tempted to say, "he agrees *in principle*"—that among a society composed of a plurality of persons, each with her or his own private vision of the good, justice demands that we let each individual act on her or his own vision—consistent only with the principle (how else could one put it?) that no individual violate the rights of another. Rorty is therefore speaking *essentially* as a liberal when he urges us "to see the aim of a just and free society as letting its citizens by as privatistic, 'irrationalist,' and aestheticist as they please so long as they do it on their own time—causing no harm to others and using no resources needed by those less advantaged."[35] This formulation can easily be read as simply offering us an updated version of John Stuart Mill's conception of liberalism—a version that incorporates the realities of the *interdependencies* that exist in late twentieth century, industrialized cultures.

In addition to updating our conception of liberalism, Rorty also provides us with an updated view of the type of citizens he thinks should now populate liberal societies. As Rorty says, *Contingency, Irony, and Solidarity* "sketches a figure whom I call the 'liberal ironist.'"[36] Ironists, roughly speaking, are those who think there is no ahistorical quality that is definitive of the self. They believe that socialization goes all the way down; that there is nothing beyond time and chance that determines who we are. Hence ironists cannot believe that humans are *inherently* rational. Liberal ironists are, according to Rorty, the natural inhabitants of a "liberal utopia"—a *liberal* place "in which ironism, in the relevant sense, is universal."[37] In more mundane terms, a liberal utopia would be a liberal "postmetaphysical culture." It would be a culture that saw liberalism (i.e., its own political practices) not as something in tune with a facility common to all humans, but rather as just the sort of thing we liberals do. It would be a culture whose citizens refused even to attempt to *justify* their practices to themselves or to nonliberals. Such a culture seems to Rorty "no more impossible than a postreligious one, and equally desirable."[38]

---

35. Rorty, *Contingency, Irony, and Solidarity*, xiv.
36. Ibid., xv.
37. Ibid.
38. Ibid., xvi.

In its most basic sense, Rorty's reformulation of liberal political philosophy raises two essential and very much related questions. The first is whether the figure of a liberal ironist is theoretically tenable, whether it is logically possible (let alone desirable) for the same person to be both a liberal and an ironist. The second question can be put in pragmatic terms. Are liberal societies best served by embracing or rejecting a foundationalist vocabulary? The present essay attempts to shed light on both of these questions. I begin in chapter 1 by attempting to connect Rorty's later political philosophy to his earlier work. Chapters 2 and 3 then address, respectively, the two questions I have just raised. Finally, chapter 4 attempts not to *argue* about whether the liberal ironist is *theoretically* possible, but simply to "redescribe" that figure so we can see whether it is the type of figure we would wish to emulate.

BEFORE PROCEEDING to the opening chapter, I want to provide an important caveat about what the reader will *not* find in this essay. While it may be true that (as Nietzsche said), every great philosophy is "the personal confession of its author and a kind of involuntary and unconscious memoir," it certainly is not true that every critic must be a confessor.[39] Hence in the remarks that follow I have not attempted to "explain" Rorty's philosophy with reference to any particular extrinsic factor: his race, his gender, his position within the social hierarchy, his personal history, and so forth. To be sure, there is a fascinating study waiting to be written tracing Rorty's mature political philosophy to his own upbringing amid an exclusive circle of American intellectuals who made their home in New York City during the period between the two world wars. But the present essay does not constitute such a study. My concern is *solely* with the ideas expressed in Rorty's writings — in particular with the way in which these ideas do or do not "hang together." Granted, at the end of chapter 4 I *do* attempt to place Rorty within the context of his own theoretical framework, and thus to "explain" him somewhat. But this explanation is offered less as a comment on Rorty himself than as a comment on the activity of doing political philosophy in a liberal–democratic society.

---

39. See Friedrich Nietzsche, *Beyond Good and Evil: Prelude to a Philosophy of the Future*, trans. Walter Kaufmann (New York: Vintage, 1966), 13.

1

"Locating" Rorty's Utopia

The title of this chapter announces itself as a small paradox, owing to the etymology of the word "utopia." From the Greek meaning, literally, "no place," utopias seemingly cannot be "located" because they exist as concrete realities nowhere in time or space. Nevertheless, they may exist in the *writings* of political philosophers. This is surely what Leo Strauss meant when he said that Socrates' "just city" exists only in speech.[1] If this is so, it should be possible to "locate" a given political philosopher's "utopia" by tracing the pattern of thought that lead to its development. That is what I have attempted in this chapter.

Rorty's liberal utopia is more or less fully developed in *Contingency, Irony, and Solidarity*. But the groundwork for that development was laid at least a decade earlier with the publication of Rorty's first book *Philosophy and the Mirror of Nature* (1979). Accordingly, the first section of this chapter discusses Rorty's early philosophy—focusing particularly on *Philosophy and the Mirror of Nature* and some of his early writings. The second section attempts to connect this early philosophy to the philosophical *assumptions* in Rorty's later political theory. Specifically, I attempt to trace what I see as the relatively tight connection between the *new* task for philosophy sketched in the last third of *Philosophy and the Mirror of Nature*—roughly the task of merely "keeping the conversation

---

1. See Leo Strauss, "Plato," in *History of Political Philosophy*, eds. Leo Strauss and Joseph Cropsey (Chicago: University of Chicago Press, 1987), 55.

19

going"—and the *new* way of viewing our language and ourselves sketched in the first third of *Contingency, Irony, and Solidarity*—roughly the view that our language and ourselves are both *entirely and exclusively* products of the conversation. Taken together, these sections are meant to demonstrate how Rorty attempts to redescribe our culture as one that has moved (or at least *should* move) from the end of (traditional) philosophy—which focuses on showing us how to get in touch with a Truth larger than ourselves—to the beginning of irony—which urges us to drop the search for ultimate truth and simply accept the contingent nature of our existence.

The End of Philosophy

It may be true that philosophy begins in wonder. But in Rorty's view, twentieth-century, Anglo-American, analytic philosophy has ended in highly technical, intellectually sterile, socially irrelevant discussions about "*pseudo*problems"—like the problem of how *exactly* we can know the difference between a thought and the mental state that corresponds to that thought. Pseudoproblems of this type appear not only in the domain of analytic philosophy but throughout all of "constructive philosophy"—that is, philosophy that holds that knowing the Truth requires that we be in *agreement* with some *nonhuman* reality. Simply put, Rorty wants us to abandon constructive philosophy altogether. He thinks we can "slough off" the pseudoproblems that constructive philosophers have forced on us by simply sloughing off the vocabulary in which those problems are phrased. Doing this would of course put constructive philosophers *as such* out of a job. To see more clearly what types of individuals are threatened with unemployment, it might be helpful briefly to sketch the image our culture has of constructive philosophers. This image is common not only to *constructive* philosophers but, I will assert, to nearly all those within our culture who called themselves philosophers.

My guess is that for most individuals the term *philosopher* continues to conjures up the image of a serious-minded fellow toiling diligently to discover Truths about Man and Society. Again, my guess is that those who have given any thought to the question of *how* philosophers arrive at these Truths would probably say that philosophers do so by rigorously and methodically applying Reason and Logic to the important questions we humans face. The appearance of the terms *Reason* and *Logic* in this sketch draws our attention to the close connection Western culture makes between what *philosophers* do and what *mathematicians* or *natural scientists* do.[2] Each set of individuals, it is supposed, *discovers* something about our world, and does so in a specific way. Granted, philosophers differ slightly from natural scientists in that philosophy is more of an "armchair discipline." It does not require laboratories or expensive equipment, and the only experiments done are "thought-experiments." And, to be sure, philosophers also differ slightly from mathematicians in that philosophical questions are more often posed in ordinary language—although these questions usually turn out to be very abstract. Philosophers might inquire, for example, whether having the thought "turtle" is *exactly* equivalent to having the mental state that corresponds to having the thought "turtle," or whether there is more to having the thought. Or, philosophers might ask whether a ship that is brought into port and has a "few"—or "most"—or "all"—of its planks replaced and is then sent back out to sea is *essentially* the same ship that first came into port. Or, finally, philosophers might turn their attention to questions that seem to more clearly involve moral or ethical matters: Is torture ever justified? What are the requirements of a just war? Is abortion morally wrong?

Regardless of the types of questions asked, however, and despite the slight differences I have mentioned, philosophers still proceed in essentially the same manner as mathematicians or natural scientists. The first step in the process is to set aside entirely one's personal feelings, desires, and emotions. If mathematicians' deeply felt desires that Fermat's last theorem be true can in no sense affect the *actual* truth or falsity of the theorem, should we think that *philosophers'* deeply felt desires can affect the *actual* truth or falsity of questions they investigate—questions concerning, for example, the morality of abortion? On the view I am sketching, we should not. The next step is for philosophers to divide the problem they face into its component parts. This is certainly the most critical step. Philosophers must be sure to divide the problem in the way

---

2. Rorty has a tendency—in his more playful moods one supposes—to use the personal pronoun "he" to refer to "constructive philosophers," "natural scientists," "mathematicians," and the like, while using the personal pronoun "she" to refer to "nonconstructive philosophers," "literary critics," "poets," and the like. Of course, this type of playfulness inscribes its own kind of sexism: men as "hard" thinkers, women as "softer" thinkers. *Presumably* Rorty is attempting to ridicule this distinction by overusing it. I have chosen not to repeat Rorty's usage pattern, because I am not convinced that it has any positive effect.

that it should, *naturally*, be divided. They must cut the problem "at the joints"—to use a metaphor that Rorty borrows from Plato. If, for example, the question at hand concerns the morality of abortion, philosophers will, by using reason, see that this question involves relations between entities called "mothers" and entities called "fetuses" and other concepts called "rights" and "obligations." Philosophers will—again using reason—see that the question does *not* involve entities called "combatants" and entities called "noncombatants." As this process of division continues, philosophers will find themselves with a set of terms that more or less precisely represent reality. The philosophers' task is to proceed with this process, using reason and logic to locate divisions that embody finer and finer degrees of precision with respect to reality. Philosophers might further see, for example, that the entity called "fetuses" must be divided into "viable" and "nonviable" fetuses. Finally, at the conclusion of this process, philosophers are left with a set of terms that represent reality so precisely and so completely that these terms can be said to represent real-ity *as reality itself would wish to be represented*. With this accurate representation of reality in sight, answers to philosophical questions are self-evident. At this point, all that remains is for philosophers to write up their results. Using the most objective, impersonal, perspicacious prose they can manage, philosophers will show how, through the use of reason, they moved toward finer and finer divisions, coming finally to their conclusion. Since the ability to reason is supposedly "hardwired" into all humans in exactly the same way,[3] philosophers can be certain that their conclusions will fit with those of any other person—assuming, of course, that no careless errors have been made along the way. Of course, since no self-respecting philosopher of the type I have sketched would busy himself or herself with any but the most important *and complex* problems, it should not seem surprising that the language he or she uses to write up his or her results often appears recondite, at best, if not hopelessly abstruse, *to the nonphilosopher*. This is, as I have said, to be expected. Why, philosophers might ask, should one think it any easier to understand the writings of a professional philosopher on the question of

---

3. A computer analogy seems somewhat fitting here. By saying that reason is "hard-wired" into all humans, I mean that all nondefective humans are endowed with the *capacity* to reason, simply by virtue of the structure of their physiology. One could go further with this analogy and say that the capacity to reason is linked with the capacity to use language. I discuss this whole idea of reason more fully in chapter 3.

abortion than to understand the writings of a professional physicist on quantum theory? Both disciplines—philosophy and physics—are, after all, rigorous, complex, analytic, precisely ordered endeavors.

The traditional image I have just sketched—that of the philosopher as a *problem solver* using the same "tools" (i.e., Reason and Logic) as the mathematician and natural scientist—is, as I have said, one that Rorty wants to replace. He wants us instead to view the philosopher as a *conversational partner*—and a witty partner at that. Rorty's new image of a philosopher looks more like a sharp lawyer or an accomplished literary critic than a hard scientist. Rorty's nontraditional "philosophers" have an especially good way with words. Like their traditional counterparts, they *do* think that the terms that attach to any given philosophical question are of central importance. Unlike their traditional counterparts, they *do not* think that these terms attach themselves naturally. They do not think that the terms of any philosophical question are out there, in nature, waiting to be "located" by philosophers. To be sure, the *world* is out there. But, as Rorty never tires of saying, the world does not have a language. It cannot dictate its terms to us, for it has no terms. Only humans have languages; hence, only humans can decide which terms they will use to describe the world. On this view, it is no more correct to say that when philosophers address the question of abortion they should naturally speak of "mothers" and "fetuses" than it is to say that they should naturally speak of "combatants" and "noncombatants." Again, nature cannot tell us how it should be represented, for it speaks no language. So—to carry this view to its conclusion—although traditional philosophers think they are representing reality with the various divisions they *create* (not *locate* somewhere out there), they are only fooling themselves. The goal, therefore, is not for philosophers to be rigorous, for there is nothing for them to be rigorous about. Rather, the goal is to be as clever and imaginative with language as one can be. Hence, Rorty recommends the image of the philosopher as a conversational partner. For it is most often in stimulating conversation (broadly defined) that clever and imaginative uses of language appear. This view shifts the image of the philosopher (prevalent in both the culture at large, and in the universities) away from the type of practices that are supposed to go on in science and math departments and more toward the types of practices that are supposed to go on in humanities departments. According to Rorty, this shift is one we should recognize and welcome. As he says in a 1982 article entitled "Philosophy in America

Today," "We [philosophers] are not doing something different in kind from what the professor of literature or history would or could do. . . . We are just enlarging a linguistic and argumentative repertoire, and thus an imagination. Beyond this traditional humanist task, we can do only what lawyers do—provide an argument for whatever our client has decided to do, make the chosen cause appear the better."[4]

Needless to say, Rorty has some philosophers bristling at his characterization of the discipline. Those philosophers who most strongly disagree with Rorty believe that seeing themselves as problem solvers is vital to their self-image. Two examples of such philosophers come readily to mind; each has something to say about Rorty. First, Jürgen Habermas.

> Forcefully freeing himself from the straight-jacket of analytic philosophy, Richard Rorty has undertaken the most ambitious project: he wants to destroy the tradition of the philosophy of consciousness, from its Cartesian beginnings, with the aim of showing the pointlessness of the entire discussion of the foundations and limits of knowledge. He concludes that philosophers need only recognize the hybrid character of their controversies and give the field over to the practitioners of . . . politics, and daily life to be rid of the problem. Like the later Wittgenstein, Rorty sees philosophy itself as the sickness whose symptoms it previously and unsuccessfully tried to cure. But Rorty is still enough of a philosopher to give a reason for his recommendation that we avoid the *Holzweg* of philosophical justification: one shouldn't scratch where it doesn't itch. It is just this assumption, that "it doesn't itch," that I find problematic.[5]

Stephen Toulmin adopted a more whimsical tone in a lecture at Northwestern University in 1987. Toulmin confessed that, "Putting down Rorty's essays, I carry away the image of a group of ex-soldiers dis-

---

4. Richard Rorty, "Philosophy in America Today," in *Consequence of Pragmatism* (Minneapolis: University of Minnesota Press, 1982), 222. This essay was first delivered at a symposium with Alasdair MacIntyre on "The Nature and Future of Philosophy" in 1981, and reprinted in *The American Scholar* the following year.

5. See Habermas's reply to Rorty's article, "Habermas and Lyotard on Postmodernity," in *Habermas and Modernity*, ed. Richard J. Bernstein (Cambridge: MIT Press, 1985), especially pp. 193–4.

abled in the intellectual wars, and sharing memories over a glass of wine of 'old, forgotten, far off things, and battles long ago.'"[6]

These criticisms, and others, suggest that Rorty's vision of the amiable philosopher not as a problem solver per se, but rather as simply a conversational partner and fellow traveler on the road with literary critics, novelists, historians, and others, has yet to be embraced by *all* of his colleagues. Indeed, as Habermas's work makes abundantly and energetically clear, there are still some problem solvers left who believe that somewhere along the journey, and for *reasons* as opposed to matters of mere preference, the road diverges.

The question of which view of the philosopher—sober, rational, problem solver, or witty conversational partner—will win in the end is still very much open. Rorty's most detailed attempt at influencing the outcome of this contest is presented in his first book *Philosophy and the Mirror of Nature*. Accordingly, I shall devote the remainder of this section to an analysis of that work.

IN TURNING TO *Philosophy and the Mirror of Nature*, one is immediately confronted with two related questions: *What* is Rorty doing in this book, and *how* is he attempting to do it? It would be tempting to respond that *what* Rorty is doing is arguing that we should replace our current view of philosophy as "constructive," with a view of philosophy that sees it as (to use Rorty's word) "edifying"—that is, as the type of philosophy practiced by the *second* example of the philosopher in the aforementioned discussion. This would take care of the first question. One could then proceed to show *how* Rorty fashions arguments within the pages of *Philosophy and the Mirror of Nature* in order to make his case. This would take care of the second question.

The problem with these two answers is that they run the risk of missing the larger point of *Philosophy and the Mirror of Nature*. To see why, we can begin by noting that *if* one assumes (as does Rorty) that the unavoidable method by which constructive philosophy proceeds is by way of the construction of arguments based on reason, then although it makes sense to speak of arguing against *a particular claim* (or set of claims) made by a constructive philosopher, it makes no sense to speak

---

6. Stephen Toulmin, "The Recovery of Practical Philosophy," *Avalon* lecture, Northwestern University, Evanston, Ill., spring 1987.

of *arguing* against constructive philosophy *as such*. Doing so would mean that one was attempting to argue against argument, and this would involve one in a performative contradiction too severe even for Rorty to tolerate.

But if Rorty is not constructing arguments in his book, we are driven back to our initial questions: What is he doing, and how is he doing it? Rorty provides a specific answer to both of these questions when he explains that his overall approach in *Philosophy and the Mirror of Nature* will be "therapeutic rather than constructive."[7] Therapy, according to Rorty, is a process that sets aside argumentation as such in favor of redescription—that is, placing certain ideas in different contexts. The therapy in *Philosophy and the Mirror of Nature* is designed to cure us of our neurotic impulse to take certain epistemological questions (the very "pseudoproblems" I mentioned earlier) as inescapable—inescapable precisely because our answers to them form the foundation of our culture. In Rorty's view, quite literally nothing (and most certainly not philosophy) can form the *foundation* of a culture. Thus Rorty can happily offer *Philosophy and the Mirror of Nature* as therapy for his readers, who, if all goes well, will come to "glimpse the possibility of a form of intellectual life in which the vocabulary of philosophical reflection inherited from the seventeenth century would seem as pointless as the thirteenth-century philosophical vocabulary had seemed to the Enlightenment."[8]

Shifting whole vocabularies is of course no mean task. It requires the creation of a context in which old words either take on new meanings or are simply forgotten. Rorty thinks that to accomplish this one must draw on the resources of *imagination* rather than on the skills involved in *argumentation*. But I think that the distinction here is quite a bit less firm than Rorty makes it sound. Indeed, I agree with Jane Heal (one of Rorty's critics), who insists that *she* will view the Rorty of *Philosophy and the Mirror of Nature* as "proceeding in the customary fashion by offering claims and defending them with arguments," and who argues (correctly, I think) that "it is one indication of some strain in [Rorty's] position that it is extraordinarily difficult *not* to treat him as so proceeding."[9] In order then to see just

---

7. Richard Rorty, *Philosophy and the Mirror of Nature* (Princeton: University Press, 1979), 7.
8. Ibid., 6.
9. Jane Heal "Pragmatism and Choosing to Believe," in *Reading Rorty*, ed. Alan Malachowski (Oxford: Basil Blackwell, 1990), 102, emphasis in original.

how Rorty attempts to accomplish his stated task of getting us to set aside the vocabulary of constructive philosophy, I shall try *both* to reconstruct (in an extremely abbreviated way) the crucial *argument* he makes in *Philosophy and the Mirror of Nature*, and to highlight the crucial *descriptions* he provides of constructive and nonconstructive philosophy. I begin by trying to get clear on the exact nature of the neurosis for which Rorty thinks we are in need of therapy. In the opening pages of *Philosophy and the Mirror of Nature*, Rorty writes,

> Philosophy as a discipline . . . sees itself as the attempt to underwrite or debunk claims to knowledge made by science, morality, art, or religion. It purports to do this on the basis of its special understanding of the nature of knowledge and of mind. Philosophy can be foundational in respect to the rest of culture because culture is the assemblage of claims to knowledge, and philosophy adjudicates such claims. It can do so because it understands the foundations of knowledge, and it finds these foundations in a study of man-as-knower, or the "mental processes" or the "activity of representation" which make knowledge possible. To know is to represent accurately what is outside the mind; so to understand the possibility and nature of knowledge is to understand the way in which the mind is able to construct such representations.[10]

Constructing such representations has been the central concern of constructive philosophy since the time of Plato. But, Rorty notes, in the seventeenth and eighteenth centuries, discussions of the method used to create such representations crystallized around a discipline called "epistemology." Since Rorty focuses his analysis on this particular method, it would be most accurate to say that *Philosophy and the Mirror of Nature* is an attack on the discipline of epistemology as such—although, as Rorty says, his attack "strategy" can be generalized and used against all constructive philosophy. Again, that strategy involves showing how words and sentences (which, after all, are all philosophers have to work with) come to be seen as *representing* reality, instead of being seen as simply metaphors that humans create in order to help us cope with our world—metaphors that we are free to change as we see fit. With respect to epis-

---

10. Rorty, *Philosophy and the Mirror of Nature*, 3.

temology specifically, Rorty notes that seventeenth and eighteenth century philosophy came to center itself around a set of bad metaphors. Rorty claims,

> It is pictures rather than propositions, metaphors rather than statements, which determine most of our philosophical convictions. The picture which holds traditional philosophy captive is that of the mind as a great mirror, containing various representations—some accurate, some not—and capable of being studied by pure, nonempirical methods. Without the notion of the mind as mirror, the notion of knowledge as accuracy of representation would not have suggested itself. Without this latter notion, the strategy common to Descartes and Kant—getting more accurate representations by inspecting, repairing, and polishing the mirror, so to speak—would not have made sense. Without this strategy in mind, recent claims that philosophy could consist of "conceptual analysis" or "phenomenological analysis" or "explication of meanings" or examination of "the logic of our language" or of "the structure of the constituting activity of consciousness" would not have made sense.[11]

What John Dewey called the "quest for certainty" is intimately connected with the metaphor of the mind as the mirror of nature. According to this metaphor, certainty—or what Rorty more accurately calls "rational certainty"—is achieved when one finally gets clear on exactly what is reflected, or re-presented, in the mirror. "Truth" then is like an "object" to be seen. And "knowing" is the process of seeing clearly. Ocular metaphors, as Rorty and others have noted, are intrinsic to the Western notion of philosophy.[12] It is largely this set of metaphors, and all of the associations that go along with them, that Rorty wishes us to aban-

---

11. Ibid., 12.
12. Rorty makes note of this throughout *Philosophy and the Mirror of Nature*. Martin Heidegger is probably the most well known philosopher to explore the ways in which ocular metaphors have constituted Western philosophy. See especially *Being and Time*, trans. John Macquarrie and Edward Robinson (New York: Harper & Row, 1962). Jacques Derrida also devotes one of his most interesting essays to an examination of metaphors connected with "light" and "seeing" in Western philosophy. See his "White Mythology: Metaphor in the Text of Philosophy," trans. F.C.T. Moore, *New Literary History* (autumn 1974), 5–74.

don. He wants us to stop thinking of "Truth" as an object that *imposes* itself on our mind's eye, and start thinking of "truth" as a term we assign to a category of sentences—some to be found in the realm of mathematics and science, but also, some to be found in the realms of art, morality, religion, politics, and so forth—which help us cope with our world. In my reading, Rorty's philosophy makes the most sense, and is most appealing, if we understand it as saying that, in almost every case, the best way of coping with our world is by *talking* with other individuals. One need *not* see the world this way. One could imagine that coping must be largely, if not entirely, a *private* act. On this second view, coping is more a matter of introspection than conversation. But Rorty's view of the philosopher is *not* that of a taciturn scholar, a modern-day Descartes, ensconced in his private study. Rather, as I have said, Rorty envisions the philosopher as a witty conversational partner.

It will immediately be objected that this vision of philosophy is untenable. It forces us to abandon the quest for certainty altogether. For if certainty is *just* a matter of conversation, then anything that can be said can be true. Rorty would probably not disagree with this point, although he would clarify it by noting that, while anything that can be said is indeed a *possible* candidate for a true statement, one can decide if it *is* true *only* by engaging in more conversation. In Rorty's view, this applies to *all* statements (all possible candidates for truth), even statements in the realm of mathematics or science—statements that constructive philosophers have always believed to be true *of necessity*. This claim is central to Rorty's philosophical thinking, and it is indeed quite dramatic. This is how Rorty puts it, in what I take to be perhaps the most important passage in *Philosophy and the Mirror of Nature*:

> It is so much a part of "thinking philosophically" to be impressed with the special character of mathematical truth that it is hard to shake off the grip of the Platonic Principle [i.e., the principle "that differences in certainty must correspond to differences in the objects known"]. If, however, we think of our certainty about the Pythagorean Theorem as our confidence, based on experience with arguments on such matters, that nobody will find an objection to the premises from which we infer it, then we shall not seek to explain it by the relation of reason to triangularity. Our certainty will be a matter of conversation between persons, rather than a matter

of interaction with nonhuman reality. So we shall not see a difference in kind between "necessary" and "contingent" truths. At most, we shall see differences in degree of ease in objecting to our beliefs. We shall, in short, be where the Sophists were before Plato brought his principle to bear and invented "philosophical thinking": we shall be looking for an airtight case rather than an unshakable foundation. We shall be in what Sellars calls "the logical space of reasons" rather than that of causal relationships to objects.[13]

Although it is generally my purpose in this section to *describe* rather than *critique* Rorty's philosophy, I cannot let this passage go without some critical comment. At best, I think that the language Rorty uses here tends to obscure a very important, and valid, distinction. Although I think it would be a mistake to do so, Rorty *can* be read as arguing that the premises (i.e., the *axioms*) from which we infer the Pythagorean Theorem are exclusively matters of argument within the conversation, and *therefore* our certainty about the Theorem is *exclusively* a matter of our certainty (still within the conversation) about these axioms. But this way of describing the situation is only half right. We can perhaps argue about whether (as a *practical* matter) we should accept a certain set of axioms as "true." When we argue in this way, our arguments turn on the question of how much precision we require to meet our practical purposes. For example, if one wanted to survey a particular piece of land for the purpose of building a house, the set of axioms that defines Euclidean geometry would be quite adequate for the job. If, however, one wanted to describe interstellar space in a way that accurately related the mass of large bodies to the gravitational fields they produce, one would need to use a different geometry—that is, a geometry that was defined by a different set of axioms—if one wanted a *useful* description. But once one has accepted a given set of axioms as true, one's certainty about the truth of theorems logically derived from these axioms becomes a matter for reason, not for conversation. Rorty is surely correct to assert that Plato believed that the axioms of Euclidean geometry really existed in some "ideal" realm beyond human sensory perception. But mathematicians have now freed themselves of any such assumption. Since at least the late nineteenth century, mathematicians have come to see the difference

---

13. Rorty, *Philosophy and the Mirror of Nature*, 157.

between necessary and contingent truths, not as the difference between "things" that correspond to reality and "things" that do not, but as the difference between statements that follow *logically* from a given set of assumptions and statements that do not. Albert Einstein can help clarify this point. In his introduction to *Relativity: The Special and the General Theory*, Einstein explains,

> Geometry sets out from certain conceptions such as "plane," "point," and "straight line," with which we are able to associate more or less definite ideas, and from certain simple propositions (axioms) which, in virtue of these ideas, we are inclined to accept as "true." Then, on the basis of a logical process, *the justification of which we feel ourselves compelled to admit*, all remaining propositions are shown to follow from those axioms, i.e., they are proven. A proposition is then correct ("true") when it has been derived in the recognized manner from the axioms. The question of the "truth" of the individual geometrical propositions is thus reduced to one of the "truth" of the axioms. Now it has long been known that the last question is not only unanswerable by the methods of geometry, but that it is in itself entirely without meaning. We cannot ask whether it is true that only one straight line goes through two points. We can only say that Euclidean geometry deals with things called "straight lines," to each of which is ascribed the property of being uniquely determined by two points situated on it. The concept "true" does not tally with the assertions of pure geometry, because by the word "true" we are eventually in the habit of designating always the correspondence with a "real" object; geometry, however, is not concerned with the relation of the ideas involved in it to objects of experience, *but only the logical connection of these ideas among themselves.*[14]

I want now to suggest that we *should* read the aforementioned passage by Rorty as chiming with the point Einstein is making here about mathematics—the point that "true" statements in mathematics should not be thought of as true *because* they *correspond* to something "real."

---

14. Albert Einstein, *Relativity: The Special and the General Theory*, trans. Robert W. Lawson (New York: Crown Publishers, 1961), 1–2, emphasis added.

Rorty should *not* be read as trying to deny that *once one has accepted a particular set of axioms or assumptions* there is *still* no difference between necessary and contingent truths. He should *not* be read as denying that there are such things as logical contradictions. Rather, his claim that our certainty about all possible statements ultimately comes down to a matter of conversations between persons should be taken to mean that since theorems in mathematics, as well as statements in philosophy and many statements in everyday life, ultimately rest on a particular set of axioms or assumptions that themselves do not correspond to anything "real," our certainty about such statements is ultimately contingent upon our acceptance of a particular set of axioms or assumptions. But, to repeat, nothing outside of the conversation *compels* this acceptance.

Suppose one were to accept Rorty's view that, in the final analysis, all we really have is the conversation. Would such acceptance bring about the "end" of constructive philosophy by allowing us finally to end the *philosophical* search for some nonhuman reality to which we humans must be responsible? In a last-ditch effort to keep their view of the discipline alive, clever constructive philosophers might answer "no" and might simultaneously invoke the memory of Kant. It was Immanuel Kant who moved constructive philosophy from a focus on "outer" reality to a focus on "inner" reality. Kant shifted constructive philosophy's emphasis from the "objective" world to the "subject," which represents that world to itself in its consciousness. Kant's transcendental project attempted to reconstruct the a priori conditions of consciousness that make possible the subject's knowledge of any and all reality. With knowledge of such a priori conditions, the subject could generate, in a purely procedural way, *substantive* knowledge of its world. Importantly, this substantive knowledge was understood by Kant as imposing itself on the subject in the same way that earlier philosophers saw the objective world as imposing itself on the subject. Unfortunately, as his critics pointed out, Kant's own project flounders on the self-referential paradox, for it is not at all clear how a subject can reconstruct the a priori conditions of its consciousness without some a priori knowledge of those a priori conditions. Kant seems to be in something of the same situation as that faced by the hapless individual who insists that he will not go into the water until he has learned how to swim.

Still, despite its apparent problems, Kantian constructivism is alive and well in much twentieth-century philosophy. The John Rawls of *A Theory of Justice* can, for example, be read as attempting to derive *substantive* claims about just practices in a democratic society by analyzing the purely procedural workings of an ideal bargaining game played by imaginary citizens of such a society. In a somewhat similar vein, although at a much higher level of generality, the Jürgen Habermas of A *Theory of Communicative Action* can be read as attempting to derive *substantive* claims about ethical norms by analyzing the purely procedural workings of an "ideal speech situation"—a situation in which conversation is undistorted by any of the normal, real-world problems of communication. For those concerned with Rorty's work, Habermas's philosophy is particularly interesting, because it seems to foreground that very activity Rorty sees as all important: the conversation.

But there is a critical difference. As Rorty points out, Habermas's work is yet one more failed attempt to rework Kantian philosophy. It is one more failed attempt philosophically to pull ourselves up by our own bootstraps. Habermas, like constructive philosophers before him, still wants to find some knowledge to which humans must be responsible. For Kant, this knowledge existed *within* the subject. For Habermas, it exists *between* conversing subjects. But both approaches are equally flawed, and for the same reason. As Rorty notes,

> Habermas thinks Kant was right in his aims, but wrong in his strategy. He thinks we can still get what Kant hoped for, so long as we give up the "philosophy of subjectivity" which Kant and Hegel shared, and instead develop a "philosophy of intersubjectivity." Habermas is urging a return to good old-fashioned universalistic Kant-style philosophy. He thinks that what was wrong with Kant was not—as all us Young Hegelians have been taking for granted for the last hundred and fifty years—his *Enlightenment rationalism*, but rather what all the rest of us had thought was just German philosophy's special, funny little God-surrogate "The Subject" (a quasi-person which constitutes the phenomenal world, gives itself the moral law, gradually becomes identical with The Object, continually overcomes itself, shepherds Being, deconstructs itself etc., as required). Habermas thinks we can revive Enlightenment rationalism as long as we use intersubjectivity instead of subjectivity as our philosophical starting point.[15]

---

15. Richard Rorty, "Posties," *London Review of Books*, 3 September 1987, 11, emphasis added.

Rorty believes that intersubjectivity is bound to fail, just as Kant's earlier attempts failed, for Rorty does not think that "intersubjective validity" is a concept we can know anything about—except, of course, through conversation with other persons. But, conversation about conversation is still, in Rorty's view, *only* conversation. Simply put, for Rorty there is no way of getting outside of the conversation.

That last sentence, phrased in just that way, sounds suspiciously like Derrida's proclamation that "There is nothing outside of the text." The suspicion is quite justified. Both Derrida and Rorty share a similar "philosophical" attitude toward constructive philosophy. Both think that the constructive philosopher's pretensions about getting in touch with "Truth" or "Reality" need to be deconstructed. And both go further by cautioning us against trying to construct *new* philosophical structures on the rubble of previous philosophical systems. For both Derrida and Rorty, what we are left with at the end of philosophy is simply the possibility for endless dialogue: endless conversation for Rorty, endless writing for Derrida.

Endless, perhaps, but neither meaningless nor frivolous. As Rorty claims in a 1978 essay entitled "Philosophy as a Kind of Writing: An Essay on Derrida," deconstruction is best seen *not* (as many have seen it) as a philosophy of language that purports to demonstrate that all writing is ultimately meaningless. Oddly, viewing deconstruction in this way would turn it into constructive philosophy by saddling it with claims about the nature of language and meaning. Rather, in Rorty's view, we should read Derrida as having little if anything to tell us about language as such, but a great deal to tell us about philosophy. What Derrida tells us is that philosophy is not a privileged form of language, it is simply one more kind of writing. At his best, Derrida's own writings are often virtuoso attempts to persuade us that (to use Rorty's words) there is no such thing as "a good piece of writing which is not an occasion for a better piece."[16]

But—a constructive philosopher might object—how can we know that a piece of writing is "better" if we do not have some *standard* by which to judge it? And must not such a standard for "better" ultimately include the notion of what is "best"? Yet if this is so, we are faced with the following dilemma. We may either admit a standard for what is "best"

---

16. Richard Rorty, "Philosophy as a Kind of Writing: An Essay on Derrida," *New Literary History* (autumn 1978): 159.

and thereby admit that *in principle at least* there must be an end to the conversation—although, in practice, that end may take an infinite amount of time to achieve. Or, we may reject the notion that there is a standard for what is "best" and in so doing find ourselves unable to say what is "better."

It might he supposed that Rorty, good pragmatist that he is, would simply grasp the first horn of this dilemma and allow the constructive philosophers to have their "theoretical" standard for what is "best," while insisting that since we can never attain such a standard in practice it does not have any *practical* relevance in the real world. Doing so, however, would put Rorty in the position of having to concede to the constructive philosophers their most important point—that is, that there is one correct theoretical vocabulary to be used when talking about "Man" or "Society" or simply "Reality," a vocabulary that is correct because it describes reality as reality wishes to be described. Constructive philosophers will argue that even if this vocabulary is (in some everyday sense) impractical, it still provides something of a *focus imaginarius* that we can use to guide our efforts. But, as we have seen, Rorty insists that the universe does not have a language, only humans have languages. This, however, lands us right back in the middle of the dilemma, for (again) how are we to determine when something (a piece of writing, a law, a scientific theory, or whatever) is better than something else of its kind? Rorty can only answer by insisting that we make this determination by conversing with our fellows as to what *we* want to define as "better." In other words, in Rorty's view, since we cannot look to "reality" for help in describing itself, we must look to our fellow interlocutors. Or, as the Greek Sophist Protagoras said, in a similar vein, "Man is the measure of all things."

To be sure, it takes a certain *kind* of philosopher to feel *satisfied* with this last statement. Constructive philosophers—who can trace their lineage back to Plato—are not of this type. What Rorty calls "edifying" philosophers are. In the last third of *Philosophy and the Mirror of Nature*, Rorty sketches the job description of the edifying philosopher. That description has quite a bit to do with simply keeping the conversation going. As Rorty notes,

> . . . I shall use "edification" to stand for [the] project of finding new, better[!], more interesting, more fruitful ways of speaking. The attempt to edify (ourselves or others) may con-

sist in the hermeneutic activity of making connections between our own culture and some exotic culture or historical period, or between our own discipline and another discipline which seems to pursue incommensurable aims in an incommensurable vocabulary. But it may instead consist in the "poetic" activity of thinking up such new aims, new words, or new disciplines, followed by, so to speak, the inverse of hermeneutics: the attempt to reinterpret our familiar surroundings in the unfamiliar terms of our new inventions. In either case, the activity is (despite the etymological relation between the two words) edifying *without being constructive*. . . .[17]

In other words, edifying philosophers converse in several different vocabularies without attempting to *privilege* one vocabulary over any other. And, since edifying philosophers love novelty, they also attempt to make all of their vocabularies as new as possible. Both of these gestures work to ensure (as much as that is possible) that the conversation will *continue without repeating itself.* If philosophy does have any sort of end, or telos, *that* is precisely what it is for Rorty. In what amounts to a final parting shot—an infuriating shot—at constructive philosophers, Rorty closes *Philosophy and the Mirror of Nature* with this last sentence: "The only point on which I would insist is that philosophers' moral concern should be with continuing the conversation of the West, rather than with insisting upon a place for the traditional problems of modern philosophy within that conversation."[18]

Again, I imagine that outraged constructive philosophers will rightly object by asking how Rorty—whose *only* concern seems to be with keeping the conversation going—can now speak of that concern as a *moral* concern. Constructive philosophers would point out that, while it is one thing to say that "continuing the conversation" amounts to an aesthetic or even a practical concern, it is another thing altogether to say—no, rather to *insist*—that this activity should be given the status of a moral concern. Where, they may rightly ask, does this concept of morality come from? Presumably it must be generated from the conversation—from Rorty's conversation, or from the conversation of

17. Rorty, *Philosophy and the Mirror of Nature*, 360, emphasis in original.
18. Ibid, 394.

others. But if this is so, might we not be justified in supplementing Rorty's last sentence in the following way? "The only point on which I would insist is that philosophers' moral concern should be with continuing the conversation of the West, rather than with insisting upon a place for the traditional problems of modern philosophy within that conversation, and (ultimately) I insist this be a moral concern *just because*, after conservation with others, I have decided to insist this be a moral concern." Rorty's typical, deflationary response to this point would surely be something like, "Of course you would be justified in pointing out that my insistence that continuing the conversation be seen as a moral concern is, ultimately, based solely on an understanding of morality I have come to by way of that very conversation. What else could it be based on? What else could anyone's insistence about anything be based on?"

What else, indeed. The worldview proffered in the last section of *Philosophy and the Mirror of Nature*—the view that all we have is the conversation, and that we should face up to this situation and not long for something more—may seem *less* dramatic than it actually is, simply because it is presented as the conclusion of a book whose main parts center around highly technical questions within the relatively specialized domain of analytic philosophy. In *Philosophy and the Mirror of Nature*, Rorty does not speak explicitly to the social and political import of his challenge that we become edifying philosophers. He does, however, take up just such a discussion in *Contingency, Irony, and Solidarity*.

The Beginning of Irony

As a way of connecting what I have said so far about Rorty's philosophical outlook with the emerging lines of his later political philosophy—a philosophy that I am not *yet* ready to critique *in depth*—I shall devote the following section to an examination of the critically important similarities that exist between the sketch of the "edifying" philosopher, provided in *Philosophy and the Mirror of Nature*, and the sketch of the "ironist," provided a decade later in *Contingency, Irony, and Solidarity*. Let me begin, where Rorty begins in the opening pages of that book, with a definition. He writes, "I use 'ironist' to name the sort of person who faces up to the contingency of his or her own most central beliefs and desires— someone sufficiently historicist and nominalist to have abandoned the idea that those central beliefs and desires refer back to something beyond the reach of time and chance."[19]

Because humans (ironists or otherwise) are symbol-using animals, and because language is our most pervasive and sophisticated symbol system, we can think of our "beliefs and desires" as represented by, or even constitutive of, the "vocabulary" we use to express our "selves." One's most *central* beliefs and desires will be represented by what Rorty calls his or her *"final* vocabulary."

> These are the words in which we formulate praise of our friends and contempt for our enemies, our long-term projects, our deepest self-doubts and our highest hopes. They are the words in which we tell, sometimes prospectively and sometimes retrospectively, the story of our lives.[20]

This vocabulary will be final, in the sense that it embodies one's most important set of beliefs and desires, a set of beliefs and desires that one literally cannot think of *being* without. It will also be final, as Rorty notes, "in the sense that if doubt is cast on the worth of these words, their user has no noncircular argumentative recourse. Those words are as far as he can go with language; beyond them there is only helpless passivity or a resort to force."[21] Lastly, the most interesting parts of one's final vocabulary will contain what Rorty calls "thick," "rigid," and "parochial" terms like *Christian, Englishman, Radical Feminist,* or the like.

Given this terminology, we can now ask the following critical question: What is the precise relationship between an *ironist* and his or her final vocabulary? To answer this question, I need to quote Rorty at some length. His answer provides, I think, an excellent sense of the type of *character* he takes an ironist to be. In Rorty's view, an ironist is one about whom we can say the following:

> (1) She has radical and continuing doubts about the final vocabulary she currently uses, because she has been impressed by other vocabularies, vocabularies taken as final by people or books she has encountered; (2) she realizes that arguments phrased in her present vocabulary can neither

---

19. Richard Rorty, *Contingency, Irony, and Solidarity* (Cambridge: University Press, 1989), xv.

20. Ibid., 73.

21. Ibid.

underwrite nor dissolve these doubts; (3) insofar as she phi-
losophizes about her situation, she does not think that her
vocabulary is closer to reality than others, that it is in touch
with a power not herself. Ironists who are inclined to philoso-
phize see the choice between vocabularies as made neither
within a neutral and universal metavocabulary nor by an
attempt to fight one's way past appearances to the real, but
simply by playing the new off against the old.

I call people of this sort "ironists" because their realiza-
tion that anything can be made to look good or bad by being
redescribed, and their renunciation of the attempt to formu-
late criteria of choice between final vocabularies, puts them in
the position which Sartre called "meta-stable": *never quite
able to take themselves seriously* because always aware that the
terms in which they describe themselves are subject to
change, always aware of the contingency and fragility of their
final vocabularies, *and thus of their selves.*[22]

If all of this sounds thoroughly relativistic, it is. If it also sounds precisely like the type of worldview one would expect someone with Rorty's
philosophical outlook to construct, it is that too. But notice: If one accepts
the "end-of-philosophy" philosophical outlook that I discussed in the previous section, then the characterization of Rorty's worldview as "relativistic" (as opposed to something else) becomes *simply* a description, and *not*
a condemnation. In fact, in Rorty's view, there are no nonrelativistic
worldviews since, *in the final analysis,* there are no noncircular arguments one could use to justify such worldviews. And again, we could
rachet this point to an even higher level of complexity by noting that *ultimately* there are no noncircular arguments one can make to prove that
there are no noncircular arguments. Again, *all* we have is the conversation. Rorty is still a shrewd enough analytic philosopher to recognize that
these paradoxes exist. Hence, he does not represent himself as attempting
to argue for an ironist worldview, nor does he contend that such a worldview can be grounded on any type of firm foundation. He attempts, simply, to reject the vocabulary of argument and grounding altogether.

I can sharpen this last point by noting that Rorty, an exemplary ironist, is also the dialectical opposite of the "metaphysician." At the level of

---

22. Ibid., 73–74, emphasis added.

philosophy, the opposition looks like this: The metaphysician is one who believes that humans are ultimately accountable to some higher, non-human reality—God, or Reason, or Natural Law, or some analogous "Truth." This belief is what allows, in fact compels, the metaphysician to adopt the vocabulary of grounding. Notice that *all* constructive philosophers are, therefore, metaphysicians. The ironist, on the other hand, is one who believes that humans are not responsible to anything outside of or inside themselves. He or she wishes, therefore, to replace the vocabulary of grounding with the vocabulary of self-creation. In this sense, the ironist finds his or her paradigmatic expression in Nietzsche's Zarathustra, a figure who embodies Blake's maxim (quoted approvingly by Rorty): "I must Create a System, or be enslav'd by another Man's."[23] All edifying philosophers are, therefore, ironists.

I now want to argue that the description of the ironist I have just provided will seem persuasive *only* to the extent that one accepts the view of *contingency* that Rorty offers. Or, to put the point slightly differently, the ironist will appear a plausible character only to the extent that one *rejects* the notion that "chance" is "*unworthy* of determining our fate"— a notion that Rorty, following Freud, argues that we should reject.[24] But, again, perhaps "argues" is not the right word. To make the case for contingency—and thus for the ironist—Rorty invokes the method of redescription, not argumentation. He attempts to describe a fully contingent world—a world in which we are content to see our *language* and *ourselves* simply as products of time and chance. He tries to do this type of redescribing most explicitly in the first two chapters of *Contingency, Irony, and Solidarity*. Since Rorty's understanding of irony depends so heavily on his view of contingency, I turn now to a detailed analysis of these two chapters. After this analysis is completed, I will conclude this section with some comments on the figure of the ironist.

I THINK IT is remarkable how exceptionally close the first chapter of *Contingency, Irony, and Solidarity*—entitled "The Contingency of Lan-

---

23. Blake, quoted in Rorty, *Contingency, Irony, and Solidarity*, 109. As Rorty points out, the next line of Blake's poem *Jerusalem* is "I will not Reason or Compare; my business is to Create."
24. Sigmund Freud, Standard Edition (S.E.), XI, 137, quoted in *Contingency, Irony, and Solidarity*, 31, emphasis added.

guage"—tracks the closing chapters of *Philosophy and the Mirror of Nature.* Writing about the relationship between truth and language, Rorty essentially repeats, but also generalizes, the point he made in his first book, by once again insisting that

> We need to make a distinction between the claim that the world is out there and the claim that truth is out there. To say that the world is out there, that it is not our creation, is to say, with common sense, that most things in space and time are the effects of causes which do not include human mental states. To say that truth is not out there is simply to say that where there are no sentences there is no truth, that sentences are elements of human languages, and that human languages are human creations.
>
> Truth cannot be out there—cannot exist independently of the human mind—because sentences cannot so exist, or be out there. The world is out there, but descriptions of the world are not. Only descriptions of the world can be true or false. The world on its own—unaided by the describing actives of human beings—cannot. . . .
>
> The world does not speak. Only we do. The world can, once we have programmed ourselves with a language, cause us to hold beliefs. But it cannot propose a language for us to speak. Only other human beings can do that.[25]

Just as *Philosophy and the Mirror of Nature* was written with the intention of being "therapeutic rather than constructive," so too *Contingency, Irony, and Solidarity* is written with therapy in mind. As I have noted many times, Rorty would insist that we *not* read the aforementioned passage as an attempt to *argue* that Truth does not exist. Rather, he would say that we should read this passage as an attempt to persuade us, by way of redescription, to see the world in a certain way. Once again, the difference in *method* is between argumentation and redescription; and once again, it may be difficult to see this putative difference as making that much of a difference—at least in practice. Still, Rorty is very conscious that he not appear to contradict himself by seeming to argue for the ultimate truth of the claim that there is no ultimate truth. Hence, he asserts that

---

25. Rorty, *Contingency, Irony, and Solidarity,* 5, 6.

To say that we should drop the idea of truth as out there waiting to be discovered is not to say that we have discovered that,
out there, there is no truth. It is to say that our purposes would
be served best by ceasing to see truth as a deep matter, as a
topic of philosophical interest, or "true" as a term which repays
"analysis." "The nature of truth" is an unprofitable topic,
resembling in this respect "the nature of man" and "the nature
of God," and differing from "the nature of the positron," and
"the nature of Oedipal fixation." But this claim about relative
profitability, in turn, is just the recommendation that we in fact
say little about these topics, and see how we get on.[26]

When Rorty says, "Our purposes would be served best by ceasing to
see truth as a deep matter," I take it he means by the phrase "our purposes" the set of goals and aspirations that attaches to liberal democracy.
These purposes do not get discussed explicitly in chapter 1 of *Contingency, Irony, and Solidarity*, but they do get spelled out in significant
detail in Rorty's writings throughout the eighties. Briefly, they amount to
the protection and expansion of the standard liberal–democratic ideals
(free speech, equality under the law, due process of law, and so forth),
and—more to the point for Rorty's purposes—the willingness to work
toward a decrease in the level of cruelty and humiliation within our society. Indeed, it would be fair to say that the advancement of *these* purposes
is the very reason *Contingency, Irony, and Solidarity* was written. With
this in mind, notice how much weight now falls on the word "best" in the
aforementioned quotation. Rorty seems to be saying not only that liberal
democracy *can* survive a vocabulary shift that dispenses with "deep" discussions about topics like "the nature of man," but, in fact, that it would
be *enhanced* by just such a shift. By making this strong claim, Rorty is
clearly siding with John Rawls—one of his favorite contemporary, liberal,
political philosophers. In his book, *Political Liberalism*, Rawls advises
that (in the political realm, at least) "we try to bypass religion and philosophy's profoundest controversies" so as to enhance the possibility of
bringing about (once again in the political realm) an "overlapping con-
sensus" between individuals who hold very different views on "deep"
questions like "the nature of man."[27] At one level, Rawls is simply coun-

---

26. Ibid., 8, emphasis in original, footnote omitted.
27. See John Rawls, *Political Liberalism* (New York: Columbia University Press, 1993),
    especially pp. 133–72.

seling an allegiance to good, old-fashioned, liberal tolerance. But there may be a problem with the *way* in which both Rawls and Rorty think this tolerance is best secured. The attempt to "bypass" philosophy's profoundest questions by simply not saying anything about them may run the risk of creating a philosophical "vacuum" within our cultural vocabulary—a vacuum that other, antiliberal individuals will be all too ready to fill with their philosophical ideas. I think it is still very much an open question whether a culture can ever "evade" the "deep matters" to which Rorty refers.

But for the present I will leave this question aside and pursue a question more critically related to the point of this section—a question about the relationship between language and language users.[28] Specifically, I wonder what role, exactly, the human agent *qua agent* plays in a world where language is *fully* contingent. By the very fact that he is engaging in persuasion, this question is directly implicated in Rorty's work. To say that we "should drop" part of the vocabulary we are presently using and replace it with something else (or decide simply not to replace it) sounds as though we have a *choice* in the matter. Furthermore, to say that after we alter our vocabulary we should then judge this alteration by simply trying to "see how we get on" sounds as though we really can "see" what our situation is, apart from any language we use to describe that situation. (Notice the reliance on an ocular metaphor in Rorty's suggestion that we should "*see* how we get on.") The problem, *as Rorty points out*, is precisely that we cannot judge a situation apart from the language that describes it. When we look to see how we are getting on, are we to look through the lens of our old vocabulary (the one we wish to drop), or through the lens of our new vocabulary (the one we wish to evaluate)? And how do we decide *this* question? Do we do so from within the perspective of still a third vocabulary, which is somehow neutral with respect to these old and new vocabularies?

Perhaps it will be responded that I am being unfair to Rorty by posing the previous set of questions. After all, he insists that he is not arguing. So attempts to show that he is in some way inconsistent may not be on point. In fact, by refusing to fashion *arguments* for his position, Rorty may be demonstrating a perfect consistency with the method of redescription. As he says, "Conforming to my own precepts, I am not

---

28. In chapter 3 I shall return to the question of whether cultures can evade "deep matters" like the foundations of their own legitimation.

going to offer arguments against the vocabulary I want to replace. Instead, I am going to try to make the vocabulary I favor look attractive by showing how it may be used to describe a variety of topics."[29]

My problem here is with the phrase "look attractive." This seems to imply some standard of attractiveness for vocabularies. As far as I can see, Rorty does not provide any such standard, nor could he, for any standard by which we were to judge vocabularies would already be compromised by being a part of some vocabulary. Rorty might respond that attractive vocabularies are those that can be "used to describe a variety of topics." But why is this evidence of attractiveness, as opposed to evidence of an unsightly imprecision within the vocabulary?

The larger issue I am pressing here is simply this: How do we move from one vocabulary to another? This is in no way a trivial issue. It goes to the heart of some "deep" questions about the relationship between language and language users. Of course, these are *precisely* the types of questions Rorty would like us simply to drop. Yet, following Heal's comment in the previous section, it is some significant evidence of a strain in Rorty's own position that *he* cannot simply drop these questions. They are, in proper Derridian fashion, always already entangled in his own discourse. In a 1987 article entitled "Non-Reductive Physicalism," Rorty acknowledges, and then seeks to escape, something very much like this theoretical entanglement. He begins by suggesting that instead of viewing the "self" in the "traditional" way as something with a stable "core" that is independent of its language, we should view the "self" as "a network of beliefs and desires which is continually in the process of being rewoven (with some old items dropped as new ones are added). This network is not one which is rewoven by an agent distinct from the network—a master weaver, so to speak. Rather, it reweaves itself, in response to stimuli. . . ." But Rorty then immediately concedes that, "This picture is hard to reconcile with common speech, according to which the 'I' is distinct from its beliefs and desires, picks and chooses among them, etc. *But we must think with the learned while continuing to speak with the vulgar.*"[30]

Suffice it to say, I find this attempt at evasion rather less than persuasive. In a sense, it is the internal coherence of Rorty's redescription

---

29. Rorty, *Contingency, Irony, and Solidarity*, 9.
30. Rorty, "Non-Reductive Physicalism," in *Objectivity, Relativism, and Truth: Philosophical Papers, Volume I* (Cambridge: University Press, 1991), 123, emphasis added.

of language that is at stake here. Do we create our language, or does it create us? Or is there some mysterious third alternative at work in the universe? As I have noted, at various times Rorty wants to describe his own endeavors as attempts to persuade us to substitute a "better" vocabulary for the one we are presently using. But at other times, Rorty's redescription of language serves to problematize his description of his own linguistic behavior. Consider that just a few *paragraphs* before the passage in which Rorty tries to persuade us that we "should drop" parts of our current vocabulary and adopt a new one, he seems to imply that we have no choice with respect to which vocabulary we use. "Europe," he writes,

> did not *decide* to accept the idiom of Romantic poetry, or of socialist politics, or of Galilean mechanics. That sort of shift was no more an act of will than it was a result of argument. Rather, Europe gradually lost the habit of using certain words and gradually acquired the habit of using others.[31]

To bolster this reading, Rorty turns to Donald Davidson, another of his favorite contemporary philosophers. In Rorty's view, Davidson's importance is that he finally breaks completely with the idea that language should be seen *either* as a medium by which we *represent* a reality outside of ourselves, *or* as a medium by which we *express* a "reality" inside ourselves. So, several pages after his comment concerning European habits about language, Rorty notes that it is Davidson who

> lets us think of the history of language, and thus of culture, as Darwin taught us to think of the history of a coral reef. Old metaphors are constantly dying off into literalness, and then serving as a platform and foil for new metaphors. This analogy lets us think of "our language"—that is, of the science and culture of twentieth-century Europe—as something that took shape as a result of a great number of sheer contingencies. Our language and our culture are as much a contingency, as much a result of thousands of small mutations finding niches (and millions of others finding no niches), as are the orchids and the anthropoids.[32]

---

31. Rorty, *Contingency, Irony, and Solidarity*, 6, emphasis in original.
32. Ibid., 16.

This allows Rorty to conclude that

> for all we know, or should care, Aristotle's metaphorical use of
> *ousia*, Saint Paul's metaphorical use of *agapē*, and Newton's
> metaphorical use of *gravitas* were the results of cosmic rays
> scrambling the fine structure of some crucial neurons in their
> respective brains. Or, more plausibly, they were the result of
> some odd episodes in infancy—some obsessional kinks left in
> these brains by idiosyncratic traumata. It hardly matters how
> the trick was done. The results were marvelous. There had
> never been such things before.[33]

Once again, it is difficult to know how we should interpret the
penultimate sentence in this passage. It is difficult to see how, for Rorty,
the "winning" results (the metaphors that survive) could ever be anything *other* than marvelous. Indeed, on this point, Rorty's philosophy
sounds suspiciously like the kind of philosophy Voltaire satirizes in *Candide*. Not completely unlike Rorty, Voltaire's fictional character Doctor
Pangloss—a practitioner of "metaphysico–theologo–cosmolonigol-
ogy"—has a particular knack for demonstrating that, since things could
not be otherwise than they are, "this is the best of all possible worlds.[34]

On that slightly unfair comment, we arrive at the end of my abbreviated sketch of the first chapter of *Contingency, Irony, and Solidarity*,
and we find ourselves confronted with a seemingly problematic
redescription of language. Simply put, Rorty's redescription of language
leaves no place for the *consciousness* of the redescriber. Yet Rorty himself
is very explicitly and very consciously engaging in redescription. This
paradox arises out of *any* philosophical inquiry into the relationship
between language and the self. Do we create language, or does it create
us? Rorty wants simply to evade this paradox by advising us to "think"
with the learned, even if we must "speak" with the vulgar. But does this
then imply that we can *think* something we cannot *say*?

Rather than pursue this paradox further, I will conclude, where
Rorty does at the end of chapter 1, by asking what type of character
would feel most comfortable with the view of language he presents. As
we saw in the previous section, the "edifying philosopher" was most

---

33. Ibid., 17.
34. See Voltaire, *Candide*, in *The Portable Voltaire*, ed. Ben Ray Redman (New York:
Penguin Books, 1977), 230.

comfortable with a view that held that all we have is the conversation. At the conclusion of the first chapter of *Contingency, Irony, and Solidarity*, the figure of the edifying philosopher is transformed, not yet explicitly into an "ironist," but into someone very similar: the "poet," or more accurately, the "strong poet."[35] Importantly, just as the edifying philosopher was (at least implicitly) held up as a cultural ideal at the conclusion of Rorty's first book, so too the figure of the strong poet is now recommended as our most important cultural asset. Hence, Rorty concludes his discussion of the contingency of language by asserting that, "A sense of human history as the history of successive [contingent] metaphors would let us see the poet, in the generic sense of the maker of new words, the shaper of new languages, as the vanguard of the species."[36]

That quotation sounds suspiciously like the famous closing line of Percy Bysshe Shelley's essay "A Defense of Poetry." Like Rorty, Shelley boldly avows that, "Poets are the unacknowledged legislators of the world."[37] But there is a crucial difference between Rorty's and Shelley's view of the poet. To be sure, both see the poet as "legislating" through the process of handing down to us our words and our languages. But for Shelley, the process is really more like *discovery* than creation, since poetical imagination puts the poet in touch with something larger than himself or herself.

> A poet participates in the eternal, the infinite, and the one; as far as relates to his conceptions, time and place and number are not. The grammatical forms which express the moods of time, and the difference of person, and the distinctions of place, are convertible with respect to the highest poetry without injuring it as poetry; and the choruses of Aeschylus, and the book of Job, and Dante's "Paradise," would afford, more than any other writings, examples of this fact, if the limits of this essay did not forbid citation.[38]

---

35. Rorty explicitly adopts Harold Bloom's description of the "strong poet." For a discussion of this type of character, see, especially, Harold Bloom, *The Anxiety of Influence* (Oxford: University Press, 1973).

36. Rorty, *Contingency, Irony, and Solidarity*, 20.

37. Percy Bysshe Shelley, "A Defense of Poetry," in Hazard Adams, *Critical Theory Since Plato* (New York: Harcourt Brace Jovanovich, 1977), 513.

38. Ibid., 500–01.

Shelley's comment captures, quite perfectly, the spirit of romanticism. By the early nineteenth century, the romantic poets were eagerly laying claim to the gift that Kant had, probably inadvertently, given them a
few decades earlier. In his *Critique of Judgment*, Kant argues that it is only
the Poet—and not the Philosopher or the Scientist—who can peer behind
the veil of appearances and glimpse the noumenal realm. For Kant, the
poets alone are the *true* "children of Nature." They are able to apprehend
directly the noumenal realm, and they are able to *translate* what they find
there into *art*, which all humans can *appreciate*, but only artists can *create*.

Rorty, of course, will have no truck with any of this. He wants to
deromanticize romanticism. This, in turn, is simply a part of his larger
project of "de-divinizing" the world, and "de-divinizing" the self. In place
of a world where Truth is out there, and in place of a "self" that has a stable "core," Rorty wants to substitute (across the board) the idea of contingency: the contingency of language, developed in chapter 1, and the
contingency of selfhood, developed in chapter 2 of *Contingency, Irony,
and Solidarity*. Rorty's point, as I understand it, is that by seeing our language and our selves as fully contingent creations, we are somehow better able to avoid "metaphysical" conundrums, and better able to sidestep
"deep" philosophical questions that only serve to waste our time. In the
second chapter of *Contingency, Irony, and Solidarity*—to which I now
turn—Rorty develops his redescription of the fully contingent self with
the help of three important intellectual figures: Friedrich Nietzsche, Sigmund Freud, and Harold Bloom.

To BEGIN, once again, at the beginning, recall my earlier invocation of
Aristotle's famous remark that philosophy begins in wonder. That "wonder," as Rorty correctly points out, is the awe of "finding oneself in a
world larger, stronger, nobler than oneself."[39] Rorty—following Nietzsche, and especially Harold Bloom—argues that poetry begins in fear,
specifically the fear that one will end his or her days in the world without having contributed anything of distinction, without having been *creative*. The strong poet's "anxiety of influence"—to use Harold Bloom's
terminology—is precisely the poet's "horror of finding himself to be only
a copy or a replica."[40] This, in turn, is precisely the poet's fear of finding

---

39. Rorty, *Contingency, Irony, and Solidarity*, 29.
40. Harold Bloom, *The Anxiety of Influence* (Oxford: University Press, 1973), 80.

that his or her most important creations (in art, politics, science, religion, or whatever) are not really his or her creations at all, but are instead the inevitable by-products of the unconscious *impressions* left on his or her mind by yet another, stronger, more *impressive* poet. Simply put, the strong poet is continually anxious about his or her *self*—specifically about the impressions left on that self by others. The strong poet wants to be free of the impressions of others; to then create his or her own impressions; and finally (as I will shortly argue), to impress *those* impressions on others. As Rorty (here following Nietzsche) points out, the process of becoming free of the impressions of others, and of thereby tracing home all the various idiosyncracies of one's individual self

> is identical with the process of inventing a new language—
> that is, of thinking up some new metaphors. For any *literal*
> description of one's individuality, which is to say any use of an
> inherited language-game for this purpose, will necessarily fail.
> One will not have traced [one's] idiosyncrasy home but will
> merely have managed to see it as not idiosyncratic after all, as
> a specimen reiterating a type, a copy or replica of something
> which has already been identified. To fail as a poet—and thus,
> for Nietzsche, to fail as a human being—is to accept *somebody*
> *else's description of oneself* [my emphasis], to execute a previ-
> ously prepared program, to write, at most, elegant variations
> on previously written poems.[41]

The invocation of Nietzsche here is crucial, for (on Rorty's account) it was Nietzsche who first explicitly suggested that we see our-selves not as *truth-seeking* animals, but rather as *self-creating* animals. If we accept this Nietzschean shift in perspective, we are then able to redescribe Western thought just as Rorty wants to redescribe it—along the lines of contingency as opposed to necessity. Notice how, in the fol-lowing two paragraphs, Rorty attempts to tie together his views on the contingencies of language and the self, with a Nietzschean view of phi-losophy and life.

> It was Nietzsche who first explicitly suggested that we drop the
> whole idea of "knowing the truth." His definition of truth as a
> "mobile army of metaphors" amounted to saying that the

---

41. Rorty, *Contingency, Irony, and Solidarity*, 27–28, emphasis in original.

whole idea of finding a single context for all human lives should be abandoned. His perspectivism amounted to the claim that the universe had no . . . determinate length. He hoped that once we realized that Plato's "true world" was just a fable, we would seek consolation, at the moment of death, not in having transcended the animal condition but in being that peculiar sort of dying animal who, by describing himself *in his own terms*, had created himself. More exactly, he would have created the only part of himself that mattered by constructing his own mind. To create one's mind is to create one's own language, rather than to let the length of one's mind be set by the language other human beings have left behind. . . .[42]

To put the same point in another way, the Western philosophical tradition thinks of a human life as a triumph just insofar as it breaks out of the world of time, appearance, and idiosyncratic opinion into another world—into the world of enduring truth. Nietzsche, by contrast, thinks the important boundary to cross is not the one separating time from atemporal truth but rather the one which divides the old from the new. He thinks a human life triumphant just insofar as it escapes from inherited descriptions of the contingencies of its existence and finds new descriptions. This is the difference between the will to truth and the will to self-overcoming. It is the difference between thinking of redemption as making contact with something larger and more enduring than oneself and redemption as Nietzsche describes it, "recreating all 'it was' into a 'thus I willed it.'"[43]

At this point one should be able to discern a relatively firm theoretical distinction between the philosopher and the strong poet. Very simply put, the one sees a world of necessity, the other a world of contingency. This distinction implies, in turn, a distinctive attitude toward the world on the part of each figure. The one seeks to be clear, candid, and morally straightforward. The other seeks (perhaps deliberately) to be enigmatic, clever in perhaps something of an evasive sense, and therefore (perhaps) morally ambiguous. But these distinctions in attitude, as real as they are,

---

42. Ibid., 27, emphasis added, footnote omitted.
43. Ibid., 29.

should not obscure some interesting similarities. In particular, it is interesting that the philosopher and the strong poet would, I suspect, each adopt the same attitude toward the other, and ultimately for the same reason. The philosopher would feel toward the strong poet a sense of disgust, engendered by what the philosopher would perceive as the strong poet's failure as a human being. In the philosopher's view, to reject the idea that humans must be responsible to a higher Truth, and to see one's moral language and one's self as products of contingency, is to adopt an attitude toward life so weak and irresponsible as to be both worthless and dangerous. Philosophers of the type I have been sketching (who obviously would have no use for Nietzsche) can sometimes be found suggesting that it is precisely the "Nietzschean" attitude toward life that is responsible for the Hitlers of the world and the sociopaths among us—not to mention the much less dangerous, though still despicable, garden-variety prevaricators, confidence men, and swindlers. The strong poet, on the other hand, would feel toward the philosopher a sense of disgust, engendered by what the strong poet would perceive as the philosopher's failure as a human being. In the strong poet's view, to embrace the idea that humans must be responsible to a higher Truth, and to see one's moral language and indeed one's very self as created by another (*even* by God or Nature), is to adopt an attitude toward life so weak and irresponsible as to be both worthless and dangerous. Where the philosopher might speak of the Nietzschean attitude toward life as productive of the Hitlers of the world, the strong poet will speak of the philosopher's attitude toward life as productive of the dogmatic, unreflective, "good soldiers" in Hitler's army. The strong poet will also point out that it is at least an open question as to whether dogmatists or relativists have, on the whole, wreaked more havoc on the planet. I can sum up my point in the following way: To adopt a worldview that holds that humans are responsible to some higher Truth, and then to adhere to that view (especially in the face of adversity), is indeed to merit a degree of respect, if not (in rare cases) a heroic status. Robert Bolt's "fictional" character Sir Thomas More is perhaps a paradigm case of a hero who is put to death precisely because he will not cease to believe that he is responsible to a higher Truth.[44] But—and this is the crucial point—to adopt a worldview that holds that humans are not responsible to some higher Truth—to believe, in other words, that humans must create their own truths—and then to adhere to this view (especially in the face of

---

44. I expand on this point in section 3 of chapter 2.

adversity), is indeed to merit an *equal* degree of respect, if not (in rare cases) a heroic status. The problem, of course, is that heroes (and even just respectable individuals) of the second sort tend not to be members of large, traditional communities, and so it might be difficult for those of us in such communities to afford them the respect they deserve. In fact, these second sort of individuals tend to be alienated from most communities, and especially from the communities into which they were born. Often, in the late twentieth century, they tend to be artists. (I imagine that many such artists find solace in the belief that prophets are indeed without honor in their own land.) To be sure, today artists rarely live in fear of their lives.[45] But it may sometimes be easier to die as a member of a particular community than to live as a member of no particular community.

If, then, one *does* decide to stand apart from his or her community, and to attempt (as Nietzsche exhorts) to recreate himself or herself, one may naturally ask how, *exactly*, does a self create itself? To the extent that all selves are socialized into a particular language and a particular culture, and to the extent that Western culture is still largely foundationalist and metaphysical, are we Westerners not all condemned by birth to be common philosophers, as opposed to uncommon strong poets? Perhaps not. And, if not, it is (on Rorty's account) Sigmund Freud whom we have most to thank. For, as Rorty puts it, "Freud's importance is that he helps us accept, and put to work, [the] Nietzschean and Bloomian sense of what it is to be a full-fledged human being." He helps us do this precisely because "[h]e de-universalizes the moral sense, making it as idiosyncratic as the poet's inventions. He thus lets us see the moral consciousness as historically conditioned, a product as much of time and chance as of political or aesthetic consciousness."[46] Rorty goes on to claim that the *specific* utility of Freud adheres in the fact that

> [h]e helps explain how someone can be both a tender mother and a merciless concentration-camp guard, or be a just and temperate magistrate and also a chilly, rejecting father. By associating conscientiousness with cleanliness, and by associating both not only with obsessional neurosis but (as he does elsewhere) with the religious impulse and with the urge to con-

---

45. But one should not forget the tragic case of author Salman Rushdie. Strong poets would undoubtedly point out that it is often philosophers, and especially religious fundamentalists, who do the most persecuting.

46. Rorty, *Contingency, Irony, and Solidarity*, 30.

struct philosophical systems, he breaks down all the traditional distinctions between the higher and the lower, the essential and the accidental, the central and the peripheral. He leaves us with a self which is a tissue of contingencies rather than an at least potentially well-ordered system of faculties. . . .

. . . Further, he gives each of us the equipment to construct our own private vocabulary of moral deliberation. For terms like "infantile" or "sadistic" or "obsessional" or "paranoid," unlike the names of vices and virtues which we inherit from the Greeks and the Christians, have very specific and very different resonances for each individual who uses them: They bring to our minds resemblances and differences between ourselves and very particular people (our parents, for example) and between the present situation and very particular situations of our past. They enable us to sketch a narrative of our own development, our idiosyncratic moral struggle, which is far more finely textured, far more custom-tailored to our individual case than the moral vocabulary which the philosophical tradition offered us.[47]

Two aspects of the above quotation are striking, and both have to do with Rorty's exclusively *private* and *individualistic* reading of Freud. Consider first Rorty's claim that Freud provides us with the "equipment to construct our own private vocabulary of moral deliberation." I take it by this he means to imply a strong distinction between our private image of ourselves and our public acts. If he does mean to imply this, he is being perfectly consistent with a 1986 article he wrote entitled "Freud and Moral Reflection." There he said, "Freud, in particular, has no contribution to make to social theory. His domain is the portion of morality that cannot be identified with 'culture': it is the private life, the search for a character, the attempt of individuals to be reconciled with themselves (and, in the case of some exceptional individuals, to make their lives works of art)."[48]

Now consider that something very similar to this public/private distinction is implied in Rorty's reading of how Freud helps to supplant our older moral traditions. Specifically, where the Judeo–Christian tradition

---

47. Ibid., 32.
48. Richard Rorty, "Freud and Moral Reflection," in *Essays On Heidegger and Others: Philosophical Papers, Volume II* (Cambridge: University Press, 1991), 154.

asserts that we are all sinners, Freud asserts that we are all neurotics. But the *crucial* difference—if I understand Rorty correctly—is that the Judeo–Christian tradition thinks of sin as merely an irrational expression of our *common, undifferentiated,* base passions, while Freud thinks of neuroses as complex phenomenon that serve to make us who we are as *distinctive* individuals. Additionally, the Judeo–Christian tradition wants to see the moral struggle as carried on between a facility called reason (which comes from above, and therefore understands the higher, intellectual, aspects of life) and passion (which comes from below, and therefore understands nothing that we should call intellectual or complex). Rorty's Freud, on the other hand, wants to level the distinction between reason and passion, and thus sees the moral struggle not so much as a struggle, but rather as a way of accommodating various different, competing interests, none of which have an a priori claim to moral superiority. On this view, Freud rejects the simplistic notion that morality involves a straightforward battle between a disembodied intellect and a mindless passion. Instead, he sees the intellect (or reason) as much less disembodied than we might wish to think, while he simultaneously sees the passions as always more richly complex than we can intellectually understand. As Rorty points out (quite correctly, I think), what is so interesting and valuable about Freud is that he "spends his time exhibiting the extraordinary sophistication, subtlety, and wit of our unconscious strategies. He thereby makes it possible for us to see science and poetry, genius and psychosis—and, most importantly, morality and prudence—not as products of distinct faculties but as alternative modes of adaptation."[49]

One of the nice aspects of Rorty's interpretation of Freud is that it focuses our attention on the individual *qua* individual. Certainly another equally nice aspect of this view is that, by positing a complex and sophisticated unconscious, it allows us to answer the question I posed earlier—specifically, how can any of us hope to become strong poets when we are socialized into a boring, foundationalist culture? On Rorty's reading of Freud, the answer is that, by virtue of our creative unconscious, we already *are* strong poets, we are just not conscious of this. This allows Rorty to sum up his entire discussion of Nietzsche, Freud, and strong poets in the following way:

---

49. Rorty, *Contingency, Irony, and Solidarity,* 33.

What makes Freud more useful and more plausible than Nietzsche is that he does not relegate the vast majority of humanity to the status of dying animals. For Freud's account of unconscious fantasy shows us how to see every human life as a poem—or, more exactly, every human life not so racked by pain as to be unable to learn language nor so immersed in toil as to have no leisure in which to generate a self-description. He sees every such life as an attempt to clothe itself in its own metaphors. As Philip Rieff puts it, "Freud democratized genius by giving everyone a creative unconscious."[50]

On that happy note, we come to the end of Rorty's discussion of the contingency of selfhood, and we find that, once we dispense with Judeo–Christianity's banal vocabulary of virtue and vice, and once we conflate reason and passion, we all possess a creative unconscious that makes us the equal of poets past. Surely no theory that so easily exalts its believers (or at least their unconsciouses) will lack for believers. And, as one reviewer of *Contingency, Irony, and Solidarity* has put it, Rorty is sure to have many believers.[51]

But things may not be quite as ideal as they seem. Up to this point I have attempted to recount and explain Rorty's notion of contingency as he details it in the first two chapters of *Contingency, Irony, and Solidarity*. For the most part, my intention has not been explicitly critical, although we have seen how certain problems in Rorty's theory present themselves, without much effort on the part of the critic, almost as soon as the theory is explained. With respect to the contingency of language, we encountered the problem of accounting for the human agent *qua* agent. It was hard to understand how Rorty could say we "should drop" various large and abstract ideas within our language, when he simultaneously seemed to be suggesting that we do not (at least consciously) decide to use or abandon these very same ideas. Simply put, he cannot seem to decide whether we speak languages, or languages speak us. Rorty, of course, would attempt to evade this admittedly "metaphysical" conundrum by labeling it an "unprofitable" topic for discussion. Perhaps it is. But I do not think that Rorty can so easily evade "metaphysical" questions that

---

50. Ibid., 35, footnote omitted.
51. See Jenny Teichman, "Don't Be Cruel or Reasonable" a review of *Contingency, Irony, and Solidarity*, in *New York Times Book Review*, April 23, 1989, p. 30.

specifically implicate our view of ourselves. These seem to demand closer scrutiny. I want, therefore, to pay special *critical* attention to Rorty's discussion of the contingency of selfhood. Specifically, I would like now to raise some objections to Rorty's view—objections that I think go a long way in calling into question the persuasiveness of his redescription.

To begin with, recall Rorty's Nietzschean assertion that the strong poet can *only* become free of the impressions of others—can only claim his or her individuality—by "inventing a new language." "For," as Rorty says, "any *literal* description of one's individuality, which is to say any use of an inherited language-game for this purpose, will necessarily fail." I take Rorty at his word here. It is he who emphasizes the term *literal*. I find it passing strange, then, that Rorty would recommend Freud to prospective strong poets. Surely *all* of Freud's "metaphors"—his descriptions of the Oedipal complex, of psychic defense mechanisms like reaction-formation or sublimation, and so forth—have become *completely* literalized in late twentieth century Western culture. Once again, it is Rorty himself who explicitly recognizes this fact when he writes, "It is unlikely that Freud's metaphors could have been picked up, used, and *literalized* at any earlier period."[52] Literalization is, of course, largely a function of time. There was undoubtedly a time—at the turn of the century, and perhaps for some decades afterward—when the Oedipal complex had strange and fascinating connotations. But today, in a culture dominated by what Alasdair MacIntyre has described as the Rich Aesthete, the Manager, and the *Therapist*, no self-respecting strong poet would dream (no pun intended) of describing himself or herself as the product of such a literalized metaphor.[53]

Another way of putting this point is to say that the contingency of self demands much more of the self than Rorty seems to think. It is instructive that Rorty swerves from the Nietzschean implications of the

---

52. Rorty, *Contingency, Irony, and Solidarity*, 39, emphasis added.

53. See Alasdair MacIntyre, *After Virtue* (Notre Dame: University of Notre Dame Press, 1984), especially 30–35. On whether a culture dominated by the types of individuals MacIntyre sketches is desirable, Rorty writes, "I would welcome a culture dominated by 'the Rich Aesthete, the Manager, and the Therapist' so long as *everybody* who wants to gets to be an aesthete (and, if not rich, as comfortably off as most—as rich as the Managers can manage, guided by Rawls' Difference Principle)" (Rorty, "Freud and Moral Reflection," 159, emphasis in original). As far as I can see, this does nothing to answer my argument that a truly strong poet could never describe himself or herself in Freud's literalized metaphors.

contingency of self—implications that would demand a more radical view of this contingency—toward a more comfortable, Freudian view. Indeed, Rorty's view comes perilously close to reflecting little more than his own leisured, liberal, agnostic view of the world—a view enjoyed (and perhaps only enjoyable) by relaxed intellectuals who, having given up on religion, have instead taken to the comforts of analysis to help them "find" themselves. Gone in all of this is the struggle—the *agon*— as Bloom puts it, which is the true distinguishing mark of the strong poet.

If what I have said so far is correct, Rorty's discussion of Freud—a discussion that comprises fully half of the second chapter of *Contingency, Irony, and Solidarity*—is at best irrelevant and at worst counter to his central thesis about contingency and the strong poet. But what if we just set Freud aside? What if we return to Rorty's main point, that strong poets must become individuals, and they must do so *on their own terms*? Would such a move rescue the persuasiveness of Rorty's description of the contingency of selfhood?

I think not, for I think that Rorty fundamentally misunderstands the way in which a self (contingent or otherwise) becomes a self. Again, the *agon* is crucially relevant here. To see why, recall my earlier assertion that the strong poet wants to be free of the impressions of others; to then create his or her own impressions; and finally to impress those impressions on others. Rorty seems to follow this description until the last part—the part about the strong poet needing to impress his or her impressions on others. In the very last sentence of the second chapter of *Contingency, Irony, and Solidarity*, Rorty acknowledges "the conscious need of the strong poet to *demonstrate* that he is not a copy or replica," and then argues that this need is merely a "special form" of the unconscious need of the rest of us to "come to terms with" the various contingencies that made us who we are.[54] But Rorty seems to think that there is not very much (of a struggle, at least) involved in the process of demonstration. To the contrary, I would argue that to demonstrate one is not a copy or a replica—indeed, even just to come to terms with who one is— is inextricably connected with the process of forcing others to see one as one wants to be seen. Again, Rorty's privatized, minimalist view of Freud seems unhelpful with respect to this struggle—although I am far from convinced that Rorty interprets Freud correctly. In regard to the relationship between Freud and Nietzsche, and with respect to the general

---

54. Rorty, *Contingency, Irony, and Solidarity*, 43.

question of identity, I tend to follow Camille Paglia, the provocative disciple of Harold Bloom. In her 1990 book *Sexual Personae*, Paglia writes, "As Freud, Nietzsche's heir, asserts, *identity is conflict.* Each generation drives it plow over the bones of the dead."[55] What Rorty seems not to appreciate is that this conflict must be social, and not merely private, precisely because language is a social creation. Examples of identity struggles within cultures are almost literally infinite. To demonstrate my Paglian point against Rorty, I will select, and very briefly describe, one such struggle in our own culture.

Consider, then, the case of contemporary feminism, and specifically one of its most prominent strong poets, Catharine MacKinnon, about whom Rorty has written somewhat extensively.[56] MacKinnon's determined attempts materially to eliminate, and socially to "delegitimate," pornography would resemble attempts by conservatives and religious leaders to censor pornography, *but for* MacKinnon's unique and critically important focus on what pornography does to the identity of women *as* women. MacKinnon is wholly unconcerned with what pornography does to the state of men's souls—which, as she correctly points out, is usually the only concern that conservatives and religious leaders bring to the pornography debate. Her work, as she says, "is not about good and evil or virtue and perversity but about power and powerlessness."[57] The power on point is the power to construct one's own iden-

---

55. Camille Paglia, *Sexual Personae: Art and Decadence From Nefertiti to Emily Dickinson* (New Haven: Yale University Press, 1990), p. 2, emphasis added. Richard King, in an article responding to Rorty's "Freud and Moral Reflection," makes something of the same point, but specifically with respect to Rorty. King writes, "As it stands, Rorty takes the bite out of Freud's description of the self. Where Rorty sees a conversationally pluralist self as the basis for an analogous political and cultural order, for Freud, the conflicted self mirrors a conflict-ridden political and cultural order. The pathos of the relationship Freud sees between the individual and the collective consists in the difficulty the self has in participating in the conversation that should be at the center of our common life" (see Richard King, "Self-realization and Solidarity: Rorty and the Judging Self," in *Pragmatism's Freud: The Moral Disposition of Psychoanalysis*, eds. Joseph H. Smith and William Kerrigan [Baltimore: Johns Hopkins University Press, 1986], 41).

56. See Richard Rorty, "Feminism and Pragmatism," *Michigan Quarterly Review* (spring 1991): 231–58.

57. Catharine A. MacKinnon, "'More Than Simply a Magazine': Playboy's Money," in *Feminism Unmodified: Discourses on Life and Law* (Cambridge: Harvard University Press, 1987), 135.

tity. In MacKinnon's view, pornography strips women of that power. As she says, "Men treat women as who they see women as being. Pornography constructs who that is. Men's power over women means that the way men see women defines who women can be." And she continues, "Pornography dispossesses women of the power of which, in the same act, it possesses men: the power of sexual, hence gender, definition. Perhaps a human being, for gender purposes, is someone who controls the social definition of sexuality."[58]

Now, if one wanted to personalize the struggle over pornography from roughly the mid-fifties to the present, one could view it as a battle between two strong poets: Catharine MacKinnon and Hugh Hefner. In addition to creating the magazine, Hefner "treated" readers of *Playboy* to a series of editorials, run in the early sixties, which described in detail the "Playboy Philosophy." Reading the first lines of the first editorial, one is struck by the almost lyrical way Hefner describes his endeavor. He begins by noting that *Playboy* magazine was "forged with much youthful zeal by a small group of dedicated iconoclasts who shared a publishing dream. . . ."[59] He then goes on to define the term *playboy*—and in so doing, of course, to define the larger terms *men* and *women*. MacKinnon argues that both Hefner's "philosophy" and his magazine explicitly subordinate women by helping to construct a social reality that defines them as beings that enjoy sexual submission. Unfortunately, as MacKinnon concedes, *Playboy* magazine is widely accepted in our culture, and this acceptance augments its power, in an ever-increasing, vicious spiral. As MacKinnon succinctly puts it, "Playboy is pornography and makes pornography legitimate."[60] That is why I earlier described MacKinnon's project as an attempt materially to eliminate, and socially to delegitimate, pornography. MacKinnon, at least, recognizes that her project requires the *destruction* of the social reality that *Playboy* magazine helps maintain. It requires the death (by delegitimation) of Hugh Hefner *as a strong poet*. Again, MacKinnon states, "I want to increase women's power over sexuality, hence over our social definition and treatment. I think that means decreasing the pornographers' power over it."[61]

In a narrow sense, I hope that the foregoing discussion has at least demonstrated that MacKinnon's philosophy and Hefner's own playboy

---

58. MacKinnon, "Not a Moral Issue," in *Feminism Unmodified*, 148, 158.
59. Hugh M. Hefner, "The Playboy Philosophy," pt. I, *Playboy*, December 1962, 73.
60. MacKinnon, "'More Than Simply a Magazine': Playboy's Money," 137.
61. Ibid., 140.

"philosophy" cannot peacefully coexist in the same culture. Each seeks the other's destruction. It is not just a private matter. It is a social "war" over the identity of women and men. Rorty, following Nietzsche, agrees that we must escape other individuals' (or, more generally, society's) literal descriptions of ourselves in order to be a self. MacKinnon believes that the society in which she presently lives quite literally describes her as simply a sex object. To be sure, this description may very well be the result of (or at least sustained by) a number of "sheer contingencies"—like, perhaps, the infantile state of Hugh Hefner's psyche, the concentration of wealth and power in the hands of males, and so forth. Nonetheless, MacKinnon feels she must (at least) be free of *this* particular description in order to have a self. And, in her view, being free of this description requires that others not describe her in ways she does not wish to be described. Otherwise put: Coming to terms with who she is requires that others adopt her important terms.

This leads to a broader claim that I hope also to have illustrated with this example: Not everyone can be a strong poet. Even if we all do possess a wonderfully creative unconscious, most of us still define ourselves in terms that others have created. We define ourselves as, for example, "Christians" or "liberals" or "playboys" or "feminists," not to mention "men" or "women." These terms are, in turn, given meaning through the struggle among strong poets—the makers of our language—the very individuals Rorty calls the vanguard of the species. I am not necessarily applauding this fact. But given that language is a social creation, it does not seem that it could be otherwise. I propose, then, that we see Rorty's interpretation and invocation of Freud as merely an intellectual wrong turn down a descriptive path that ultimately leads nowhere, and now return to Rorty's more accurate interpretation and invocation of Nietzsche. In so doing, I do not think we *must* relegate the vast majority of humanity (i.e., those who are not strong poets) to the status of dying animals, as did Nietzsche. But we must realize, as Rorty seems not to, that self-creation is in large measure a struggle for public recognition. On that somewhat restrained note, I conclude this brief critique of Rorty's notion of the contingency of selfhood and turn now to some final remarks about the ironist.

EARLIER I NOTED that the strong poet is someone very similar to the ironist. Rorty says essentially this when he notes that ironists "take naturally to the line of thought developed in the first two chapters of [*Contingency,*

Irony, and Solidarity]."[62] Both the strong poet and the ironist (and, to be sure, the edifying philosopher) take the view that language is fully contingent. This leads naturally to the view that our very selves—our final vocabularies—are also fully contingent. But *this* view might threaten to obliterate completely the self. Under the white-hot scrutiny of this theoretical view, it might seem that the human subject simply melts away and is gradually replaced by an enormously expansive view of *language*. Rorty's intense emphasis on the *conversation,* and the post–structuralist's equally intense emphasis on the *text,* might be seen as working to advance this very end. But now I want to argue that Rorty actually resists the *complete* dissolution of the subject. His chapter on the contingency of self turns us back, in an odd way, toward the individual. By locating that chapter around the Nietzsche–Freud–Bloom axis, Rorty preserves some important measure of the autonomy of the self. For none of the three figures Rorty draws on would—properly interpreted—have much use for the radical post–structuralist abandonment of the subject. This may be especially the case with Harold Bloom. As James Aune explains in a very interesting comment,

> Bloom is *not* to be classed with people such as Paul de Man and Jacques Derrida, who contend that linguistic meaning is fundamentally undecidable. Rather, Bloom argues that meaning, any meaning, occurs as part of an agon or struggle with previous meaning. He thus does not take part in the post–structuralist attempt to eliminate the human subject from the "human sciences." Bloom is the quintessential Emersonian American in that he wishes to restore the priority of the individual speaking voice and its attempt to create the saving illusion of self-reliance.[63]

I think Rorty wants something similar to this. His description of the ironist is, after all, designed to clear some imaginative space *for the individual.* But—once again, and finally—Rorty ignores, or drastically minimizes, the *agon,* the central metaphor in Bloom (and perhaps in Nietzsche and Freud). In an attempt to make the world safe for ironism, Rorty swerves from the essentially social character of the struggle to

---

62. Rorty, *Contingency, Irony, and Solidarity,* 74.
63. James Arnt Aune, "Burke's Late Blooming: Trope, Defense, and Rhetoric," *Quarterly Journal of Speech* 69 (1983): 329, emphasis in original.

become a self, and instead provides us with a privatized vision of irony, wherein our struggle is now located on the couch, with the aid of a comforting therapist. In the final analysis, then, Rorty's vision of ironism asks relatively little of us. His vision of *liberalism*, however, asks much more. It is to a critique of that vision that I now turn.

2

Liberalism

Above and Below the Surface

To my mind, there is simply no escaping the fact that in writing *Contingency, Irony, and Solidarity*, Richard Rorty has committed an act of political philosophy. Now some political philosophies, like John Rawls', are elegant in the *forceful simplicity* of their key idea. Other political philosophies, like Alasdair MacIntyre's, derive their persuasive appeal from the *august traditions* with which they associate themselves. Still other political philosophies, like Roberto Unger's, gain an appreciative hearing because of the *productive novelty* they bring to old questions. Finally, some political philosophies, like Rorty's own, capture our attention through the *sheer audacity* of their redescriptive endeavors. For the past two and a half centuries, liberalism has been the defining political tradition in the West. Liberalism has been described in a number of ways throughout these centuries, but never quite in the way Rorty redescribes it. In the Introduction, I provided a brief sketch of some of the central principles of liberalism. It shall be my purpose in this chapter to provide an in-depth explanation and critique of Rorty's specific redescription of what it means to be a liberal. In section 1, I examine Rorty's provocative claim that liberalism consists *principally* in the desire not to be cruel. I argue that this definition works only if one understands cruelty in a physical, as opposed to a psychological, sense. In other words, Rorty's definition works only if we "stay on the surface." I conclude the first section by

demonstrating that Rorty refuses to do just this. Section 2 then takes up
the consequences of moving below the surface. I argue that Rorty's linkage of liberalism with the desire to avoid engaging in acts of humiliation
renders his political philosophy theoretically incoherent. Finally, section 3 attempts to bring together some of the larger ideas in these first two
chapters by examining the relationship between liberalism and ironism.

Liberalism and Cruelty

In the introduction to *Contingency, Irony, and Solidarity*, Rorty offers a
somewhat particular definition of liberalism that is, however, apparently
shared by at least one other philosopher. Rorty writes, "I borrow my definition of 'liberal' from Judith Shklar, who says that liberals are the people who think that cruelty is the worst thing we do."[1] I presume that Rorty
has borrowed this definition from Shklar's 1984 book *Ordinary Vices*. In
what I consider the relevant passage, Shklar writes, "It seems to me that
liberal and humane people, of whom there are many among us, would,
if they were asked to rank the vices, put cruelty first. Intuitively they
would choose cruelty as the worst thing we do."[2] Immediately after asserting this, Shklar adds that once such liberal and humane people had
made this choice, "[t]hey would then quickly find themselves faced with
all the paradoxes and puzzles that Montaigne encountered."[3] The sixteenth-century French philosopher Montaigne is something of a "hero"
in *Ordinary Vices*, largely because he made the investigation into cruelty
an important part of his philosophy. Primary among the puzzles and
paradoxes Montaigne encountered in his investigations is the still unresolved question: What does it mean to be cruel? Shklar advances something of a working definition when she notes that cruelty is "the willful
inflicting of physical pain on a weaker being in order to cause anguish
and fear."[4] Rorty seems implicitly to accept this working definition. But
he supplements it by including as acts of cruelty the willful infliction of
a certain kind of nonphysical pain called *humiliation*. As I have said,
Rorty's *specific* understanding of the link between cruelty and humilia-

---

1. Richard Rorty, *Contingency, Irony, and Solidarity* (Cambridge: Cambridge University
   Press, 1989), xv.
2. Judith N. Shklar, *Ordinary Vices* (Cambridge: Harvard University Press, 1984), 44.
3. Ibid.
4. Ibid., 8.

tion is both the central, and indeed the most problematic, aspect of his notion of liberalism. For now, however, I want to remain focused on the *general* aspects of Rorty's liberalism—a liberalism that has at its core the simple desire to avoid cruelty (in whatever form it takes).

It strikes me that this definition of liberalism amounts, ultimately, to little more than a platitude; but, as platitudes go, a very powerful one. To appreciate the strategic advantage Rorty gains with this redescriptive maneuver, one might begin by asking: If a liberal is one who believes that it *is* the case that "cruelty is the worst thing we do," then is a nonliberal one who believes that it *is not* the case that "cruelty is the worst thing we do"? Strictly speaking (that is, speaking like an analytic philosopher), yes. But it is unsophisticated, and just plain silly, to think that what distinguishes liberals from *most* others who would not call themselves liberals (and, indeed, whom Rorty would not call liberals) is the fact that, in the end, liberals are most worried about not being cruel, and nonliberals are most worried about something else. Rather, it is more likely the case that (again, for most individuals) the dividing line is over the unresolved question I alluded to earlier: What (*exactly*) does it mean to be cruel?

One could imagine Rorty responding to this by insisting that it is *not* a definitional question about what counts as a particular act of cruelty *as such*, but rather a question of final vocabularies. A liberal, he might persist, is one for whom the avoidance of cruelty *is an end in itself*. On this view, the nonliberal—say, a Christian—is one for whom the avoidance of cruelty *could* in some cases be subordinated to some higher goal like (in this case) obtaining salvation for oneself or another. The suggestion that Christians can be seen as non (if not *anti*) liberal may strike the modern Western reader as at least highly questionable, and perhaps insulting. In using this example, I am following Shklar, who follows Montaigne, who, of course, was writing during a time when Christians were doing, in retrospect, some pretty nasty things. We modern Westerners are heirs to what is now a largely secular (in the narrow sense of nonreligious, not in the broader sense of antifoundationalist) culture, and so we no longer burn heretics. But to imply, as do Rorty, Shklar, and (in a slightly different sense) Montaigne, that there is, or can be, an interesting difference between Christians and liberals on the question of cruelty, is simply to misunderstand the intelligent Christian's position. For there could *only* be a difference here if the Christian could *imagine* responding affirmatively to the question, "If you knew *for certain* that an act of cruelty toward another would bring about his or her salvation, would you undertake such an act?" Far from responding affirmatively to this question, the Christian *qua* Christian could not even make sense of it. This is so, because for the Christian, the Platonist, or any other "metaphysician," what is ultimately desired (salvation, the just society, or something else) is, by definition, good (hence not cruel), *and* what is cruel is, by definition, not good and hence not ultimately desired. Which is a complicated way of saying that for most people, when you come right down to it, Truth and Goodness are one.

To drive home this point, consider Shklar's ill-phrased assertion that, "A benevolent, medicinal, kindly meant cruelty is, moreover, a Christian duty, especially when used to return the wayward to the true faith."[5] Now, I am not sure if Shklar thinks that today's Christians include such "kindly meant cruelty" among their worldly duties, or whether she is restricting this assertion to Christians of the past. I am sure that whichever she means, she is wrong on both counts. Recall that in Shklar's own definition (and here I am being *extremely* charitable in my interpretation of this definition), an act is cruel *only* if *any* of the reasons for which it is done includes the desire to produce anguish and fear in a weaker being.[6] Given this definition, it would be convenient for our three self-professed liberals (Shklar, Rorty, and Montaigne) if the Christian were to say something like, "I am willfully inflicting physical pain on this weaker being in order to cause anguish and fear, and in the further hope that, in so doing, I can cause this wayward soul to return to the true faith." Arguably—on the basis both of the charitable interpretation of Shklar's definition of cruelty presented earlier and on Rorty's linkage of this definition with liberalism—such a remark could be seen as evidence of a nonliberal nature on the part of the Christian. After all, by putting it in just this way, the Christian has conceded that the use of physical pain to induce anguish and fear is an acceptable means to some desirable end. This is something a liberal could not say. But it is odd to think that a Christian would (or could) put it just that way. Surely Saint Ignatius Loyola, for example, was as subtle a thinker as Montaigne—or for that matter, Rorty and Shklar. Indeed, I imagine that what *was* said went something like, "Because it is self-

---

5. Ibid., 240.
6. It is not clear from Shklar's definition whether she means to include as acts of cruelty only those acts that are undertaken (against a weaker being) for the *sole* purpose of producing anguish and fear, and for no other reason. Or, whether she means to define cruelty in the broader sense, as I have in my interpretation.

evidently cruel to stand by while an individual deprives himself or herself of the opportunity of salvation, I am willfully inflicting physical pain on this weaker (in several senses) being, not because I wish to cause him or her anguish and fear, but rather because I wish to return him or her to the road to salvation." The claim that this second sentence more accurately reflects what the sixteenth-century Christian *really* thought is certainly debatable. But it is not a claim with which Rorty—and here we must be careful to restrict the discussion to Rorty only—would disagree. Indeed, Rorty would probably concede that many sixteenth-century Christians sincerely believed that their treatment of heretics was not cruel. Just as he would (I think) concede that, say, devout Muslims in this century believe that it is not cruel (indeed it is in their minds an expression of love) to mete out to "those who have gone astray" the just punishments prescribed in the Quar'an. Are such individuals (the sixteenth-century Christians and the present-day Muslims) then liberals? Based upon what has been demonstrated so far—that is, based upon Rorty's acceptance of Shklar's definition of cruelty—Rorty would be forced to answer "yes." All of which suggests, at this point in my explication, that particular acts of cruelty simply are not central to Rorty's (and Shklar's) notion of liberalism. Rather, the *intentions* of an individual who engages in acts that we suspect may be cruel—questions about whether such an individual actually desires to induce anguish and fear—appear to be what is at issue for liberals.

Appearances, of course, can be deceiving. In a moment we shall see how Rorty attempts to slip free of the position he is put in by adopting Shklar's definition of cruelty. For now, however, it seems that we must invite into the fold of liberals all *devout* Christians and Muslims, as well as all *genuine* Platonists and any other *sincere* metaphysicians whose worldviews link the True with the Good. But such a move would so attenuate the definition of a liberal as to render it almost useless. *It would become a definition that did not define.* With these inclusions granted, the only individuals who would now count as nonliberals would be those whose ultimate vision of themselves and their world—whose final vocabulary—was so structured as to *preclude* any connection between their desires and the good of their fellows. The portrait of a totally self-obsessed artist, particularly as a young man, might be an instance of nonliberalism. But, fortunately, there are few of these people around. Certainly a more common personality type within the cultures Rorty is addressing—advanced capitalist societies like our own—is that of the self-obsessed "young urban professional." Notice, however, that such an individual would, under Rorty's definition, qualify as a liberal if, as is *surely* the case for those who came to political consciousness under the reign of Reaganomics, he or she could sincerely tell himself or herself some story about the world that tied his or her own personal gain into some larger gain for society. We could easily imagine such "liberals" arguing against welfare programs, affirmative action, and the like, all because, to those thoroughly schooled in Reaganomics, these programs really are cruel. After all, such programs only foster dependency and thereby rob recipients of their dignity. Similarly, one could image a "liberal" arguing (as does Ambrose Evans–Pritchard in a provocative article in *The National Interest*) that nineteenth-century imperialism was indeed a benevolent undertaking on the part of Westerners, because it saved the savages from themselves.[7] Obviously the point I am raising here has nothing to do with the question of whether any of these beliefs is correct in some moral or ethical sense. My point is that if these individuals can qualify as liberals, it is hard to see who would not. Even the *totally* self-obsessed artist who *completely* identified his or her own good with some cosmic good would qualify as a liberal. Simply put, if we accept Rorty's definition (as he borrows it from Shklar) there will be *very* few *self-professed* nonliberals around.

I conclude from all of this that Shklar's definition of cruelty cannot do the work Rorty wishes it to do. It cannot be used to make any meaningful distinctions. So it seems, *pace* Shklar, that the *real* issue in the whole debate between liberals and nonliberals is not about believing or not believing that cruelty is the worst thing we do. Rather, the real issue is still what it has been for two and a half millennia—namely, what counts as being cruel. Any effort to answer this question will necessarily involve one in an examination of various "metaphysical" issues: What is the relationship between the mind and the body? What does this relationship imply about our human capacity to feel pain? What are our obligations toward others with respect to alleviating their pain? And so forth. Rorty's attempt to opt out of this discussion by appropriating Shklar's definition strikes me as, at best, an attempt to substitute platitudes and slogans for well thought out philosophical ideas. At worst, it strikes me as a clever ploy to seize the redescriptive "high ground," so to speak. "We liberals," one can imagine Rorty confidently saying, "just loathe

---

7. See Ambrose Evans–Pritchard, "A Good Word for Imperialism," *The National Interest* (fall 1989): 63–70.

being cruel. Others? Well. . . ." What tempts me to think that Rorty is being disingenuous in his use of the term *liberal* is the fact that, while energetically linking liberalism to Shklar's strategically powerful definition of cruelty, he refuses to embrace the implications of this definition. Specifically, he refuses to include as liberals many of the individuals mentioned earlier—sixteenth-century Christians, for instance, and Loyola, by name. But his refusal to grant these figures liberal status is not based on any coherent interpretation of Shklar's definition of cruelty. Indeed, in my reading, there could not be any coherent interpretation of this definition that successfully managed to *exclude* the individuals just mentioned. Rather, Rorty's refusal to see these figures as liberals is plainly based on a rejection of Shklar's definition—in particular, on a rejection that *intentionality* should play a part in determining whether one's actions are cruel.

To GET CLEAR on this last point, I turn now to an examination of two *distinct* versions of liberalism that coexist (not always peacefully) in Rorty's political philosophy. The first version, the one based on Shklar's definition of cruelty, purports to tell us something essential about the mind-set of liberals: they put the avoidance of cruelty first. This version provides Rorty with a powerful redescriptive "stick" with which to beat unsuspecting nonliberals. The second version pretty much dispenses with questions of *intentionality* altogether, to the extent that such questions arise in the public realm. This more prosaic version provides Rorty with the ability to do the mundane but necessary work of determining, within a reasonable degree of specificity, just which *actions* should be allowed in a liberal society, and which should not.

Unfortunately, these two versions are often at odds. The conflict comes over the issue of intentionality. Version one, the version Rorty develops from Shklar's definition, tells us that one is cruel *if and only if* one inflicts physical pain (on a weaker being) while *consciously intending* to cause that being anguish and fear. But this definition is far too broad. It excludes almost no one, because almost everyone can (and sincerely does) construct for himself or herself a final vocabulary in which his or her own "well intentioned" actions are not seen as cruel.[8] Here,

---

8. Recall, from chapter 1, that *everyone* constructs a final vocabulary. This applies to metaphysicians as well as ironists. Ironists, however, have continuing *doubts* about their vocabulary.

"well intentioned" means something like "properly constructed, so as not to seem inconsistent or aberrational with the remainder of the vocabulary." So, for example, a devout Christian who killed someone *while in a fit of passion* would *not* be performing a well intentioned act within his Christian final vocabulary. On the other hand, the same Christian who killed someone *while participating in a "just war"* might be performing a well intentioned act.

Version two gets around this problem of overbreadth by simply dismissing questions of intentionality altogether. It is this version that has been adopted (more or less) by Western societies since the Enlightenment. It brackets questions of intentionality and says that certain actions are cruel, regardless of the intentions of the actor who undertakes them.

In his recent political writings, including *Contingency, Irony, and Solidarity*, Rorty can often be found defending this second, more traditional, view of liberal politics. His defense is grounded upon the thoroughly pragmatic argument that a liberalism so conceived has at least one major advantage over other political theories: it works in large pluralistic societies like our own. It works precisely because, in Rorty's view, we can, for the purposes of social arrangements, make a coherent distinction between actions and the intentions behind these actions. Once this distinction is made, intentions can, again in Rorty's view, be "privatized" in a way that actions like cruelty toward another cannot. Obviously, this view requires, in turn, that we can make a reasonably coherent distinction between the public and private realm. To be sure, this is not always an easy task. Indeed, modern societies have become so interdependent that distinguishing the public from the private has become a matter of fine distinction. But—paradoxically—it is just because modern societies are so interdependent that such a distinction has become even more important. At any rate, once this distinction *is* made, *all* intentions (which, by definition, are wholly within the private realm), as well as those actions that are also wholly within the private realm (if indeed *any* action can be said to be wholly a private matter), simply drop out. Those remaining actions that *do* fall within the domain of the public realm are now all we need to consider for the purposes of maintaining social order.

When Rorty is defending this second version of liberalism, we hear him sounding very much like a nineteenth-century liberal with the social conscience of a late twentieth-century, bourgeois intellectual. We catch him making statements like: We "liberals" should "see the aim of a just and free society as letting its citizens be as privatistic, 'irrationalistic,' and aestheticist as they please so long as they do it on their own time—causing no harm to others and using no resources needed by those less advantaged."[9] Or, we might catch him explaining that the "ideal [liberal] society" will "equalize opportunities for self-creation and then leave people alone to use, or neglect, their opportunities."[10] Or we might find him offering his "hunch, or at least hope" that liberal society "is gradually coming to be structured around the idea of freedom—of leaving people alone to dream and think and live as they please, so long as they do not hurt other people. . . ."[11] Again, when Rorty is defending this second version of liberalism, we find him naturally referencing, or quoting with approval, traditional nineteenth- and twentieth-century liberal political theorists like Thomas Jefferson, Emerson, J.S. Mill, and (in this century) Isaiah Berlin. The following concise assessment of John Stuart Mill's political philosophy nicely sums up the point I have been making about Rorty's defense of this second version of liberalism. Rorty says, "J.S. Mill's suggestion that governments devote themselves to optimizing the balance between leaving people's private lives alone and preventing suffering seems to me pretty much the last word."[12]

Notice that this version of liberalism enables one to, in Rorty's words, "stay on the surface" psychologically and philosophically. It enables, indeed compels, one to stay out of another individual's private life, and to refrain from questioning that individual's final vocabulary to the extent it is publicly known. Such a view is clearly at odds with Shklar's definition of cruelty and, by extension, Rorty's first version of liberalism. For as we have seen, this first version of liberalism forces one to ask questions about another individual's final vocabulary, since it is that final vocabulary, rather than an individual's actions *as such*, that determines whether the individual is indeed cruel.

My reading of Rorty's work during the past ten years or so convinces me that he understands and takes seriously the point I have just raised. In particular, he takes seriously the charge that he appears, at least, to be caught on the horns of a dilemma. It seems Rorty can either remain on the surface and dispense with Shklar's definition of cruelty, or, he can

---

9. Rorty, *Contingency, Irony, and Solidarity*, p. xiv.
10. Ibid., 85.
11. See Richard Rorty, "Truth and Freedom: A Reply to Thomas McCarthy," *Critical Inquiry* 16 (spring 1990): 635.
12. Rorty, *Contingency, Irony, and Solidarity*, 63.

embrace this notion of cruelty, complete with its focus on the intentionality of the actor, and thereby obligate himself to get below the surface
and inspect final vocabularies. One gets a vastly different sense of how
Rorty approaches this dilemma, depending upon which work (or part of
a work) by Rorty one reads. In a critically important 1988 article entitled
"The Priority of Democracy to Philosophy," Rorty resolves the aforementioned dilemma by simply, and firmly, grasping the first horn.[13] He
maintains that certain actions just are cruel, regardless of the intentions
of the actor who undertakes them. This approach requires, of course,
that Rorty adopt some standard of cruelty that is independent of final
vocabularies. Or, to put this point in slightly different terms, this
approach requires that Rorty forthrightly adopt *one* final vocabulary as
dominant over all others. This he does by arguing that those views on
cruelty that are incompatible with liberal democracy are simply not ones
we liberal democrats should worry about taking seriously. Saying this
does not, in Rorty's view, compel us liberal democrats to make a moral
or ethical judgment about those who hold these incompatible views. It is
all simply a pragmatic exercise. So, for example, we liberal democrats
should not see Saint Ignatius Loyola as being wrong, or worse, as being
evil. We should see him simply as being "mad" — in the narrow sense that
his views are so incompatible with ours as to appear *to us* not to fit in any
conceivable way with the social order *we* want to maintain.[14] To the
extent that we can continue productively to converse with him, we
should. But when discourse becomes unproductive, when Loyola
becomes "fanatical" about his views, we liberal democrats are justified in
preventing him (by force if necessary) from *acting* on these views. Specif-

---

13. See Richard Rorty, "The Priority of Democracy to Philosophy," in *The Virginia
    Statue of Religious Freedom*, eds. Merrill Peterson and Robert Vaughan (Cambridge:
    Cambridge University Press, 1988), 257–88. This article is reprinted in *Reading
    Rorty*, ed. Alan Malachowski (Oxford: Basil Blackwell, 1990), 279–302. It is also
    reprinted in Rorty, *Objectivity, Relativism, and Truth: Philosophical Papers, Volume
    I* (Cambridge: University Press, 1991), 175–96. I quote from the article in *Objectiv-
    ity, Relativism, and Truth*.
14. Rorty follows Rawls in describing Loyola as "mad." As Rorty puts it, "we heirs of the
    Enlightenment think of enemies of liberal democracy like Nietzsche or Loyola as,
    to use Rawls's word, 'mad.' We do so because there is no way to see them as fellow
    citizens of our constitutional democracy, people whose life plans might, given inge-
    nuity and good will, be fitted in with those of other citizens." See Rorty, "The Prior-
    ity of Democracy to Philosophy," 187.

ically, in regard to those instances where Loyola does not understand cruelty as we liberal democrats do, we are again justified in preventing him from performing acts that *we* feel are cruel. In a sense, we liberal democrats have no choice but to act this way.

Some might object that there is something potentially very cruel in forcing an individual to adopt (or at least to live by) a particular view of cruelty that is not his or her own. But *that* cruelty—the cruelty of forcing an alien view of cruelty upon another—is presumably the one exception to the liberal's claim to see cruelty as the worst thing we do. Again, we liberals have no choice but to act this way. Faced with this apparent paradox, Rorty would assert that, for practical political purposes, we liberals should simply ignore the self-referential nature of the aforementioned objection.

To purse this last point a bit further, let us look again at the type of cruelty liberals are accused of inflicting upon those like Loyola. This cruelty appears—appears to us liberals, of course—not to be of the same *type* as Loyola would wish to inflict upon heretics. We liberals wish only to prevent Loyola from inflicting *physical pain* on another. Even if, in very extreme cases, we need *incidentally* to inflict physical pain on him in order to prevent him from inflicting physical pain on others, we liberals are not (and, as liberals never should be) concerned with making an attempt, through the use of physical pain, to cause Loyola to alter his own final vocabulary.[15] *That* attitude marks the *difference* between us and him. We liberal democrats wish always to stay on the surface. He does not. We wish to maintain a firm distinction between the public and the private. He does not.

Of course, Loyola might respond that in preventing him from inflicting physical pain upon others we were *de facto* altering, *perhaps*

---

15. In saying that we liberals may, in extreme cases, need incidentally to inflict physical pain on Loyola for the purpose of preventing him from inflicting physical pain on others, I am thinking of a case, for example, in which we needed (for simply pragmatic reasons) to jail Loyola in a prison cell that has been determined by us liberals to be a physically painful environment (perhaps because it was overcrowded). Of course, we liberals alone could make this determination. If Loyola were in a cell we determined (by exhaustive scientific analysis) was not physically painful, and yet he thought it was, we liberals would be justified in disregarding his assertion that he was in pain. Also, if we liberals did determine that Loyola was in a physically painful environment, we should (as liberals) work as hard as possible to eliminate the conditions that cause the environment to be painful. We would not want to cause Loyola physical pain; his present, physically painful condition would be an incidental, not an inherent, feature of our system.

even causing him to alter, his final vocabulary. There is some justification for this view. A belief that can never be practiced may eventually
cease to be a belief. Indeed, by 1992, Rorty comes around to maintaining *exactly* this position. But, in the late eighties, Rorty had apparently
not yet come to this new understanding. So, in 1988, in response to Loyola's claim that he was in pain, Rorty would say that we liberals need to
insist that, for practical political purposes, it is still best to remain on the
surface and consider only *physical* pain. To back up this response, Rorty
might further note that it does not seem *necessary* to probe a person's private self, his final vocabulary, in order to prevent that person from inflicting physical pain on another, even though that act of prevention on our
part may *incidentally* cause a change in the person's final vocabulary.
Again, the relevant point here is that we liberals wish (as far as it is possible) to remain on the surface. We put the desire to remain on the surface first, so to speak. Loyola would not.

But Saint Ignatius Loyola, nimble metaphysician that he was,
might have had another response that, as far as I can see, Rorty has not
explicitly considered. Suppose Loyola were to say, "Let us compare the
two possible worlds, two final vocabularies, we have here. Consider that
in your 'liberal' world, you liberals are not suffering cruelty, *but I am*. But
in my world, you liberals would not be suffering cruelty (after you were
converted) nor, of course, would I. If you liberals are serious about seeing cruelty, in all its forms, as the worst thing you do, you would select
one nonliberal final vocabulary (mine, or any other suitably metaphysical, nonliberal vocabulary) and help to impose that vocabulary on *everyone*. In the end, after the conversion, no one would be a *systematic* victim
of cruelty, no one would suffer as a result of an *inherent* aspect of the ruling political theory (as I am suffering now under liberalism). There is,
then, a strong argument that sincere liberals (those who take their own
view of liberalism seriously) should prefer a nonliberal political system."

Here I need to pause briefly to discuss what will be the obvious,
even reflexive, response to Loyola's position. It is a response I find insuf-
ficient. It will be argued that the "conversion" process necessitated by
any forceful shift in final vocabularies, any shift of the type that seems
necessitated by Loyola's argument, is automatically ruled out by us liberals. We wish always to remain on the surface, and so we could never
advocate such a conversion process, *regardless* of the ends it might
achieve. And surely a good liberal could point to numerous historical
examples of conversion processes in which the means have been tragi-

cally ill-fitted to the ends. But my hunch is that Rorty, and certainly other liberals like Jefferson and Mill, would not be comfortable with this argument alone. For such an argument, offered by itself, would not defeat the more serious charge by Loyola that liberalism is, in fact, *internally inconsistent*. Someone like Rorty, who thinks that J.S. Mill has offered us "the last word" on political theory, should wish for a stronger argument to use against Loyola than the means/end conversion argument offered earlier. So would others. Ultimately, in terms of consistency and rationality, we liberals should at least insist that our system be (to us in our vocabulary) on a par with other systems, while recognizing that no system could be seen as being better than any other.

To put liberalism back on an even footing with other final vocabularies, to see it as no worse than other political systems, we need to ask, where is the theoretical flaw in Loyola's argument? It must surely be in his assertion that "you liberals are not suffering, *but I am*." Remember, we liberals can only think of "suffering" in *our* vocabulary. Since *we* maintain a public/private split, as long as we do not inflict *physical* pain upon Loyola, we do not see any suffering. *He* may think he is suffering some form of cruelty (some form of mental anguish, if you will) by being prevented from inflicting physical pain on others, but *we* do not think he is. We only see the physical pain on the surface. To the extent that we cannot see any *physical* pain, as far as we can see he is not suffering. And even if we were to inflict physical pain on Loyola for the purpose of preventing him from inflicting physical pain on others, our act of inflicting that pain upon him would be only an incidental aspect of liberalism. As I mentioned before, as good liberals, we should continuously be working to change whatever material conditions might make it incidentally necessary for us to inflict physical pain on others. The infliction of such physical pain is in no way an *inherent* aspect of a liberal political order. The key point in this response to Loyola rests on a relativistic claim with which Rorty would be in full agreement. The point is to insist that there is, ultimately, no way to *compare* final vocabularies. For someone like Rorty, it is in the nature of final vocabularies that there are no external standards to which these vocabularies must be responsible, and hence no external standards that could serve as the basis for comparison between any two vocabularies. Recall Rorty's earlier point, that if doubt is cast on one's final vocabulary, one has no "noncircular argumentative recourse" by which these doubts can be answered. Presumably, then, any final vocabulary worth that name must be both internally consistent and stable. It will be stable in the sense that there will be no theoretical way of producing reasons *from within that vocabulary* that would require one to abandon the vocabulary. Now I maintain that *the insistence on a firm distinction between the public and the private, coupled with the desire always to remain on the surface, is a necessary condition for the stability of the liberal's final vocabulary.*

Notice that in remaining on the surface, we liberals, to the extent we act exclusively as liberals, could only be concerned with getting clear on exactly what constitutes physical pain. The goal of preventing or eliminating physical pain would become, to us liberals, synonymous with the goal of achieving a well-ordered society. It would be the only *joint* goal we liberals could undertake. This, it seems, is precisely how Rorty ultimately understands liberalism. He evidences this understanding when, for example, he notes with approval that J.S. Mill's paramount goal (quoted earlier) was that of "optimizing the balance between leaving people's private lives alone and preventing suffering." I suggest that we must now interpret the phrase "preventing suffering" only in its physical sense, for only in this sense can we remain on the surface.

And notice, finally, that this liberal goal of eliminating physical pain chimes well with Rorty's pragmatic, antitheory, antimetaphysical biases. For in determining who is suffering physical pain, all we need to do is make careful observations, and then apply the relatively straightforward standards of everyday science. We do not need to start asking questions about a person's final vocabulary, much less about the nature of the "self." In other words, when we remain on the surface, biology, not psychology, is the science with which we are concerned. I imagine Rorty would prefer this, since fewer "deep" questions about the notion of the "self" arise in the realm of biology.

As I said earlier, there is a certain unarguable political stability to this version of liberalism. We can indeed see this version of liberalism as embodying a final vocabulary that represents the "last word." Of course, it will represent this last word only in the relativistic sense that *any* consistent final vocabulary will represent to its users the last word. And yet, that should be good enough for people like Rorty, who say they wish finally to get away from the impossible dream of synthesizing all final vocabularies. So, we seem now to have a stable, internally consistent theory of social order that allows us to dispense with the need for further theorizing and enables us to get down to the practical business of determining who is suffering and what (within our system) can be done about that physical suffering.

But, alas, Rorty still refuses to leave well enough alone. Specifically, he refuses to stay on the surface. Instead, he plunges us below the surface (below the epidermis, as it were) by noting—no, rather by *insisting*—that the most important form of cruelty involves a certain special, *nonphysical*, type of pain called *humiliation*. By including—or rather, by *focusing on*—the question of humiliation in *Contingency, Irony, and Solidarity*, Rorty drastically problematizes the version of liberalism handed down to us by thinkers like Jefferson, Mill, and Berlin. To see why, recall that before this focus on humiliation we liberals were justified (under our vocabulary) in simply ignoring Loyola's claim that he was suffering, when that claim was made in the absence of any physical condition we could detect as the cause of such suffering. But, with the inclusion of humiliation as a form of suffering, we liberals can no longer ignore this claim. We must now concern ourselves with alleviating Loyola's "pain," even though that pain is in no way the result of any physical contact between us and him. Indeed, it may be the very absence of such physical contact that is causing this special kind of nonphysical pain! As one can readily imagine, myriad problems lurk on the horizon of this new version of Rortyian liberalism, problems associated with the ability (or inability) adequately to describe emotional states, with the theoretical problem of defining concepts like dignity and respect, with the even more vexing theoretical problem of splitting one's final vocabulary into a public part and a private part, and so forth.

It perhaps bears repeating that these problems did not plague Rorty's liberal heroes: Jefferson, Mill, and others. These liberals did not evaluate the avoidance of humiliation, as opposed to physical cruelty, to the same level as does Rorty. And, not surprisingly, neither did Montaigne. As Shklar notes, "Painful as humiliation is, it does no bodily damage. Montaigne was well aware of moral cruelty [e.g., humiliation], and saw it as a personal danger, but he never confused it with physical brutality."[16] Granted, this passage does indicate that Montaigne cared about not humiliating others; but he did not confuse that desire with the belief that cruelty in its physical form is the worst thing we do. What Mon-

---

16. Shklar, *Ordinary Vices*, 36. Rorty footnotes this same page in reference to a discussion of humiliation [*Contingency, Irony, and Solidarity*, 89, note 9], but he does not seem to recognize the tension between his view of cruelty as *necessarily* including humiliation, and (at least on my reading) Montaigne's view of cruelty as only *incidentally* including humiliation.

taigne (and, I would argue, all of Rorty's liberal heroes) saw was this: The avoidance of physical cruelty can be just a matter of tolerance. It does not *require* that we liberals rework our own final vocabulary. And such avoidance of physical cruelty is the only goal of a liberal society. But the avoidance of humiliation may indeed require that we reform our own final vocabulary, our own beliefs and desires, so that those beliefs and desires do not put us at odds with another's final vocabulary. This, at least, is the argument I will now examine.

Liberalism and Humiliation

My purpose in this section is to show that there exists a fundamental and unalterable tension between the Jeffersonian view of liberalism that enjoins us to leave people alone (a view we would today most closely associate with libertarianism) and Rorty's *new* injunction that we liberals must also refrain from humiliating others. The strategy I shall adopt in pressing this claim is, I think, simple and direct. I shall argue that in order to refrain from humiliating others, we liberals must simultaneously grant these others some measure of dignity or respect. In other words, to one who understands fully the nature of final vocabularies, it makes no sense to speak of *merely refraining* from humiliation. Final vocabularies (according to Rorty's own definition) are not isolated entities. As I pointed out in the previous chapter, such vocabularies can emerge and develop *only* in conversation (and perhaps *confrontation*) with others. In an important sense, then, the "pain" of humiliation is different from physical pain. The avoidance of humiliation requires a *positive* act of conferring respect upon another. But if such an act is not to be a mere "pose" — if it is to confer a *genuine* measure of respect — it must be based on a true understanding of the person toward whom that respect is directed. Respecting another involves more than simply saying the right words; it involves saying the right words, to the right person, in the right context, at the right time. In short, it involves "knowing" another person, and specifically, knowing that person's final vocabulary. Certainly the best and perhaps the only *true* way of getting an understanding of another's final vocabulary is by inquiring of the source. Such inquiries require that we *not* leave our fellow citizens alone. Indeed, in a broad sense, Rorty's injunction that we all must avoid humiliating our fellows requires a kind of cheerful sociability. In other words, the avoidance of humiliation requires that *all* individuals within a given society be willing and able to engage in open and honest and equal conversations about their respective final vocabularies. And it requires more than *just* that. Since humiliation is of such a deeply personal nature, its avoidance requires that the conversations we have with our fellows embody an ethic of what one might call "full disclosure." Only such full disclosure about our final vocabularies can *guarantee*—if indeed anything can guarantee—that humiliation be avoided. For in the end, final vocabularies are, by their nature, delicate, complex, and idiosyncratic constructions. To fit them together in a well-ordered society with any success at all requires that, in the words of contemporary feminists, we see the personal as political. Another way of putting this is to say that the vision I have just sketched of a society honestly and perhaps *primarily* concerned with the avoidance of humiliation looks more like the type of republic Plato had in mind, or the type of *polis* Aristotle pictured, than the type of society Jefferson made the focus of his experiments.

This is not to suggest that Jefferson or his Enlightenment companions were in any way more callous toward their fellows than Plato or Aristotle. Rather, it is to suggest that Enlightenment liberals thought that the avoidance of humiliation played no *political* role in the advancement of liberalism *as such*. Once again, Rorty wants to have it both ways. He wants to retain the Enlightenment vision of liberalism, a vision which enjoins us simply to leave people alone (if they wish to be left alone), and which therefore gets around the enormously intricate problem of fitting together competing final vocabularies by insisting that the *only* goal of politics is to create a society relatively free of the threat of *physical* harm (to one's person or one's property) from another. But at the same time, Rorty envisions a society of "liberals" whose *overriding* goal is to avoid committing acts of humiliation, and, *perhaps*, who are *also* committed to preventing *others* from engaging in such acts. Unfortunately, there is no way to bring about the second goal without vitiating the first. Jefferson's republic and Plato's republic are worlds apart. The attempt to fit them together produces an irresolvable tension.

To appreciate fully the precise nature of this tension, we need to get clear on exactly how Rorty understands the notion of humiliation. Surprisingly, although this term plays such a decisive part in Rorty's overall view of liberalism, he fails to define it explicitly until the penultimate chapter of *Contingency, Irony, and Solidarity*, the chapter on George Orwell. And when Rorty does come around to defining humiliation in this chapter, he does so within the larger context of a discussion about torture. In the section immediately following this one, I shall undertake a detailed analysis of Rorty's reading of Orwell. But for now it should suffice to point out that the extreme and malevolent form of humiliation upon which Orwell focuses in his novel *1984* is not the form that most directly concerns us North American and Western European liberals. Both as potential victims and potential perpetrators, *we* are more directly susceptible to a much less drastic, much more prosaic form of humiliation. While always mindful of the not inconceivable savagery Orwell depicts, we liberals are more immediately faced with the type of humiliation that occurs, not infrequently, in large, pluralistic, liberal societies when one final vocabulary incidentally or necessarily bumps up against another, different final vocabulary. Such collisions need not always be humiliating to both parties, or even to one party. But sometimes they are humiliating, at least to one of the parties involved. In chapter 4 of *Contingency, Irony, and Solidarity*—entitled "Private Irony and Liberal Hope"—Rorty gives us a glimpse of the type of actions he feels can produce humiliation. He writes

> [T]he best [i.e., most effective] way to cause people long-lasting pain is to humiliate them by making the things that seemed most important to them look futile, obsolete, and powerless. Consider what happens when a child's precious possessions—the little things around which he weaves fantasies that make him a little different from all other children—are redescribed as "trash" and thrown away. Or consider what happens when these possessions are made to look ridiculous alongside the possessions of another, richer, child. Something like that presumably happens to a primitive culture when it is conquered by a more advanced one. The same sort of thing sometimes happens to non-intellectuals in the presence of intellectuals. . . . Redescription often humiliates.[17]

There are at least two important points to note about this account of how persons can be humiliated. Perhaps the key point is that the act of humiliation necessarily involves redescription. When we characterize someone, or his or her actions, in *our* final vocabulary as opposed to *his or hers*, we may run the risk of humiliating that person. Of course, the tendency to describe someone in our final vocabulary as opposed to his

---

17. Rorty, *Contingency, Irony, and Solidarity*, 89–90.

or hers will be much greater if his or her final vocabulary is either inconsistent with our own final vocabulary or simply is one we do not care to use. But then, if his or her final vocabulary is so configured we are almost *assured* of humiliating him or her—unless, of course, we persuade the individual in question that his or her vocabulary is actually harmful *to himself or herself*. Such an act of persuasion would be an example of attempting to *convert* this individual to *our* final vocabulary. As Rorty himself notes, if this attempt at conversion is successful, then the *newly* converted individual would not feel humiliated but rather "empowered."[18] He or she would have *learned* to see his or her old final vocabulary as we saw it—as harmful to everyone, including himself or herself.

Of course, not all conversion attempts are successful. But even the successful attempts require actions on the part of the "converter," which are antithetical to the injunction that we should leave people alone (if they wish to be left alone). Notice that *before* his or her conversion, the *potential* convert will generally want nothing to do with those who wish to convert him or her. The potential convert *may* wish to be left alone. But to those who wish to convert him or her, this behavior on the part of the potential convert only evidences his or her desperate need to be converted, to be "educated." Naturally, then, those who attempt to convert a wayward soul would never describe their *own* actions as attempts at humiliation. Rather, these actions would be described (and intended) as attempts at education or empowerment. Notice now that we seem to find ourselves in the same position with respect to humiliation as we initially found ourselves in with respect to physical cruelty. On Shklar's definition, an act was cruel only if any of the reasons for which it was performed included the intent to cause anguish and fear in a weaker being. We saw that this definition was very nearly useless because many (perhaps most) cruel individuals do not—in *their* vocabulary—intend to be cruel.

This leads directly to the second important point I want to make about the passage quoted earlier. Once again, it seems that Rorty has confused the distinction between intentional and unintentional behavior. Sometimes we do intentionally wish to humiliate another, as when

---

18. Rorty says, "Redescription which presents itself as uncovering the interlocutor's true self, or the real nature of a common public world which the speaker and the interlocutor share, suggests that the person being redescribed is being empowered, not having his power diminished" (*Contingency, Irony, and Solidarity*, 90).

we redescribe a child's toys as "trash." At other times, it is not so clear whether we wish *intentionally* to *humiliate* another. Does the fundamentalist Christian who describes the openly homosexual individual as a "sinner" intend to humiliate—or rather to educate or enlighten—the homosexual individual? For that matter, does the rich child in Rorty's example actually intend to humiliate his or her poorer counterpart? Does the member of the more advanced culture intend to humiliate the "primitive"? Does the intellectual intend to humiliate the nonintellectual? In all of these cases, I think the answer *could* be "no." This underscores the point I made earlier, that the avoidance of humiliation requires a positive act. Try saying that one should "refrain from unintentionally causing humiliation," and listen to how awkward that sounds. To put the point slightly differently, it is clear that *in Rorty's own examples,* the avoidance of humiliation requires more than simple restraint, more than mere tolerance. It requires *active acceptance,* at some level, of another's final vocabulary.

Rorty leaves no doubt that humiliation, whether intentional or not, is unacceptable in a liberal society. Speaking in the first person, he affirms that his version of liberalism *"requires* me to become aware of *all* the various ways in which other human beings whom I might act upon can be humiliated."[19] Presumably, one should then attempt, as far as possible, to avoid those acts that produce humiliation.

Although laudable, it strikes me that this is quite a heavy burden to impose upon oneself and one's fellow liberals. At a *minimum,* it is a burden that, if taken seriously, forces the liberal to remain continually within his or her community, perpetually a part of the political process. There can be no escape to Walden. For withdrawing from a particular community, *even so as not to risk humiliating members of that community,* may indeed humiliate these members if the person who seeks to withdraw has the *misfortune* of being highly esteemed by his or her fellows. In such an instance, the very act of withdrawal could logically be seen as an insult to the worth of the community. And so our liberal must remain within his or her *polis,* and he or she must dispense dignity in equal measure—as far as this is consistently possible—to any and all groups that seek it. He or she must do this because, as a good liberal, he or she is both familiar and in agreement with one of Rorty's favorite liberal heroes, John Rawls, who writes that "democracy in judging each other's aims is the *foundation* of

---

19. Ibid., 92, emphasis added.

self-respect in a well-ordered society."[20] Here I read Rawls as advancing the strong claim that, in order to maintain the self-respect of every individual in society—in other words, in order not to humiliate anyone—everyone's final vocabulary must ultimately be seen as no worse (but also no better) than everyone else's final vocabulary. One suspects that our imaginary liberal, if he or she is to live up to his or her status as a liberal, will be plagued by numerous problems.

These problems arise precisely because the avoidance of humiliation may indeed require that one reform at least part of his or her own final vocabulary, his or her own beliefs or desires, so that those beliefs and desires do not offend the dignity of another's final vocabulary. To get clear on precisely what is meant here, let us take a *concrete* example. We could well imagine one tolerating, say, the practice of homosexuality—tolerating it in the sense of not attempting actively to prohibit it by force of law—and yet, at the same time, not feeling "comfortable" around those who engage in this practice. Sincerely, perhaps even piteously, claiming that homosexuals are "deviant" or "sick," while not attempting to legislate against the practice, would be a specific instantiation of the type of behavior about which I am talking.[21] We may now ask whether individuals who admit to feeling "uncomfortable" around acknowledged homosexuals—we could call such individuals "antihomosexuals," but since that sounds both too negative and too judgmental, let us simply

---

20. John Rawls, *A Theory of Justice* (Cambridge: Harvard University Press, 1971), 442, emphasis added.

21. I have chosen the example of homosexuality because Rorty specifically argues for the *irrelevance* of sexual preference within liberal democratic societies. On at least two occasions, he maintains that "sexual matters" and "sexual preference" can be merely private concerns. In *Contingency, Irony, and Solidarity*, he argues that philosophy should put itself "*in the service* [his emphasis] of democratic politics" by providing us with one more technique "for reweaving our vocabulary of moral deliberation in order to accommodate new beliefs (e.g., that women and blacks are capable of more than white males had thought, that property is not sacred, *that sexual matters are of merely private concern* [my emphasis])" (196). In "The Priority of Democracy to Philosophy," he asserts, "It is appropriate to speak of gustatory or sexual preferences for these do not matter to anybody but yourself and your immediate circle. But it is misleading to speak of a 'preference' for liberal democracy" (187). Presumably, Rorty believes that sexual preference does not matter to anybody but yourself and your immediate circle, because he believes such preferences have no *material consequences* outside of that circle. *Even if he were correct in this belief,* my argument is that the introduction of humiliation forces us to consider myriad *non-*

call them "traditionalists"[2]—we may ask whether traditionalists who do not attempt to prohibit homosexuality by law are liberals or nonliberals. Presumably, Rorty would respond that they are nonliberals because their language and attitude can be expected, *whether intentionally or not*, to have a humiliating effect on homosexual individuals. Again, in the final analysis, intentions seem simply to drop out of Rorty's philosophy—at least when the going gets theoretically tough.

What, then, is to be done about the fact that the openly homosexual individual might be humiliated by the traditionalist? *Ideally*, the homosexual individual and the traditionalist will get together and hash out their differences in a free and open encounter. This is precisely the kind of solution Rorty continually returns to throughout his work whenever the problem of competing worldviews, or competing systems of *any* type, arises. Of course, as Rorty also likes to point out, we have no idea *beforehand* how this encounter will turn out. The homosexual individual might start off by explaining why he or she feels humiliated. He or she may then try to *educate* or *enlighten* the traditionalist by, for example, providing him or her with some literature by and about homosexual indi-

---

material consequences, hence sexual preference may very well affect society at large. Although I hope it should be obvious, I will note, for emphasis, that nothing I will say in the following discussion of homosexuality and humiliation should in any way be construed as implying or suggesting that I am in anything less than complete agreement with the principle that homosexuals should enjoy the same full and equal rights granted to all individuals in the United States.

22. The general attitude of Americans in the late 1990s toward the homosexual community is still very much an open question. On the most charitable reading, one could say that, when it comes to matters like employment, housing, credit, and so forth, most Americans probably think homosexuals should be treated like everyone else. Questions about whether acknowledged homosexuals should be able to serve in the military might seem to present a special case, but I think it probable that the courts will decide that discrimination against homosexuals by the military is illegal. Having said all of this, however, there is still the delicate question of what to do with laws that codify what we might call "traditional" values or institutions. Should homosexual individuals, for example, be allowed to marry? Opinion polls, not to mention the activities of various legislative bodies, including Congress, consistently and overwhelmingly show that most Americans would answer this question with a resounding "no." Since homosexuality seems to challenge *traditional* views—like the view of the "traditional" family as being composed of an adult male married to an adult female and the two living with their child or children—I have chosen the term *traditionalist* as the most neutral word for one who may not wish to legislate against the practice of homosexuality, but still feels uncomfortable about it.

viduals. Or, he or she might try to explain that the traditionalist's homophobic attitude reflects a classic case of "reaction-formation"—the desire to destroy outward manifestations of desires one cannot face within oneself. The traditionalist, for his or her part, will explain that it is not at all his or her *intention* to humiliate anyone, and he or she is, in fact, offended that the homosexual individual should think he or she would try to do such a thing. The traditionalist will further note that it is *he or she* who is offended by the practice of homosexuality. (Of course, it could not have been the homosexual individual's intention to offend either.) The traditionalist might then try to educate or enlighten the homosexual individual by, for example, providing him or her with some passages from the Bible discussing the unnaturalness of homosexuality. Or, he or she might try to explain that the homosexual individual's deviant behavior is, in fact, traceable to a poorly formed relationship with a parent. This conversation could, of course, go on indefinitely. It might never come to a satisfactory conclusion. But, with luck, persistence, and a good deal of hard work on both sides, a resolution just might be found such that neither party felt humiliated, and both parties felt the desire not to engage in any behavior toward the other that might be perceived as humiliating.

Now nothing I have said so far, and indeed nothing I shall say in the remainder of this section, should be taken as evidence that I am in anything less than complete agreement with Rorty that the procedure just sketched is undoubtedly the optimal way to resolve disputes. The only point on which I would insist—a point I made a few pages back— is that these encounter sessions are the very antithesis of what is involved in leaving someone alone. Both individuals in the aforementioned example would need to be deeply involved in reworking their own (and their interlocutor's) final vocabulary. But if large, pluralistic, liberal societies consisted *entirely* of individuals so motivated, there would be no need to distinguish between a public sphere and a private sphere, there would be no need to talk (as Rorty repeatedly does) of leaving people alone. Everyone would welcome togetherness. Since Rorty apparently believes that a significant number of individuals do not welcome complete togetherness, and that we should not force it upon them, he is left with the following problem: What do we do with the traditionalists who do not wish to put their final vocabulary *fully* on display—traditionalists who like a little privacy? Is there any way we can keep these traditionalists, who do not wish to engage in open, honest, and *equal* discussions with homosexual individuals, from humiliating them?

Clear thinking Jeffersonian liberals will respond to this last question by answering "no." If the traditionalist is unwilling to get together and talk openly, honestly, and equally with the homosexual individual—rather than, say, preaching *at* him or her—the best we can do, the Jeffersonian liberal will insist, is to then prevent either individual from physically harming the other, and resign ourselves to the existence of humiliating behavior within our society. Rorty, however, thinks there is another alternative. He thinks we can teach the traditionalist how to split up his or her final vocabulary, his or her very *self*, if you will, into a public part and a private part. Since the public part of one's final vocabulary is, obviously, the part that interacts with others (with the public), *only* it can be the part of one's vocabulary that *produces* humiliation in others. Rorty argues that if we could simply teach the traditionalist how to keep his or her public vocabulary in check, how to prevent it from humiliating others, the traditionalist could go right ahead and despise, in private, anyone he or she so chooses. Of course, as we have already seen, it is awkward to speak of teaching someone to "refrain" from humiliating another, since such humiliation can be unintentional. We—that is, we liberals whose behavior does not intentionally or unintentionally humiliate homosexual individuals—will need to teach the traditionalist quite a lot about what *not* to do, and what *to* do, in the presence of homosexual individuals. To get really proficient at this, the traditionalist will need to internalize a whole set of complex behaviors to the point where they become almost second nature to him or her—but only "*almost*." We would not want any of the nonhumiliating parts of the traditionalist's public vocabulary to spill over into his or her private vocabulary—which obviously desires to humiliate—since that would interfere with the traditionalist's "privacy." While this may sound hopelessly complicated, it is, nonetheless, exactly what Rorty advocates. This is how he puts it in a key passage, a portion of which I quoted earlier:

> [W]e need to distinguish between redescription for private and for public purposes. For my private purposes, I may redescribe you and everybody else in terms which have nothing to do with my attitude toward your actual or possible suffering. My private purposes, and the part of my final vocabulary which is not relevant to my public actions, are none of your business. But as I am a liberal, the part of my

final vocabulary which is relevant to such actions requires me to become aware of all the various ways in which other human beings whom I might act upon can be humiliated.[23]

The importance of this passage in Rorty's recent work *cannot* be overstated. It represents what Nancy Fraser has called Rorty's "partition position"—his attempt to escape contradictions in his view of the self by partitioning the self into a public part and a private part.[24] There are, I think, a number of good reasons for rejecting this position, with its bifurcated view of the self.

First, to see ourselves in this way would be—dare I say it?—*humiliating*. The sort of individual who, in an effort to meet the demand not to humiliate others, *is* able to perform with his or her final vocabulary the type of public/private split Rorty insists upon would be "two faced" in the *worst* sense of that term. He or she would appear a facile, politic character in public, while in private he or she would nurture *necessarily* illiberal thoughts. We know that the private part of his or her final vocabulary would be illiberal because, if it were not, there would be no reason for him or her to wish to keep it to himself or herself. The society that emerges from this is one in which we would never know when another individual was being sincere. Of course, Rorty might argue that we can never know such a thing *for certain* in our present society. Still, the situation seems worse in the kind of society Rorty imagines, for in such a society individuals would be encouraged, as a matter of social norms, to misrepresent their private (and presumably most sincere) beliefs. One wonders if, in the final analysis, it would not be less humiliating to the homosexual individual for the traditionalist simply to say, "I'm sorry, I can't split my public and private vocabulary apart, and hence I can't tell you in public that I do not think your behavior is deviant, while sincerely believing, in private, that it is. But at least now you know what I honestly think about you."

What I have just said constitutes what one might call an "aesthetic" reason why we should wish to reject Rorty's suggestion that in order to avoid humiliating another we split our vocabulary up into a public and a private part. We may simply not like the "picture" that emerges of the

---

23. Rorty, *Contingency, Irony, and Solidarity*, 92–93.
24. See "Solidarity or Singularity? Richard Rorty between Romanticism and Technocracy," in Nancy Fraser, *Unruly Practices: Power, Discourse and Gender in Contemporary Social Theory* (Minneapolis: University of Minnesota Press, 1989), 93–110.

individual self if this is done. There are, however, also powerful theoretical reasons for rejecting Rorty's vision of the self. Simply put, his vision of the self is theoretically untenable. Notice: If the person doing the humiliating can be expected to split his or her vocabulary down the middle and keep the private part separate, and hence not have it interact with the public part, why cannot the victim of humiliation be expected to do the same? Now consider that if we *all* could simply split up our vocabularies into a public and a private part, and keep the private part to ourselves and our close friends, it seems that we could all be free of the possibility of being humiliated—except, of course, by ourselves or by our close friends. As far as I can see, the *only* argument Rorty could make about why the suggestion I have just made would not work is that the *victim* of humiliation cannot split up his or her vocabulary in the same manner as can the *perpetrator* of humiliation. In other words, when it comes to humiliation (and humiliation *alone*) we need to see the self as an organic, seamless whole. But for the purpose of every other behavior or emotion, we can (indeed, we must) see the self as being split into several parts. This is perhaps the most dramatic tension in Rorty's recent theoretical work. It relates directly to what it means to be a liberal, what it means to be a "self," and what it means to humiliate and be humiliated. In the next section I shall take up a detailed examination of this tension. For now, however, I want to return to the specific conflict between the traditionalist and the homosexual.

As a good pragmatist, Rorty might note that for all practical purposes, once the homosexual individual discloses his or her sexual preference to the public, his or her private vocabulary then becomes (in one important respect at least) identical to his or her public vocabulary. Hence, at that point, the homosexual individual could no longer split up the relevant part of his or her private and public vocabulary.[25] So, to be practical, Rorty might say that we need to call on the traditionalist to split up *his or her* final vocabulary. But it is hard to see how this approach would solve much. If homosexual individuals are allowed to go public with their private vocabulary—a vocabulary that may indeed offend the

---

25. Of course, the homosexual could simply decide to lie and say publicly that he or she was no longer a homosexual, while continuing in private to be one. This would then mean that the homosexual would need to say one thing in public and believe another in private. The question is: Should he or she or the traditionalist be in this position? And who decides?

traditionalists' private vocabulary—why cannot the traditionalists then go public with their private vocabulary? Does it become a matter of who is the *first* to disclose publicly his or her private vocabulary? If the traditionalist were to say, "Because of my unique, private value system, I would feel humiliated if I knew that I were a member of a society which condoned the public acknowledgment of homosexuality" *before* a given homosexual individual were publicly to disclose his or her sexual preference, should we then call on the homosexual individual to keep his or her private vocabulary private, and not publicly express his or her sexual preference?

Since this does not seem fair, perhaps the best solution is simply to enjoin *both* the homosexual individual and the traditionalist from going public with his or her respective final vocabulary. This leads to what one might call a "least-common-denominator" vocabulary that everyone must use in public. Such a vocabulary would require that everyone be enjoined to keep to himself or herself *anything* that would be likely to humiliate or offend *anyone* else. Homosexual individuals would not be allowed to go public with their sexual preference, traditionalists would not be allowed to go public with their antihomosexual attitudes, fundamentalist Christians would not be allowed to go public with their belief that they alone are saved, Jews would not be allowed to go public with their belief that they are the chosen people, wealthy individuals would not be allowed to go public with their belief that their wealth derived from their superior character, poor individuals would not be allowed to go public with their belief that the wealthy folks are greedy and self-centered, and so forth. Obviously, this approach has the effect of constricting rather than expanding the range of "public" conversation.

But perhaps an even more serious problem with this approach is that all sorts of groups within large, pluralistic, liberal societies *do not want to (or feel they cannot) keep their private vocabularies private.* Indeed, quite a few groups would argue that forcing them to keep their private vocabularies private is both humiliating and oppressive. But many of the individuals who compose these groups would also think of themselves as liberals. And lots of other liberals might agree with them.

Consider, in this regard, the debate that is presently taking place at many American universities—the very bastions of Rortyian liberalism, a liberalism that thinks that humiliation is the worst thing we do. After much debate, one university, Smith College, passed a code of conduct for its faculty and students that prohibits "oppression of those of sexual orientation other than heterosexual," and then goes on to stipulate that "this [oppression] can take place *by not acknowledging their [homosexuals', bisexuals', and so forth] existence.*"[26]

Or consider the 1989 United States District Court case of *Doe v. Michigan*, in which Judge Cohn struck down the University of Michigan's "Policy on Discrimination and Discriminatory Harassment of Students in the University Environment," on the grounds that it violated students' First Amendment rights. As Judge Cohn pointed out, among other problems the policy seemed to forbid private associations of almost any kind, unless approved by the University. As a specific example of how the policy violated students' First Amendment rights, Cohn pointed to an official pamphlet entitled "What Students Should Know about Discrimination and Discriminatory Harassment by Students in the University Environment," which was given to all students. The pamphlet was designed to clarify the University's Policy on Discrimination and Discriminatory Harassment, and to make students aware of the sanctions applied to conduct that violated the policy. In the pamphlet the following (nonexhaustive) list of presumably *actionable* conduct was delineated, under the heading "You are a harasser when":

> You exclude someone from a study group because that person is of a different race, sex, or ethnic origin than you are . . .
>
> You display a confederate flag on the door of your room in the residence hall . . .
>
> You comment in a derogatory way about a particular person or group's physical appearance or sexual orientation, or their cultural origins, or religious beliefs.[27]

Finally, let me add one more example, which is not drawn from the realm of the academy. It is again an example that focuses on homosexuality, because, as I said before, *Rorty* believes that sexual preference can be merely a private matter. However, many homosexual individuals feel that their sexual orientation must be acknowledged in public and by others. In 1994, the Supreme Judicial Court of Massachusetts apparently agreed when it upheld a lower court's order barring the Veterans Council (a private organization) from excluding what it felt were homosexual

---

26. Quoted in R. Emmett Tyrell Jr., "PC People," *The American Spectator* (May 1991): 8.

27. *Doe v. Michigan*, 721 F. Supp. at 858.

"messages" from its annual Saint Patrick's Day parade. The suit was brought by the Irish–American Gay, Lesbian, and Bisexual Group of Boston (GLIB). The Supreme Judicial Court of Massachusetts acknowledged that "GLIB's purposes are to *express* its members' pride in their dual identities as Irish or Irish–American persons who are homosexual or bisexual. . . ."[28] It then argued that members of GLIB must be allowed to march in the parade, under their own banner, because this parade was a "public accommodation," and Massachusetts law forbids discrimination based on sexual orientation in places of "public accommodation." Why, exactly, is this parade a public accommodation? Because, the court reasoned, "It is impossible to discern any specific *expressive* purpose" to the parade.[29] Apparently it was not impossible for the members of GLIB to discern just such a purpose. As Judge Nolan argued in his dissent

> [R]equiring the Veterans Council not to exclude the members of GLIB on the basis of their sexual preference may be a constitutionally valid infringement on the Veterans Council's rights; however, precluding the Veterans Council from disallowing the members of GLIB from expressing themselves as a group is not related to the State's interest, and is therefore unconstitutional. . . .
>   . . . mandating mere association in this case may be constitutional; mandating a message is not.[30]

In 1995, a unanimous Supreme Court overturned the ruling of the Supreme Judicial Court of Massachusetts and allowed the Veteran's Coun-

---

28. *Irish–American Gay, Lesbian, and Bisexual Group of Boston & others v. City of Boston & others*, 636 N.E.2d 1295, emphasis added.
29. Ibid., 1297, emphasis added.
30. Ibid., 1304. Would Judge Nolan's reasoning then mean that we must allow hotel and restaurant owners to discriminate against black individuals? I think not necessarily. To see why, start with this basic fact: There is no practical way an individual cannot *not* disclose his or her race, or gender, in public. In the case of black individuals specifically, even if "blackness," or "acting black" is a "cultural construct," skin color certainly is not. Hence, it is impossible for a black person to treat his or her "blackness" as *entirely* part of his or her "private vocabulary." At least some part of that private vocabulary will necessarily be public. In other words, a black person cannot keep his or her racial identity entirely to himself or herself. But, can we use *the same rationale* to force the Veteran's Council to acknowledge approvingly the identity of a homosexual individual? Apparently not, since sexual preference, as opposed to race, gender, or physical disability, *is* something that one can keep *entirely* to him-

cil to exclude homosexual messages from its parade. Writing for the Court, Justice Souter made it clear that, in this case, mandating that the Veteran's Council include in its parade a message with which it did not agree violated the First Amendment.[31] The Supreme Court's decision, of course, angered many homosexuals and their supporters. But it seems impossible to imagine a solution that would have made everyone happy. Indeed, as all of the previous examples make abundantly clear, *if* we concern ourselves with preventing humiliation, then somewhere along the line we still need to *choose* which private vocabularies get to be public and which do not. There is simply no way around this. Rorty's partition position simply does not work. To put this point in different terms: The right not to be humiliated includes the right *comfortably* to go public with one's private vocabulary. But, again, this involves a choice among competing private vocabularies.

It seems that Rorty has finally realized this. Indeed, the best argument against Rorty's partition position comes from Rorty himself. That is why I have saved it until last. The argument I am referring to appears in a 1992 article in which Rorty attempts to defend his pragmatic, antifoundationalist view against the charge that it is less capable than other views of producing positive social change in today's world. Rorty's defense comes in reply to an article by Lynn Baker in the *Virginia Law Review*. Baker persuasively argues that, *on strictly pragmatic grounds*, social "prophets" who wish to affect positive social change, but who almost necessarily (in our society) find themselves in positions of *relative* powerlessness—individuals like, for example, Martin Luther King Jr. or Catharine MacKinnnon—would do well to claim, in their public speeches, that they are in touch with a force (specifically Truth) larger and more powerful than themselves or their opponents.[32] Rorty is quite turned off by this obviously foundationalist rhetoric, which he argues is often employed by "authority freaks."[33] Rorty would prefer that *his*

---

self or herself. Remember, homosexual individuals were *not* barred from marching in the parade. However, *any* individual (homosexual or not) who endorsed a homosexual "lifestyle" was barred. Simply put: when it comes to designing measures to prohibit *humiliation*, society may be justified in treating "lifestyles" differently than it treats *certain* physical characteristics—that is, those characteristics one cannot change.

31. See *Hurley v. Irish–American Gay Group of Boston*, slip opinion, No. 94–749.
32. See Lynn A. Baker, "'Just Do It': Pragmatism and Progressive Social Change," *Virginia Law Review* 78 (1992): 697–718.
33. Richard Rorty, "What Can You Expect From Anti-Foundationalist Philosophers?: A Reply to Lynn Baker," *Virginia Law Review* 78 (1992): 725.

or her social prophets simply drop any foundationalist appeals (to Truth, God, Nature, or the Fatherland), and say things like, "If we try it (treating all men and women as brothers and sisters, abolishing slavery, banning pornography) we'll like the consequences."[34] But Rorty immediately acknowledges that the audience to whom a prophet appeals does not always hold the same values as does the prophet himself or herself. That is what makes life difficult for the prophets. Recognizing this, Rorty asks of his own position, "Isn't there an ambiguity between 'we, the people with power to change things' and 'we—all of us—the powerless as well as the powerful?' Doesn't my cheerful, upbeat 'liberal' use of 'we' obscure this difference?"[35] To which, Rorty replies,

> It does, but then the difference has *become* more obscure—or at least more usefully obscured—as what Nietzsche was pleased to call "slave-morality" has caught on, as the franchise has been extended, as education has become more nearly universal, etc. The rhetoric of the relatively powerful has had to change to take account of the need to use persuasion rather than force on the relatively powerless. Lately, the operations of constitutional democracy—the pressures brought by what President George Bush is pleased to call "interest groups"— have forced people to stop naked appeals to sexism and racism, and forced them to make cloaked appeals instead. A lot of things that some of the powerful believe in their hearts—e.g., that men have the right to beat up on women whenever they need to bolster their own self-confidence—are things they can no longer say in public, and can barely admit to themselves. We have a long way to go in this direction, obviously, but I see no better political rhetoric available than the kind that pretends that "we" have a virtue even when we do not have it yet. That sort of pretense and rhetoric is just how new and better "we's" get constructed. *For what people cannot say in public becomes, eventually, what they cannot say even in private, and then, still later, what they cannot even believe in their hearts* [my emphasis].[36]

---

34. Ibid.
35. Ibid.
36. Ibid., 725–26.

Even for someone like Rorty, who never seems to feel the pressure of a contradiction, I cannot see how the last sentence in the above quotation can be reconciled with the view that we could split the self up into a *private* part and a *public* part. For it *now* appears that nothing can exist in the private part of one's vocabulary *unless* it can also be made public. By 1992, at least, Rorty seems to have come around to the position I earlier ascribed to Loyola—that is, the position that a belief that cannot be practiced (in public) will eventually cease to be a belief. But the problem—as I hope to have shown in this section—is that a liberalism that concerns itself with preventing humiliation must *necessarily* regulate an almost infinite number of public actions and, therefore, private beliefs. It hardly seems that *this* version of liberalism would be very good at "leaving people alone to dream and think and live as they please. . . ." To sum up: Rorty's view of liberalism, with its *principal* injunction against humiliation, a view that he sketches in *Contingency, Irony, and Solidarity*, is in serious tension with his view of liberalism, with its *principal* injunction that we leave people alone, a view that (alas) he also sketches in *Contingency, Irony, and Solidarity*.

In the next section I try to make my point about the inability to partition the self even more clear by focusing on the relationship between liberalism and ironism. I will show that as liberals—that is, individuals who are primarily concerned with eliminating humiliation—we cannot also be ironists. For to understand the self in an ironic way would be to eliminate that self's susceptibility to humiliation. *Only a nonironist self can be humiliated.* Hence, it makes sense for liberals (like Rorty) to be concerned about humiliation *only* if they see the self in a way fundamentally opposite from the way Rorty sees the self.

My strategy in pressing this claim will be to provide a close reading of the eighth chapter of *Contingency, Irony, and Solidarity*, the chapter entitled, "The Last Intellectual in Europe: Orwell on Cruelty." This chapter and a similar chapter immediately preceding it on Nabokov form essentially the last third of *Contingency, Irony, and Solidarity*. Recalling that "liberals are the people who think that cruelty is the worst thing we do," Rorty provides these successive chapters on Nabokov and Orwell as a way of concretely dramatizing two forms of cruelty: the cruelty of *passive* humiliation displayed in the actions of Nabokov's fictional creation, Humbert Humbert; and the cruelty of *active* humiliation displayed in the actions of Orwell's fictional creation, O'Brien. I might have chosen either of these two chapters as a way of illustrating the tension between

Rorty's understanding of humiliation and his understanding of the ironist self. I have chosen the chapter on Orwell because I think it helps us see the theoretical tension I have spoken of more clearly.

Liberalism, Humiliation, and the Ironist Self

George Orwell may justifiably be said to have written the most important *political* novel of the twentieth century: *1984*.[37] He may also have created in that novel one of the cruelest characters imaginable: O'Brien, the maniacal (what word could do him justice?) Inner Party member who enjoys torturing Winston Smith, simply because he *can* torture Winston. In O'Brien's own, infamous formulation, "The object of persecution is persecution. The object of torture is torture. The object of power is power."[38] But Orwell was not the first to write a twentieth-century dystopia about a totalitarian world in which torture is the rule and liberty is unknown. That rather dubious honor probably goes to Evgeny Zamyatin, whose 1921 novel *We* resembles *1984* in many ways: both dystopias involve extraordinary *physical* brutality, the ubiquitous presence of a secret police apparatus, governmentally enforced sexual asceticism, and so forth. What, if anything, makes *1984* unique?

On Rorty's reading (and here I think he *does* have something), what makes *1984* of special interest is O'Brien, and what makes O'Brien of special interest is the type of pain he specializes in inflicting. It is of a type that may indeed be more cruel than mere physical pain. O'Brien specializes in humiliating persons—humiliating them deeply and irreparably. In the remarks that follow, I shall explore Rorty's understanding of O'Brien's methods with an eye toward seeing how such an understanding problematizes Rorty's own conception of humiliation, and of the self, and therefore, of a liberalism based on the injunction not to humiliate any fellow self.

To properly contextualize this discussion, recall a point I made earlier about the ironist self. We saw that, in Rorty's view, the ironist self "faces up to" the contingency of his or her own selfhood. But facing up

---

37. For an excellent discussion of the way in which Orwell has been "read" by various political groups in the last half century, see John Rodden, *The Politics of Literary Reputation: The Making and Claiming of "St. George" Orwell* (Oxford: University Press, 1989).

38. George Orwell, *1984* (New York: Harcourt Brace Jovanovich, 1977), 267.

to the contingency of selfhood does not mean dispensing with the notion that every human, simply by virtue of being human, can feel pain. The capacity to feel pain becomes, for Rorty, a noncontingent aspect, indeed the *only* noncontingent aspect, of our *human* nature. This capacity is noncontingent in the sense that it is not subject to time or chance; it is not something that varies among societies or cultures or historical epochs. It is constitutive of ourselves; it is embedded in the very structure of our central nervous systems. We could not *be* without it.[39] But notice that animals, creatures we *assume* to be different from ourselves *in important ways*, can *also* feel pain. If we can find nothing else that human beings share in common but the capacity to feel pain, and if we now recognize that animals too feel pain, does this mean that facing up to Rorty's "contingency of selfhood" *compels* us to see ourselves *as* selves in essentially the same way we see our pets? And if so, does this not mean that we must now recognize essentially the same level of solidarity to exist between ourselves and our pets, as that which exists between ourselves and our neighbors? Does this mean, Rorty himself asks, "that our moral vocabulary should be extended to cover animals as well as people?" That would be one way of reacting to the contingency of selfhood. But Rorty says

> A better way . . . is to try to isolate something that distinguishes human from animal pain. Here is where O'Brien comes in. O'Brien reminds us that human beings who have been socialized—socialized in any language, any culture—do share a capacity which other animals lack. They can all be given a special kind of pain: They can all be humiliated by the forcible tearing down of the particular structures of language and belief in which they were socialized (or which they pride themselves on having formed for themselves). More specifi-

---

39. On this point, consider Elaine Scarry's remark: "Terrifying for its narrowness [physical pain] nevertheless exhausts and displaces all else until it seems to become the single broad and omnipresent fact of existence. From no matter what perspective [physical] pain is approached, its totality is again and again faced. Even neurological and physiological descriptions repeatedly acknowledge the breath of its presence. Its mastery of the body, for example, is suggested by the failure of many surgical attempts to remove pain pathways because the body quickly, effortlessly, and endlessly generates new pathways." See Elaine Scarry, *The Body in Pain: The Making and Unmaking of the World* (Oxford: University Press, 1985), 55.

cally, they can be used, and animals cannot, to gratify O'Brien's wish to "tear human minds to pieces and put them together again in new shapes of your own choosing."[40]

Rorty seems to assert that the only "species universal" that we humans share is the ability to feel pain. But the *specific difference* between human pain and animal pain involves the uniquely human capacity to feel the pain of humiliation.[41] What happens when we bring together this assertion with Rorty's picture of the ironist self? Again, at first glance, it seems that O'Brien's apparently irresistible ability to humiliate anyone, any *possible* self, is incompatible with the very possibility that we could see ourselves as being what Rorty thinks we are: totally contingent selves. For, only if we *could* see ourselves as totally contingent selves could we resist O'Brien. But, to repeat: In Rorty's view, we *cannot* resist O'Brien's methods, although we *certainly* can try to prevent O'Brien from using those methods on anyone. Another way of putting this point is to say that, to the extent one *could* resist O'Brien, one would (to exactly that extent) be "inhuman," in the sense that one would *not* share with his or her fellows the only attribute Rorty feels makes us *uniquely* human—the capacity to feel the pain of humiliation.

Now, the suggestion that we *must* become inhuman to resist O'Brien's own inhuman form of torture may seem vaguely disquieting, at best, if not paradoxically terrifying, at worst. It is a suggestion, however, that seems unavoidable based on Rorty's understanding of the nature of the self, and the nature of humiliation. To understand exactly why Rorty is forced into this position, we need to get clear on O'Brien's precise method of torture. The critical scene in which this method is described comes near the end of the novel. Winston Smith, a middle-level bureaucrat and member of the Party, has been arrested for a "thought-crime."

---

40. Rorty, *Contingency, Irony, and Solidarity*, 177.
41. But consider, in this regard, the following remark by Thomas McCarthy:

> With scarcely a glance at the human sciences, Rorty assures us that the only species universal is "the ability to feel pain," to which he sometimes adds the "susceptibility to . . . humiliation" as a distinctively human form of pain. Why not also add the ability to speak, act, think, work, learn, interact, play roles, be guided by norms, have desires, and, indeed, feel feelings other than humiliation?

See McCarthy, "Ironist Theory as a Vocation: A Response To Rorty's Reply," *Critical Inquiry* 16 (spring 1990): 649, footnote omitted.

He is taken to the Ministry of Love and tortured in all of the customary ways: he is kicked, clubbed, made to endure electric shocks to his body, and so forth. Of course, he signs whatever confessions O'Brien, his very sophisticated torturer, demands that he sign, and he implicates whomever he is told to implicate in whatever crime he is told to implicate the person. Essentially, Winston *says* whatever he is told to say; he *goes through the motions* that O'Brien dictates. But through it all, the *one* thing Winston does not do is betray Julia, his lover. The word "betray" has a very precise meaning here: Winston never ceases, not even for a moment, sincerely to love Julia. For O'Brien, this simply will not do. Winston is therefore taken to Room 101 and confronted with his special, unendurable fear. In Winston's case, this is a fear of rats. He is strapped to a chair, and a cage containing live rats is placed over his head. At the crucial moment, just *before* the cage door is to be opened and the rats are to be let at Winston, he cries, "Do it to Julia," *and he sincerely means it.* He wants O'Brien to torture Julia instead. In that instant, he has betrayed Julia; he has been broken.

There is, of course, a great deal one could say about this scene. In the following passage, observe how Rorty describes the *essential* element in O'Brien's method, and observe also the conclusions about the nature of the self that Rorty draws from this description. As Rorty notes,

> O'Brien wants to cause Winston as much pain as possible, and for this purpose what matters is that Winston be forced to realize that he has become incoherent, realize that he is no longer able to use a language or be a self. Although we can say, "I believ*ed* something false," nobody can say to himself, "I am, right now, believing something false." [This, of course, would be an example of "doublethink."—EMG] So nobody can be humiliated at the moment of believing a falsehood, or by the mere fact of having done so. But people can, their torturers hope, experience the ultimate humiliation of saying to themselves, in retrospect, "Now that I have believed or desired *this*, I can never be what I hoped to be, what I thought I was. The story I have been telling myself about myself—my picture of myself as honest, loyal, devout—no longer makes sense. I no longer have a self to make sense of. There is no world in which I can picture myself as living, because there is no vocabulary in which I can tell a coherent story about myself." For Winston

the sentence he could not utter sincerely and still be able to put himself back together was "Do it to Julia!" and the worst thing in the world happened to be rats. *But presumably each of us stands in the same relation to some sentence, and to some thing.* If one can discover that key sentence and that key thing, then, as O'Brien says, one can tear a mind apart and put it together in new shapes of one's own choosing.[42]

It is important to emphasize here that Winston's betrayal of Julia was *also*, and to at least an equal degree, an act of *self*-betrayal. To underscore this point, let me turn briefly from the fictional world of O'Brien and Smith to the real world of torturers past and present as this world is sketched (with every bit as much impact as we find in Orwell) in Elaine Scarry's *The Body in Pain: The Making and Unmaking of the World.* I should mention that Rorty references with approval Scarry's analyses of torture. Consider, then, the ways in which Scarry's description of what real world torturers do to their victims—in particular, how these torturers attempt to humiliate their victims—fits with Rorty's description of what O'Brien does, and his analysis of the relationship between O'Brien and Smith. Scarry writes,

> Torture systematically prevents the prisoner from being the agent of anything and simultaneously pretends that he is the agent of some things. Despite the fact that in reality he has been deprived of all control over, and therefore all responsibility for, his world, his words, and his body, *he is to understand his confession as it will be understood by others, as an act of self-betrayal.*[43]

It would not be too much to say, I think, that there is a paradox at the very heart of this passage, a paradox so powerful that it encompasses everything that can be said about torture, humiliation, and the nature of the self. It is a paradox that Rorty seems not to understand in its fullest dimensions. We can begin to understand this paradox by noticing that, *for some inexplicable reason*, it is impossible either for Winston Smith, or for any one of the real life victims to which Scarry refers, simply to say after the torture, "Well, I was being tortured, so whatever I said simply

42. Rorty, *Contingency, Irony, and Solidarity,* 179 (emphasis added).
43. Scarry, *The Body in Pain,* 47 (emphasis added).

does not matter. I was in such agonizing pain at the time, or suffering from such dreadful fear, that I really was not myself, you know." The vaguely insouciant tone of this remark is deliberate. We shall see why shortly. For now, it is important to underscore the central element of the paradox at the very heart of this section: As far as I can see, Rorty *must* concede that neither Winston, nor any real life victim of torture, could give the type of response I have just sketched. *But, it is not at all clear why these victims could not provide exactly this response.* Indeed, in Winston's case, we should think that such a response would be the easiest thing in the world for him to utter, and sincerely to believe. O'Brien himself gives Winston the perfect "out"—so to speak. This is what O'Brien tells Winston just seconds before the torture with the rats: "[F]or everyone there is something unendurable—something that cannot be contemplated. *Courage and cowardice are not involved.* If you are falling from a height it is not cowardly to clutch at a rope. If you have come up from deep water it is not cowardly to fill your lungs with air. It is merely an instinct which cannot be ignored."[44] If O'Brien is correct here, then Winston's cry, "Do it to Julia" is *essentially* no different than the involuntary muscle contractions he undergoes during a particularly gruesome session of torture involving the use of electric shocks to his body. But, even more than that, *if* O'Brien is correct, then not only Winston's *physical* cry, "Do it to Julia," but his accompanying, quite sincere *desire* that they do it to Julia, is also *essentially* no different than those aforementioned involuntary muscle contractions. So, to repeat my earlier question, why could not Winston simply dismiss his remark about Julia as an irrelevant action (both physical and mental) in the same way he surely saw his involuntary muscle contradictions as irrelevant actions?

"Because," Rorty might insist, "he *sincerely* meant it." True. But why could Winston not simply respond, "Well, yes, of course I was being sincere when I said, 'Do it to Julia.' *But I was also being tortured.* And, as you know, anyone can be made to say, sincerely, anything under the right kind of torture. So, although what I said was quite sincere, it was also quite trivial and irrelevant." I suspect that the problem most people will have with this response is in seeing a sincerely uttered remark as trivial. There seems *ultimately* to be something nontrivial about a sincere remark, *regardless of the context in which it is uttered*. But why should this be so?

---

44. Orwell, *1984*, 287 (emphasis added).

Another way of approaching the issue that I have been posing through the previous series of questions is to reverse direction and ask, what positive *ability* would it take for Winston to manage the type of replies that I have sketched? The perfectly obvious answer is that, to reply in the ways I have sketched, Winston would need the ability to adopt toward the entire torture episode an attitude of *ironic detachment*. Could it be, then, that Winston's real problem was simply that he took himself a bit *too* seriously? The poor fellow just could not bring himself to see the utter triviality involved in betraying someone *while being tortured*. Presumably, Winston was just not enough of an ironist.

To give this argument the kind of outlandish twist it deserves—and to meet Rorty on the ground of the modern novel—let me engage in a bit of literary fantasy and imagine that O'Brien found himself about to torture not poor, old, straightforward, two and two equals four Winston Smith, but instead a truly *ironic* character, say Lord Henry Wotton of Oscar Wilde's *The Picture of Dorian Gray*. For our purposes, the plot of this nineteenth century neo-gothic novel is not important. The characterizations are, however; and, in particular, the characterization of Lord Henry. It would be fair to say, I think, that Oscar Wilde continues to represent, more or less, the type of personality traits we have come to associate with the figure of the aesthete. Wilde's creation, Lord Henry Wotton, is the literary telos of that personality type. He is the *perfect* aesthete. He is therefore a consummate ironist: a man who cannot take himself, his final vocabulary, nor indeed anyone's final vocabulary seriously. Recall here Rorty's definition of "ironists" as individuals who are "never quite able to take themselves seriously." Surely Lord Henry fits this description perfectly. As he says, "Humanity takes itself too seriously. It is the world's original sin."[45] (Presumably Lord Henry intends for this remark about the sin of seriousness to be taken seriously. But we should not get tripped up in self-referential paradoxes before we even get started.)

One could well imagine Lord Henry conversing easily with O'Brien before the torture session was to begin. Henry might say, "O'Brien old chap, those spectacles really are all the rage; I must get a pair for myself. And those black overalls which you in the Inner Party wear are also quite chic. Elegant, but understated, I would say. It shows

---

45. Oscar Wilde, *The Picture of Dorian Gray* (New York: New American Library, 1962), 56.

good fashion sense. I must congratulate B-B, if I ever see him. You know, they say clothes make the man; but, *entre nous*, I don't think *anything* makes the man. Yet if something must, why not let it be clothes? It's as good a candidate as anything, I should think.

"Now, I understand that you are about to torture me. Very well. You should know that I absolutely cannot endure so much as one ounce of physical pain. At its onset I am immediately reduced to a sniveling, grovelling lump of flesh. You should also know that I am frightened quite literally out of my wits by rats, spiders, bugs, and a whole series of other vermin, large and small. I shall make a list, if you like. Finally, you should know that there is simply nothing I cannot imagine myself not saying, and indeed not sincerely believing, while under torture. Let me be clear about this. *While under torture* I can be made to hate or despise anyone; I can be made to desire the brutal torture, or even death, of a best friend or lover; I can be made to wish for the lingering, painful death of each and every member of my family; and so forth. But this is tedious. If you still wish to torture me, please proceed. Assuming that this does not take too long—and I cannot imagine that it will—I plan to meet a couple of friends, Winston Smith and Dorian Gray, later at the Chestnut Tree Cafe. I do not wish to be late. But do your best job, old boy, for (as will happen from time to time) there has descended upon my recent conversations with Winston and Dorian a most dreadful air of *ennui*. Surely *you* know how suffocating such an air can be. We need something interesting to discuss, and my torture will certainly provide a fascinating diversion."

Of course, O'Brien is nothing if not a stubborn character. One can just see him readjusting his spectacles in that "curiously civilized" way and responding, "My dear Lord Henry, it is so rewarding to find such a prime specimen for torture. I shall enjoy humiliating you more than I enjoyed humiliating poor Winston. Now Henry—may I call you Henry?—you seem to be under the impression that I will force you to betray someone, or to wish for a friend's death, or something equally banal. But I shall do nothing of the sort. In *your* case I shall force you to believe that there *is* some noncontingent Truth—with a capital T. Perhaps I shall make you sincerely believe that there is a God, or that there is an immutable moral law, or even that there is a core, noncontingent self. Yes, that is it: I will cause you to betray yourself by torturing you into believing that there cannot be an ironist self. I shall send you out of the Ministry of Love a more serious, stouthearted, morally upright, insipid being than even you could imagine. When you look back on the facile aesthete who now stands before me you will feel deep, unelimitable humiliation. Do you deny that I *could* do that, and that by doing just that I would indeed humiliate you?"

It is time for Lord Henry's argumentative *coup de maître*. Imagine him responding, passively, of course, "O'Brien old boy, you just do not get it. Perhaps you are not the wit some, like Rorty, appear to think you are. Very well, I shall go over it one last time. Now, do pay attention. Certainly you could make me believe, while I was being tortured, that there is no such thing as an ironist self. But just as surely, neither the act of holding that belief, nor the act of having held that belief, would humiliate me. I would simply look back, after the torture, and say, 'Well, yes, I believed that, but I was being tortured.' Now, if you 'remade' me such that I could *never* look back on my torture experience and say exactly this—that is, if I could no longer exercise any degree of ironic detachment—then instead of having succeeded in *humiliating* me you would have succeeded in *converting* me. But this conversion would not humiliate me in the *totalizing* way in which you wish to humiliate me.

"Let me make this last point more clear, old chap. I do *not* deny that you could, through torture, bring me to a point at which I could no longer look back upon such torture with ironic detachment. You could, in other words, change me from an ironist to a nonironist. Or, to use Rorty's terminology, you could—through the use of torture—change me from an ironist into a metaphysician. But notice: the act of torturing me into adopting a metaphysical final vocabulary, indeed into *becoming* a metaphysician, would not be analogous to 'breaking' me in the same sense that you broke Winston by forcing him to betray Julia. The difference is that in 'breaking' me—if, indeed, we could even speak sensibly of 'breaking' an ironist—you would *not* also be humiliating me in the same totalizing way you humiliated Winston. The only way you could do to me what you did to Winston would be to take the *new* metaphysical me you created and break *that* person; for only a metaphysician can be humiliated. I submit, however, that the person you would then humiliate would in no relevant sense be me, any more than I would be the 'same' person after a frontal lobotomy.

"I perceive, O'Brien, that you wish to object to this position. I know precisely what your objection will be, for I know *you*, my friend. You see, we really are two of a kind. You wish to object that occurrences of conversion and humiliation are not necessarily mutually exclusive, as I have seemed just now to have implied. You wish to point out that we can easily imagine examples of individuals for whom a conversion experience is associated with intense humiliation: take, for instance, the Christian convert who looks back upon his or her life of sin and depravity with the most acute sense of humiliation. Such examples certainly do exist; they may in fact be numerous. And yet, it is surely beneath your dignity, O'Brien old boy, to suggest that this type of humiliation is *all* that you could hope to inflict upon me. You will notice, I am sure, the critical difference between this type of humiliation and the humiliation suffered by Winston. As I have said, Winston's humiliation was *total*. Everywhere Winston 'looked'—backward in time, forward, or to the present—he could feel nothing but humiliation. In the case we just spoke of regarding the Christian convert, the situation would be much different. When he or she looked *backward* in time he or she would indeed feel a deep sense of humiliation. But when he or she looked to the present or the future, he or she would feel a wonderful sense of pride in himself or herself, or at least contentment and solace. And from his or her present perspective, the trade-off would be well worth the pain of looking back. To purse this point a bit further, imagine the comic outcome if you were to attempt to humiliate me *merely* by changing me into a stouthearted metaphysician. After the 'conversion' I could not help but sincerely thank you for what you had done. I would then (after the 'conversion') stand in the same relationship toward you as the 'well converted' *former* heretic would have stood toward the kindly sixteenth-century Jesuit. I would *love* you, or Big Brother, in a very nonironic sense. In fact, because 'I' was now a metaphysician, I could *only* love you, or Big Brother, in a nonironic sense. But surely this is not what you want. If this type of outcome were all you ever wanted, your objective in torturing Winston would have been to force him finally to love Big Brother—in a nonironic sense. Yet, as Rorty correctly points out, you wanted nothing of the kind, and not *just* because Big Brother is unlovable in anything but an ironic sense. What you wanted in Winston's case, and what you want in my case, as in all cases, is simply to cause your victim humiliation through and through. To do that to me, you would need to convert me and *then* humiliate the convert. But I put it to you: Who or what would you then be humiliating?

    "To sum up: As long as I remain an ironist, *I* cannot be humiliated. Certainly you could torture me into becoming a metaphysician, who you could *then* humiliate. And yet, in so torturing me—the ironist me who is now speaking to you—you would in effect *destroy* me, for I am nothing if not an ironist. But notice finally: The thought that you could in this way destroy me, while a terrifying thought, and indeed a thought that I quite literally cannot endure—in the same sense that I cannot endure a bullet—is no more humiliating (or terrifying) to me than the thought that you could, right now, shoot me and thereby destroy my physical body. So, you can forget about humiliating *this* Lord Henry Wotton. You see, O'Brien, in the last analysis the torturer and the victim of humiliation are, in a strange and terrifyingly paradoxical way, complicitous. *Each* is involved in the victim's humiliation. I simply refuse to be involved. Or, in words too ironic for Winston ever to have thought, or said, 'I have beaten you, O'Brien.'"

I imagine that in the face of such a response O'Brien might just drop his spectacles. What could he do? Surely torturing Lord Henry would be quite uninteresting, for Henry *would* be completely malleable—as (presumably) we all are—*and would recognize himself to be.* Hence, he would not "resist." There would be nothing to humiliate.

It is perhaps sobering to think that the best defense against O'Brien is *not* a strong moral character—for that can always be broken—but rather, a light-minded, ironic approach toward the self. Of course, if one *is* sobered by this thought, one is presumably evidencing precisely the type of strong moral character that, it has been concluded, is problematic. So one should not find this thought sobering after all, but simply *ironic*.

That conclusion would fit Lord Henry well, but I suspect it would fall flat on very nearly everyone else. Indeed, there is a temptation—a very strong temptation—to say that characters like Lord Henry are *utterly* lacking in self-respect. And, in saying this, there is an equally strong temptation to conclude that *we* should not (or perhaps, could not) respect such figures. Again, my suspicion is that what really disturbs people about Lord Henry is not so much his inability to withstand torture, but rather his willingness to admit this inability without feeling a sense of humiliation. Lord Henry's attitude may strike most of us as being suspect, precisely because we naturally think of the self as having some *core* that, although moved about from scene to scene, *must* remain the same. This is exactly what it means to see the *self* as noncontingent. We think that anyone who does not see the self in this way—as ironists do not appear to—cannot really have *a* self to demand our respect.

Of course, *this* picture of the stable, core self is not without complications of its own. For one thing, we change selves continually—at least we *seem* to. Some of these changes obviously seem to be trivial, as when we change our preference for red wine to a preference for white wine. Some seem to be much less trivial, as when we change political affiliations. And some may seem to be definitive of our very core selves, as when we change religions or, perhaps, occupations. I would note— parenthetically—that those like Rorty who adopt the view that "social- ization goes all the way down" might point out, correctly I think, that what one sees as a "major" change in himself or herself may vary from culture to culture. With but a little imagination we could conceive of a society that placed an extraordinary emphasis on wines. In such a society, changing one's preference in wines might even be more "definitive" of the self than changing one's preferences in religions. I shall leave to the anthropologists the question of whether, in such a society, the preference for wines is merely a rechanneling of religious sentiments, or whether, in our society, the preference for religions is merely a rechanneling of sen- timents about wine, or whether some third alternative is at work.

For our purposes, the more interesting question would seem to be: How can we make sense of a self changing *itself*? In other words, how can we make sense of conversion experiences? Such experiences do happen—at least they seem to. And yet, for a self to change its *core* self would seem to necessitate a still more "central" core self to perform the change. Ultimately this paradox goes to the heart of questions involving the concept of "free will." It is a paradox that thinkers like Plato and Augustine (to select only two of the most prominent figures) grappled with throughout their philosophical lives, without definitive success. As we saw in the previous chapter, Rorty confronts (if that is the correct word) this paradox when he advises us to think of the self as "a network of beliefs and desires which is continually in the process of being rewoven (with some old items dropped as new ones are added). This network is not one which is rewoven by an agent distinct from the network—a master weaver, so to speak. Rather, it reweaves itself, in response to stimuli. . . ." Again, as we saw, Rorty is quick to add that "[t]his picture is hard to reconcile with common speech, according to which the 'I' is distinct from its beliefs and desires, picks and chooses among them, etc. *But we must think with the learned while continuing to speak with the vulgar.*"[46] For those who find Rorty's answer to this

---

46. Rorty, "Non-Reductive Physicalism," in *Objectivity, Relativism, and Truth*, 123, emphasis added.

paradox unsatisfying, let me offer another. Going back to the paradox as stated earlier, might we say that the core self is simply the *ability* to perform changes in belief systems? On this view, the core self is not constitutive of the beliefs and desire we hold; rather it *is* our ability to hold beliefs and desires.

I can sketch this view of the self in more detail by considering the example of a person who converts from Islam to Christianity. Under normal conditions, such a person could say, "I was once a Muslim, now I am a Christian." It is simply the ability to make this statement which would constitute the person's core self. But I should add here that "making" this statement involves more than merely saying the words. It involves also being able to tell oneself a coherent story about how one got from a past state to the present state. This story may seem trivial or serious or something in between; the only requirement is that it be coherent to the person telling it. In our example, the convert might say, "Well, I became a Christian because I decided it would just be too much of a bother to travel to Mecca." Or the convert might say, "I became a Christian because I finally understood that Christ *is* the Son of God." We could even imagine such a convert saying, "Now that I have found the true faith, I will be a Christian for life," and then, sometime later, converting to Buddhism. Such a person would still constitute a core self if he or she could say, for example, "Well, I had been confused by Western notions of God all my life, but now I can see the true nature of the universe more clearly." The point, to repeat, is that the ability to tell these stories constitutes the self.

To come at this point from the reverse angle, consider that under *abnormal* conditions we can imagine such a person *not* being able to say this. Perhaps the least controversial example of such abnormal conditions would involve cases of mental illness, specifically schizophrenia. In such cases we tend to speak of the patient *being* several persons. (Of course, Rorty would include torture as another abnormal condition. But then we are back to the earlier paradox: Why cannot a torture victim include the act of being tortured in a coherent story about why he or she changed his or her beliefs and desires?)

The picture of the self that I have just sketched strongly resembles Kant's deontological vision of the self. In *Liberalism and the Limits of Justice*, Michael Sandel notes that for those who adopt a deontological vision of the self, "what is most essential to our personhood is not the ends we choose but our capacity to choose them. And this capacity is located in a self which must be prior to the ends it chooses."[47] In other words, what is most essential about a person is not that he or she *is* a Christian, a Muslim, or a Buddhist, but that he or she has the ability to choose to be one of these. It was Emerson (I believe) who once said, "Choice is the ultimate fiction." One might read this remark as saying that choice is *merely* a fiction, hence we have no free will and the universe is fully determined. But it would be better to read it as saying that our ability to believe that we do have choices is ultimately the only thing that allows us to act. In this sense, the fiction of choice is *prior* to all of the other fictions we may create for ourselves.

Of course, there are also problems with *this* view of the self. For one thing, it is hard to imagine a core self that does not contain *any* beliefs or desires. Such a core self would be totally empty; it would be nothing (literally no "thing"). But in saying this we are brought back to square one, for again, how can we make sense of a self changing *itself*? To say that we can make sense of this by positing a self that is nothing does not seem to help matters.

If this is so, why have I spent so much time sketching this view of the self? Partly because I think it no *worse* than any other view, and more relevantly because I think that ultimately it comports best with Rorty's own view. Rorty would demur. In his 1988 article "The Priority of Democracy to Philosophy," he explicitly rejects this deontological view of the self. Rorty rejects this view *only* because he thinks it too *metaphysical*.[48] This, of course, places all of the weight on the term *metaphysical*. I strongly suspect that Rorty would have no problems with the deontological conception of the self if it were possible simply to drop the weightiness that is associated with this view; if, in other words, no one would insist that we take this picture of the self seriously. Of course, Rorty's point is not *just* to insist that we drop the seriousness associated with this particular view of the self. Rather, his point is that we drop the seriousness associated with *all* views of the self.

But this gets us nowhere. If one could dispense with the seriousness in all pictures of the self, one could presumably take one's own self nonseriously, and hence, one could presumably resist O'Brien. *But no one can resist O'Brien.* So it seems that one cannot *not* privilege some aspect of the

47. Michael Sandel, *Liberalism and the Limits of Justice* (Cambridge: Cambridge University Press, 1982), 19.
48. See Rorty, "The Priority of Democracy to Philosophy," especially pp. 184–86.

self. But what is a "core" self, if not precisely that privileged aspect of the self? Whether that core consists of a particular set of beliefs and desires, or whether (as on the deontological view) it is simply the ability to hold beliefs and desires, or whether it is some third "thing," the very idea of a core self seems indispensable. Even while denying this point, Rorty does indeed smuggle back into his system the concept of a core self—a concept that, as I said, looks very much like the deontological view.

To see exactly how Rorty does this, begin by recalling his discussion of the way in which Winston is finally broken. Specifically, recall Rorty's assertion that, for each and every one of us, there is some sentence the utterance of which makes it impossible for one to continue telling oneself a coherent story about oneself. This seems to imply that, in fact, there *is* a core self— that core self being defined, negatively, as whatever it is that cannot withstand the utterance of this sentence. Of course, Rorty might respond that such a core self does not really constitute a noncontingent self, since this key sentence is obviously contingent upon some historical set of circumstances and could even change over time. (This response is, of course, similar to the objection that the deontological picture of the core self is an empty one.) But I think Rorty is trying to have it both ways. One could certainly grant that this key sentence is contingent, and one could also grant that this sentence could (perhaps most likely *would*) change from time to time. But granting all this would not prevent one from asserting that what ultimately constitutes the *core* (noncontingent) self is the self's belief that it has a core—that is, the self's belief that *at any given moment* there is some sentence the utterance of which would obliterate itself. All of this is a negative way of saying that what really constituted Winston's self was not his love of *Julia* as such, but rather, his ability to *choose* to love anyone.

This view of the core self puts all of the weight on the notion of *choice*. And even if Emerson is "correct" (whatever that would mean) in his assertion that choice is a fiction, it is still an *essential* fiction. At this point, a number of threads appear to come together. Notice, for example, the connection we seem naturally to make between a person's capacity to exercise choice *over particular changes in his or her set of beliefs and desires*, and the level of respect we seem to feel is due that person from his or her fellows. *Perhaps this connection should not exist.* But it seems to, at least in our culture.[49] To say, "I am the captain of my

---

49. I need to emphasize here that my point in this section is *not* to ridicule the character of Lord Henry, or the figure of the aesthete in general. If it appears the such a fig-

soul," as does the narrator in William Ernest Henley's poem "Invictus" (the word is Latin for "unconquered"), is perhaps just a more poetic way of asserting, at least in our culture, that one is due respect from one's peers. Again, perhaps this should *not* be so. Nevertheless, from what has been said so far, I think we can pose a tentative hypothesis: Strong selves, those that we seem to agree are deserving of our respect, are selves that at least appear to be in control of the changes over their set of beliefs and desires. Weak selves, those less deserving of our respect, are selves that at least appear not to be in as great a degree of control over these changes.

If this all sounds hopelessly abstract, I can make my point a bit more concrete by juxtaposing the perhaps less than respectable character of Lord Henry with another "fictional" character, a character we *do* respect, indeed a veritable cultural hero in the West: Robert Bolt's Sir Thomas More. The hero of the play *A Man For All Seasons*, though a scholar and a wit, has not an ironic bone in his body. He is an exemplary metaphysician: one who sees the self as noncontingent, and one who certainly can imagine himself feeling the pain of humiliation. Both of these aspects of Sir Thomas's character are dramatized nicely in a scene at the end of the play. Sir Thomas has been imprisoned—essentially for refusing to take an oath declaring that the marriage of Henry VIII and Ann Boleyn is sanctioned by God. More will not take the oath, as he says earlier in the play, "because *I* oppose it—I do—not my pride, not my spleen, nor any other of my appetites, but *I* do—I!"[50] Now, at the end of the play, More's daughter Meg comes to see him in prison. She tries to convince her father to "say the words of the oath, and in your heart think otherwise." More, of course, cannot do this; Meg cannot understand why. They then talk about oaths, the nature of the self, and things that Sir Thomas is loathe to do. More says

> When a man takes an oath, Meg, he's holding his own self in
> his hands. Like water. [He cups his hands.] And if he opens

---

ure is often the object of ridicule, that may say more about our culture, *Rorty's culture*, than about anything else. Notice, however, that if I am correct in my characterization of Lord Henry, it follows that he, at least, would not be offended by anything I have said. For if Lord Henry could be offended by ridicule, he could surely be made to feel humiliation. But we already know that is impossible.

50. Robert Bolt, *A Man for All Seasons: A Play in Two Acts* (New York: Vintage Books, 1962), 71.

his fingers *then*—he needn't hope to find himself again. Some men aren't capable of this, but I'd be loathe to think your father one of them.[51]

Among other things, this passage demonstrates that there is a direct, though perhaps illusive, similarity between Sir Thomas and Winston Smith. For each man there exists one unique sentence, the sincere utterance of which would *totally* humiliate him. In Winston's case, the sentence is "Do it to Julia." In Sir Thomas's case, the sentence is "The marriage of Henry VIII and Ann Boleyn is sanctioned by God." But at this point we need to take care to describe with extreme precision exactly what thoughts and actions will cause humiliation to Winston and Sir Thomas. Notice, then, that it is not *merely* the sincere utterance of each statement that would totally humiliate our metaphysicians. Each sentence must also be sincerely uttered *in a particular context*. For Sir Thomas, the sentence must be uttered in the context of his still feeling allegiance to the Catholic Church. For Winston, the sentence must be uttered in the context of his still loving Julia. If Sir Thomas had ceased to recognize the supremacy of the Catholic Church *before* Henry VIII demanded the oath from him, he could have taken the oath (uttered the sentence) without being humiliated. Similarly, if Winston had ceased loving Julia *before* he was arrested (or indeed, anytime before the actual torture with the rats), he could have said "Do it to Julia" without being humiliated.

This focus on the context in which the key (potentially) humiliating sentence is uttered helps us see the paradox I have been emphasizing throughout this section in yet another way. Observe that both Winston and Sir Thomas must be *made* to see their respective key sentences in one context, and they must be *prevented* from seeing their respective key sentences in another context. In Winston's case, for example, it seems to matter greatly that he utters the sentence "Do it to Julia" in the context of still loving her, but it seems not to matter at all that he utters this sentence in the context of being tortured. The torturer, of course, understands this. And he or she takes advantage of our natural (how else can one explain it?) tendency to *privilege* one context over another. We tend to say, for example, "Winston should feel humiliated because he sincerely wanted rats to chew through the face of someone

---

51. Ibid., 81.

he loved." But we should say, "Winston should not feel humiliated because he sincerely desired what he desired while he was being ruthlessly tortured." And yet, even Rorty, whom we would think should have foreground Winston's torture in his mind throughout his discussion of *1984*, at times lapses into making statements that ignore the context of Winston's own beliefs and desires.

For example, in a discussion of a torture scene between Winston and O'Brien in which O'Brien forces Winston to believe that two and two equals five, Rorty has this to say: "The *only* point in making Winston believe that two and two equals five is to break him. Getting somebody to deny a belief for no reason is a first step toward making her incapable of having a self because she becomes incapable of weaving a coherent web of belief and desire."[52] But clearly Winston did not come to believe two and two equals five *for no reason*! He was, at the time, under intense physical pain. Notice that if Winston really had come to believe two and two equals five for no reason at all—no reason that he could later look back upon as a legitimate reason for changing his belief—then he would be *simply* insane. He would be like the aforementioned schizophrenic, who could not tell himself a coherent story about himself, and so could not tell what "he" was up to from one moment to next. But Winston surely did have a reason for changing his belief, hence he should have been able to weave a coherent set of beliefs and desires around his actions. The only reason he cannot weave a coherent set of beliefs and desires around his saying two and two equals five is that he cannot shake the belief that under no circumstances (i.e., for no *reason*) should he believe this—not even if he is being tortured.

Surprisingly, Rorty repeats the very same mistake I have just described, only two sentences later. He writes,

> Making Winston briefly believe that two plus two equals five serves the same "breaking" function as making him briefly desire that the rats chew through Julia's face rather than his own. But the latter episode differs from the former in being a final, irreversible unmaking. Winston might be able to include the belief that he had once, under odd conditions, believed that two and two equals five within a coherent story about his character and his life. Temporary irrationality is

---

52. Rorty, *Contingency, Irony, and Solidarity*, 178, emphasis in original.

something around which one can weave a story. But the belief that he once wanted them to *do it to Julia* is not one he can weave a story around. That was why O'Brien saved the rats for the best part, the part in which Winston had to watch himself go to pieces and simultaneously know that he could never pick up the pieces.[53]

Forget, for the moment, that Winston could not "pick up the pieces," again, only because he was insufficiently ironist. Notice instead Rorty's characterization that Winston came to believe two and two equals five *under odd conditions*, and that this belief could be seen by Winston as merely a case of "temporary irrationality." First, it is surely odd to say that the conditions under which Winston's beliefs were induced were "odd." The conditions were brutal. They were not conditions Winston would have found even slightly puzzling at the time. Nor could he be confused about these conditions when he reflected on them afterward. Again, if Winston really were to have changed his beliefs for reasons *he* thought odd, then we should speak of him as, at least, confused. Second, on the question of the role rationality could have played in helping Winston put himself back together, Rorty has it exactly backwards. The real problem, as before, is simply that Winston could not bring himself to see the utter triviality (though consummate *rationality*) of believing anything *while being tortured*. The only truly odd aspect of Winston's plight was his inability to see his utterance "Do it to Julia" as a completely rational response to an inescapable situation, though, precisely because of this rationality, as a completely meaningless response also.

And yet this oddity is necessarily common to all torture victims who are made to suffer humiliation, which brings us back to the paradox I have been pressing throughout this section, and to the final question: Why is it the case that the torturer can successfully humiliate his or her victim in the (presumably intelligent) victim's full knowledge that he or she is being tortured? The only answer I can come up with that makes any sense at all is simply that the ironic detachment demonstrated by Lord Henry is, in reality, *not* possible. Indeed, Rorty's *insistence* that we are *all* potential victims of humiliation drives this point home. We are, therefore, led inescapably to the following conclusion: Since, in the final analysis, we *must* see our "selves" as potential victims of humiliation, we

---

53. Ibid., emphasis in original.

cannot see our "selves" as ironists. Further, since liberal *solidarity* consists *solely* in our ability imaginatively to identify with other potential victims of the cruelty of humiliation, such solidarity is impossible to bring together with an ironic attitude toward ourselves or others. More simply put: Rorty's vision of liberalism and his vision of irony are fundamentally incompatible. This is so not *just* because the liberal wishes the desire to avoid acts of cruelty (in particular acts of humiliation) to be an invariant part of everyone's final vocabulary, while the ironist rebels against the suggestion that any part of anyone's final vocabulary should be seen as invariant. Rather, and more importantly, these two visions are fundamentally incompatible because Rorty's vision of liberalism, with its focus on humiliation, obliterates any meaningful distinction between the public and private. That one distinction, however, is *all* Rorty provides as a way of keeping the "privatistic, 'irrationalistic,' and aestheticist" impulses inherent in irony from turning around and destroying liberal solidarity.

Such is the position we find ourselves in at the conclusion of these first two chapters. In the next chapter I discuss the second major theoretical distinction that Rorty attempts to defend in his recent political philosophy—the distinction between persuasion and force. As we shall see, Rorty's inability to firm up this distinction also threatens to destroy the coherence of his vision of liberalism.

3

Sticks and Speech
Is There a Difference?

The question I pose in the title of this chapter is perhaps the most important question liberal political philosophy must answer. Put less colorfully, the question amounts to this: Can we draw a meaningful distinction between persuasion and force? Or, to return to my metaphorical phrasing, when we use speech to win an argument are we doing anything *essentially* different from what we do when we use sticks or guns to "win" an argument? Rorty's answer to the previous questions would be yes and no. He would argue that, yes, when we use persuasion we are doing something different from what we do when we use force, but, no, this difference is not an essential one, because there *are* no *essential* differences. In short, Rorty thinks that liberal societies should simply draw a firm distinction between persuasion and force, and then not worry about the status of this distinction—whether it is essential or accidental, natural or unnatural, or whatever. I will argue that, as liberals, unless we can tell ourselves a coherent story about why persuasion is essentially different from force, we are necessarily left with a poorer view of ourselves and our society than we might otherwise be able to envision. By "poorer" I mean, specifically, less capable of helping us get what we want as liberals and less capable of helping us hang on to what Rorty calls our Western "culture of hope."[1]

---

1. Rorty develops this notion of our Western culture of hope by a comparison to what he

115

To develop this argument, section 1 begins with an attempt to refute what I see as one of the most persuasive arguments *against* the claim that we can draw a firm distinction between persuasion and force. My refutation hinges on the assertion that, in order to continue seeing ourselves as we wish to see ourselves (including as those who wish to abandon this distinction *still* wish to see *themselves*), we must believe certain things about the way in which persuasion and force are essentially different. This claim, in turn, hinges on a point that Rorty often repeats: having certain beliefs often necessitates having lots of other beliefs. In section 1 I further claim that to have certain beliefs about the possibility of making a distinction between persuasion and force, we must have cer-

---

calls Eastern cultures of resignation. In an article entitled "A Pragmatist View of Rationality and Cultural Difference," Rorty argues that

> [John] Dewey would entirely agree with [the Indian philosopher Ashis] Nandy that "only by retaining a feel for the immediacy of man-made suffering can a utopia sustain a permanently critical attitude toward itself and other utopias." But he would argue that the West is likely to be, relatively speaking and despite its manifest cruelties, pretty good at retaining such a feel. He would base his argument on the fact that the West has developed a culture₁ of hope—a hope of a better world as attainable here below by social effort—as opposed to the cultures₁ of resignation characteristic of the East. (590, footnote omitted)

In his article, Rorty distinguishes three different senses of the word "culture." What he calls culture₁ "is simply a set of shared habits of action, those which enable members of a single human community to get along with each other and with the surrounding environment as well as they do. In this sense of the term, every army barracks, academic department, prison, monastery, farming village, scientific laboratory, concentration camp, street market, and business corporation has a culture of its own" (582). Rorty also distinguishes several senses of the term *rationality*. The sense of the term he likes best is the sense in which rationality is understood as

> roughly synonymous with tolerance—with the ability not to be overly disconcerted by differences from oneself, not to respond aggressively to such differences. This ability goes along with a willingness to alter one's habits—not only in order to get more of what one previously wanted but also in order to reshape oneself into a different sort of person, one who wants things that are different from what one had before. It also goes along with a reliance on persuasion rather than force, an inclination to talk things over rather than to fight, burn or banish. (581)

This sense of rationality is similar to but not nearly as well developed as the sense I discuss in section 2 of this chapter. See Richard Rorty, "A Pragmatist View of Rationality and Cultural Difference," *Philosophy East and West* 42 (1992): 581–96.

tain beliefs about the ability of reason to bring about a just society. Section 2 then undertakes a detailed analysis of what these beliefs about reason must entail. Finally, section 3 attempts to dramatize the difference between my view of liberalism and reason and Rorty's view by asking which view better equips us to take up a challenge Rorty thinks we cannot (unfortunately) avoid—the challenge of "answering Hitler."

Before I get into the particulars of my argument, however, I need to offer one crucial caveat about the remarks that follow. For the most part, when I use terms like *persuasion, force, freedom of speech, liberal democracy,* and so forth, I shall attempt to keep the discussion on the level of the individual. In other words, I shall assume that it is possible to say something meaningful about the notion of freedom of speech without getting caught up in questions of "political economy": questions like who *really* controls the major television networks, or what the New Information Order portends for First World governments. For theoretical clarity, I shall be adopting a very *idealized* view of liberal democracy—a view also adopted by one of Rorty's favorite liberal heroes, Alexander Meiklejohn.[2] To be sure, there is a universe of difference between Meiklejohn's "town meeting"—a heuristic device he uses to sketch the principles of democratic government and the notion of free speech—and the realities

---

2. In a 1976 article entitled "Professionalized Philosophy and Transcendentalist Culture," Rorty has the following to say about the state of American philosophy in the period between the world wars—what he calls the "heroic period of Deweyan pragmatism":

> When, during the Depression, Stalinism recruited whole battalions of highbrows, a small circle around Sidney Hook—Dewey's chief disciple—kept political morality alive among the intellectuals. Philosophers like Max Otto, Alexander Meiklejohn, and Horace Kallen offered their students the possibility that "America's ruling passion, the love of business" might be transformed into a love of social reconstruction. Having sat at their feet, a whole generation grew up confident that America would show the world how to escape both Gradgrind capitalism and revolutionary bloodshed. In the years between the wars, American philosophy not only escaped from the genteel tradition but provided moral leadership for the country. For the first time, American philosophy professors played the sort of role which Fichte and Hegel had once played in Germany. (63)

> See Richard Rorty, "Professionalized Philosophy and Transcendentalist Culture," in *Consequences of Pragmatism* (Minneapolis: University of Minnesota Press, 1982), 60–71.

of communication in advanced capitalist societies like the United States.[3] In following Meiklejohn, I am following Rorty, who keeps his own discussions of persuasion and force almost exclusively at the level of the "town meeting." For this, Rorty has been severely criticized. An exasperated Thomas McCarthy has written, "[Rorty] nowhere provides a satisfactory analysis of free *encounters* or *political* freedom, for the simple reason that his account of freedom moves almost exclusively at the level of the isolated individual and scarcely thematizes structures of intersubjectivity or *institutional* arrangements."[4] McCarthy is quite correct. Rorty obstinately refuses to get dragged into debates about large governmental structures and huge social institutions. He refuses because he is an Emersonian, which is to say, he is an *American*. The political rhetoric of America has always been, and continues to be, structured around the individual, as though the "town meeting" really were a proper analogue for what takes place when our politicians and special interest groups try to agree on (for example) a health care bill. Rorty's own position clearly opens him up to critiques that theorize persuasion and force at the level of the institution rather than the individual. Thomas McCarthy has sketched what such a critique might look like, as has Nancy Fraser.[5] Although I often find what McCarthy and Fraser have to say quite stimulating, I am simply not interested in carrying on such a critique in this chapter. Indeed, my approach throughout this book has been to critique Rorty *on his own ground*. So I too shall attempt to keep my discussions of persuasion and force at the level of the individual.

Liberalism and Reason

To begin our discussion of the *connection* between liberalism and reason, it is appropriate to focus first on the *distinction* between persuasion and force. Now, on the question of whether liberal societies *should* make such a distinction, Rorty is unequivocal. He notes that a "liberal society

---

3. For a discussion of Meiklejohn's concept of the "town meeting," see Alexander Meiklejohn, *Political Freedom: The Constitutional Powers of the People* (New York: Harper & Brothers, 1960), especially pp. 8–28.
4. Thomas McCarthy, "Ironist Theory as a Vocation: A Response to Rorty's Reply," *Critical Inquiry* 16 (spring 1990): 648, emphasis in original.
5. See her essay "Solidarity or Singularity? Richard Rorty between Romanticism and Technocracy," in *Unruly Practices: Power, Discourse, and Gender in Contemporary Social Theory* (Minneapolis: University of Minnesota Press, 1989): 93–109.

is one whose ideals can be fulfilled by persuasion rather than force," and that such a society "has *no* purpose except to make life easier for poets and revolutionaries, while seeing to it that they make life harder for others *only by words, and not deeds*."[6] He generalizes this point somewhat by arguing that, in the political realm, the *only* important distinction is "that between the use of force and the use of persuasion."[7] Now consider his contention that, "It is central to the idea of a liberal society that, in respect to words as opposed to deeds, persuasion as opposed to force, anything goes," and his further claim that, "[A]n ideal liberal society is one which has no purpose except freedom, no goal except a willingness to see how such [free and open] encounters go and to abide by the outcome."[8] Taken together, these statements, all of which appear in *Contingency, Irony, and Solidarity*, give us a pretty good idea of where Rorty is coming from. In an exchange with Thomas McCarthy, which appeared a year after that work was published, Rorty reaffirmed his conviction that, once again in the *political* realm, "what is really important to think about is what makes an encounter free from the influence of force."[9] Notably, this injunction to keep encounters free from the influence of force seems to apply universally—not just to us comfortable citizens of North American and European democracies. In an article examining the political theory of the Brazilian-born philosopher Roberto Unger, Rorty has rather boldly stated that in *desperate* political circumstances—that is, circumstance in which individuals are "on the barricades" and political revolutionaries need to get things done—concepts like ideology, political theory, *and just about everything else* become irrelevant. But, *crucially*, "[w]hat remains relevant is, roughly, freedom of speech."[10]

Statements like the ones I have quoted—and in particular that last remark about freedom of speech—chime very well with the rhetoric of good, liberal politics—especially *American* politics. Such statements harken back to the rhetoric of those who founded liberal polities—men

---

6. Richard Rorty, *Contingency, Irony, and Solidarity* (Cambridge: University Press, 1989), 60–61, emphasis added.
7. Ibid., 84.
8. Ibid., 51–52, 60.
9. Richard Rorty, "Truth and Freedom: A Reply to Thomas McCarthy," *Critical Inquiry* 16 (spring 1990): 634.
10. Richard Rorty, "Unger, Castoriadis, and the Romance of a National Future," in *Essays on Heidegger and Others: Philosophical Papers, Volume II* (Cambridge: University Press, 1991), 190.

like Thomas Jefferson and James Madison, who gave us the First Amendment and the document to which it is appended—and those upon whom these "founders" built—men like John Locke, John Milton (author of the *Areopagitica*), and various members of the Enlightenment.[11] What all of these individuals had in common (albeit to varying degrees) was a belief that a polity that allowed its citizens to speak their minds freely was ultimately the best hope we have of achieving a just society—where a "just society" was defined as one that maximized tolerance, minimized suffering, and allowed for the fullest degree of individual liberty. More than two centuries after the First Amendment was ratified, most Americans probably still take for granted the belief that freedom of speech is a *necessary* part of any just society. But if one critically examines this belief, it is not immediately obvious why free speech must always advance the cause of justice. It is not immediately obvious, for example, why allowing the American Nazi Party to march down the streets of a neighborhood composed largely of survivors of the Holocaust does not, in fact, *undermine* the goal of maximizing tolerance and minimizing suffering.[12] Nor is it immediately obvious why allowing the sale of pornography does not *decrease* the individual liberty *of women*. So perhaps, *pace* Rorty, it is not correct to say that, "[i]t is central to the idea of a liberal society that, in respect to words as opposed to deeds, persuasion as opposed to force, *anything goes*. . . ." Perhaps allowing *some* words to be spoken or allowing *some* forms of persuasion to be enacted would be *bad* for liberal societies. But again, *pace* Rorty, this would seem to negate the claim that a "liberal society is one whose ideals can be fulfilled by persuasion rather than force. . . ."

For more than two centuries the liberal response to the claim that some words and some forms of persuasion are bad has been to insist not

---

11. I have in mind such "enlightened" philosophers and critics as Voltaire, Dennis Diderot, Jean Le Rond d'Alembert, Immanuel Kant, and David Hume. For a good discussion of these and other figures connected with the Enlightenment, see Peter Gay, *The Enlightenment: An Interpretation*, vol. 1, *The Rise of Modern Paganism* (New York: W.W. Norton & Co., 1977).

12. I refer to the case of *Collin v. Smith*, 578 F.2d 1197 (7th Cir. 1978), in which a federal judge struck down (on First Amendment grounds) an ordinance passed by the Village of Skokie, Illinois, which made it a misdemeanor to disseminate material (defined to include the "public display of markings and clothing of symbolic significance") that tended to promote or incite racial or religious hatred. The Village attempted to use the law to prevent the NSPA, a Nazi organization, from peacefully marching down one of its main streets. Although the ordinance was struck down, the group decided not to march in Skokie.

on censorship but on the faith embodied in Justice Brandeis's assertion that "the fitting remedy for evil counsels is good ones."[13] In other words, with respect to questions of free speech, liberal political philosophers must believe in something like the *reverse* of Gresham's Law. Liberals must believe that good persuasion drives out bad persuasion. I now want to argue that to believe *this* we must *also* believe something about ourselves and about the moral universe we inhabit. Specifically, we must believe that 1) as "symbol-using animals" our response to persuasion is free and unforced in a way that our response to other physical stimuli is not, and 2) that the unforced force of reason can ultimately guarantee a minimally just society as previously defined. I want now to examine both of these beliefs, in turn, as a way of better understanding the connection between liberalism and reason.

THE FIRST OF THESE beliefs asserts that there is something to human beings that cannot be reduced to the merely physical. It is precisely this belief that allows us to use terms like *freedom* and *responsibility* in a meaningful way. For if there is no distinction between symbolic *inducements to action* and nonsymbolic *causes of action*—no distinction between persuasion and force—then there can be no meaningful notion of human freedom. But if there is no meaningful notion of human freedom, there can be no meaningful notion of "responsibility," since responsibility assumes freedom of choice is possible.

Interestingly, in the name of "freedom" and especially "responsibility," a number of legal scholars and First Amendment theorists have recently argued that symbolic action is essentially no different from any other form of action, and that, therefore, the *symbolic* component of symbolic action should be subject to regulation *in just the same way* that all other forms of action are subject to regulation.[14] This is a complex, overly theoretical way of saying that *speech* should be subject to governmental regulation in just the same way that *action* is subject to governmental

---

13. *Whitney v. California*, 47 S.Ct. 648.
14. As examples of such theorists, see Stanley Fish, *There's No Such Thing as Free Speech, and It's a Good Thing, Too* (New York: Oxford University Press, 1994), especially pp. 102–33; Kent Greenwalt, *Speech, Crime, and the Uses of Language* (New York: Oxford University Press, 1989); and Catharine A. MacKinnon, *Feminism Unmodified: Discourses on Life and Law* (Cambridge: Harvard University Press, 1987), especially pp. 127–213.

regulation. Again, the rationale for this position hinges on the claim that speech and action are *essentially* indistinguishable.

Plainly, theorists who hold this view cannot be liberals, because they make no distinction between persuasion and force. I imagine that Rorty might wish to banish such "antiliberal" theorists from *his* liberal utopia, just as Plato banished the poets from his utopia. Plato, however, was not a liberal. As liberals *we* are precluded from banishing (i.e., censoring) those who hold antiliberal positions, for to do so would be to contradict our own principles. The best we can do, then, is attempt to provide the most persuasive response we can to the antiliberal position. Such a response may or may not persuade antiliberals to change their own position. But, at the very least, it will help clarify what we, as liberals, believe.

Perhaps the best way to get clear on the liberal position with respect to the distinction between persuasion and force is to examine a very well thought out antiliberal argument against this distinction. Such an argument is provided by Stanley Fish in his 1994 book, provocatively entitled, *There's No Such Thing as Free Speech, and It's a Good Thing, Too*. In the central essay of this book—the essay from which the title of the book is taken—Fish argues that attempts to draw a firm distinction between speech and action (between persuasion and force) are both theoretically and practically impossible. He provides some initial plausibility for this claim by noting that the First Amendment, which purportedly draws just such a distinction by guaranteeing "freedom of speech," has never been held to mean *exactly* what it says. As Fish puts it,

> Despite the apparent absoluteness of the First Amendment, there are any number of ways of getting around it, ways that are known to every student of the law. In general, the preferred strategy is to manipulate the distinction, essential to First Amendment jurisprudence, between speech and action. The distinction is essential because no one would think to frame a First Amendment that began "Congress shall make no law abridging freedom of action," for that would amount to saying "Congress shall make no law," which would amount to saying, "There shall be no law," only actions uninhibited and unregulated. If the First Amendment is to make any sense, have any bite, speech must be declared not to be a species of action, or to be a special form of action lacking the aspects of

action that cause it to be the object of regulation. The latter strategy is the favored one and usually involves the separation of speech from consequences.[15]

This passage is a bit confusing because it begins with an assertion that would only be employed by the censor (only a censor would claim that the First Amendment is *not* absolute), and ends by discussing the arguments that would be used by one who wished to *avoid* being censored (only such an individual would attempt to separate speech from consequences). But the passage becomes more understandable when we see that *both* parties are really doing the same thing: manipulating the distinction between speech and action. So, for example, if one is a state official who wishes to prohibit (i.e., censor) the act of burning the American flag, one will argue, as did Chief Justice William Rehnquist in his dissent in *Texas v. Johnson,* that "flag burning is the equivalent of an inarticulate grunt or roar that, it seems fair to say, is most likely to be indulged in *not to express any particular idea,* but to antagonize others."[16] On the other hand, if one is a disaffected young man who wishes to burn the American flag as part of a protest, one will argue, as did Justice Brennan for the majority of the Court in the same case, that "[t]he expressive, overtly political nature of this conduct [flag burning] [is] both intentional and overwhelmingly apparent," and for this reason deserving of First Amendment protection, since, "[i]f there is a bedrock principle underlying the First Amendment, it is that the Government may not prohibit the expression of an idea simply because society finds *the idea itself* offensive or disagreeable."[17]

Fish is arguing, really, that when we manipulate the distinction between speech and action, that distinction easily collapses, and everything is seen as what it truly is, *action.* But notice, if we could not make a meaningful distinction between speech and action, it does not seem that there could be any point to the First Amendment. Fish would agree, "[I]nsofar as the point of the First Amendment is to identify speech separable from conduct and from the consequences that come in conduct's wake, *there is no such speech* and therefore nothing for the First Amendment to protect."[18] This is the nub of Fish's argument. He is claiming

---

15. Stanley Fish, *There's No Such Thing as Free Speech, and It's a Good Thing, Too,* 105.
16. *Texas v. Johnson,* 105 L Ed. 2d 342, emphasis added.
17. Ibid., 354, 360, emphasis added.
18. Fish, *There's No Such Thing as Free Speech, and It's a Good Thing, Too,* 106, emphasis added.

that, insofar as every action that is meaningful is consequential, speech that *is* completely separate from any consequence would indeed be free, but also, by definition, *inconsequential*, hence, ultimately meaningless. But since we do not want to see speech (certainly our own speech) as meaningless, we must view it as consequential, and hence, *not* free. So there is no such thing as free speech. This is a good thing, of course, because it means that all speech matters. Fish puts this point the following way at the conclusion of his essay:

> [T]he thesis that there is no such thing as free speech . . . is not, after all, a thesis as startling or corrosive as may first have seemed. It merely says that there is no class of utterances separable from the world of conduct and that therefore the identification of some utterances as members of that nonexistent class will always be evidence that a political line has been drawn rather than a line that denies politics entry into the forum of public discourse. . . . The good news is that precisely *because* speech is never "free" in the two senses required— free of consequences and free from state pressure—speech always matters, is always doing work; because everything we say impinges on the world in ways indistinguishable from the effects of physical action, we must take responsibility for our verbal performances—*all* of them—and not assume that they are being taken cares [sic] of by a clause in the Constitution.[19]

Not to belabor the point, but again the essence of Fish's argument is that since all meaningful speech must be consequential, we can draw no real distinction between speech and action, hence there is no such thing as free speech.

But, quite obviously, Fish reasons invalidly from the premise that all meaningful speech must (*in some way*) be consequential, to the conclusion that we can make no principled distinction (*at all*) between speech and physical action that is not speech. And let there be no mistake, this is exactly what Fish concludes. Recall his assertion that *"everything* we say impinges on the world in ways *indistinguishable* from the effects of physical action. . . ."* But if this were so, there would, quite literally, be no place for human consciousness in the world. In other words, Fish's world is a completely mechanistic world. It is a world in which

---

19. Ibid., 114, emphasis in original.

human *action* is reduced to physical *motion*. It follows that there is no place in this world for a distinction between persuasion and physical force. Ironically, in Fish's world there really would be no such thing as free speech, not because all speech would have consequences, but rather because there would be no such thing as freedom. Simply put, a world in which one cannot conceive of a meaningful distinction between persuasion and physical force is a world in which one cannot conceive of a meaningful notion of human freedom. Kenneth Burke puts this point succinctly, and (dare I say?) persuasively, when he writes, "Persuasion involves choice, will; it is directed to a man only insofar as he is *free*."[20]

If, then, we conclude that in order to preserve a meaningful notion of human freedom, we must preserve a meaningful distinction between persuasion and physical force, how can we square this conclusion with Fish's quite justifiable assertion that all meaningful speech must have consequences? We can do so by seeing that meaningful speech, as distinguished from other forms of physical action, is associated with its "consequences," only in a *mediated* way. In other words, when I speak meaningfully, my words will have consequences (some intentioned, some not intentioned, some predictable, some not predictable, and so forth) precisely because these words are received and then "processed" in the mind of another in myriad, complex, never *completely* explainable ways. This, at least, is a point upon which liberals must insist. We must insist (and seek to persuade others) that Fish is wrong in asserting that everything we *say* operates in the world in ways *indistinguishable* from everything we *do*. For if this were true, then there would be no difference between *character* assassination and (I am tempted to say) *real* assassination; no difference between libeling the president and shooting him. There is a difference *just because* we can distinguish words from acts; and we can do this *just because* we can distinguish humans from trained animals or machines. So, when Catharine MacKinnon argues that pornography should be censored in part because it *causes* men to rape women, and then draws an analogy by asking, "[W]hich is saying 'kill' to a trained guard dog, a word or an act?" we need to insist that there is a meaningful difference between guard dogs and humans.[21] In sum, we need to insist (and, as liberals, to believe) that, as inducements to action (or

20. Kenneth Burke, A *Rhetoric of Motives* (Berkeley: University of California Press, 1969), 50, emphasis in original.
21. See Catharine MacKinnon, "Not a Moral Issue," in *Feminism Unmodified*, 156.

sometimes *inaction*) symbols (i.e., speech, writing, visual images, and so forth) can be resisted in a way that a bullet, for example, cannot.

Granted, the *extent* to which symbols can be resisted will depend upon our view of the nature of the self. As a political philosophy, liberalism requires that we adopt a relatively strong view of the self. In chapter 2 I quoted the line "I am the captain of my soul" from William Ernest Henley's poem *Invictus*. To my mind, this bit of pithy poetical verse captures very well one of the central assumptions upon which liberalism is founded.

Of course, one need *not* agree with this strong view of the self. From his discussion of the way in which words do their "work" in the world, I take it that Fish views the self as a relatively powerless entity, bent this way and then that, as a weak reed in the onrushing stream of speech. Although I find this view fundamentally at odds with liberalism, I can perhaps accept it as a consistent, philosophical, *anti*liberal position. What I find difficult to accept, however, is the use (or rather misuse) of the term *responsibility*, by one who holds this view. Recall here Fish's injunction that, because speech is not free, "we must take responsibility for our verbal performances—*all* of them. . . ." I wonder what exactly *Fish* means by the term *responsibility*. It is difficult to understand how any notion of responsibility can stand once the distinction between speech and action falls. Put otherwise, it is difficult to understand, given Fish's worldview, why *any* individual could not automatically excuse his or her wicked actions (including wicked verbal performances) by pointing out that these actions were simply the *consequence* of *another's* wicked verbal performances. Of course, this "other" will simply point out that his or her wicked verbal performances were simply the consequence of still another's wicked verbal performances, and so on, *ad infinitum*. It seems, then, that in order to use the term *responsible* in a responsible manner, one must assume that some actions are not the *direct and unmediated consequence* of some prior verbal behavior on the part of another. One must assume, as Fish seems not to, that some *meaningful* speech *is* different from action.

The logical problems with Fish's view put him in somewhat of a difficult position. It seems that he cannot quite figure out where to lay the considerable blame for the many evils he finds in the world. To lay the blame on society in general seems too easy. To lay the blame on individuals seems hypocritical, if one is simultaneously arguing (as Fish does) for a position that undermines any meaningful notion of individual responsibility. Yet when forced to choose, as choose he must, Fish shows little reluctance to blame individuals for failing to act responsibly. So, for example, Fish can charge the editors of Duke University's student news-paper, the *Chronicle*, with acting irresponsibly and even *immorally* when, in line with what they saw as First Amendment principles, they accepted for publication an advertisement denying that the Holocaust occurred. In Fish's view, the fact that the advertisement was "pernicious and false" (*and agreed to be so by the editors*) should have compelled a decision *against* publication, the First Amendment notwithstanding. As Fish puts it,

> [W]hen it happens that the present shape of truth is com-pelling beyond a reasonable doubt, it is our *moral* obligation to act on it and not defer action in the name of an interpreta-tive future that may never arrive. By running the First Amend-ment up the nearest flagpole and rushing to salute it, the student editors defaulted on that obligation and gave over their responsibility to a so-called principle that was not even to the point.[22]

Although I certainly agree with Fish that the advertisement in ques-tion was both false and pernicious (and reprehensible for other reasons too), I find his moralistic condemnation of the student editors very odd. Presumably Fish believes that the student editors erred in running the advertisement because it was false and *pernicious*. And, presumably, Fish believes that it was pernicious because he believes that the consequence of the advertisement would be to cause individuals to act in a pernicious manner (either by being intolerant of Jewish individuals, or by partici-pating in hate crimes with neo-Nazi groups, or in an infinite number of other ways). But when we apply Fish's speech/action (non)distinction in this case, we find that the very individuals who acted perniciously because of the advertisement could not be responsible for their actions, because these actions were a direct consequence of the advertisement—this very directness being, simultaneously, the reason 1) why the individ-uals who acted because of the advertisement could not be responsible for their actions, and 2) why the individuals who published the advertise-ment could not *not* be responsible for their actions. Now, to repeat my

---

22. Fish, *There's No Such Thing as Free Speech, and It's a Good Thing, Too*, 113, empha-sis added.

earlier point: it is not clear why the student editors could not have escaped responsibility by simply claiming that their own behavior was the consequence of some other individuals' verbal performances — say those of Thomas Jefferson or John Stuart Mill. Fish cannot have it both ways. He must either cease using terms like *responsibility* and *moral obligation* or come up with a different reason than he has yet presented as to why there is no such thing as free speech.

I conclude from all of this that Fish's notion of responsibility is *formally inconsistent* with his own arguments about free speech. This is so because his view of the way in which words do their work in the world implies a completely mechanistic world in which there is no place for human action or will. But, as we are liberals, this view of ourselves is unacceptable. It follows, then, that in order to see ourselves as we wish to see ourselves — as free individuals capable of taking responsibility for our actions — we must reject Fish's arguments and instead insist that there is an essential distinction between speech and action, between persuasion and force. But that is only half of the story.

EARLIER I NOTED that as liberals we must also believe that the unforced force of reason can ultimately guarantee a minimally just society. As a way of connecting this belief with what I have just said about the need to maintain a distinction between persuasion and force, I want now to examine briefly the work of Franklyn Haiman, one of the most ardent defenders of freedom of speech. In his book *"Speech Acts" and the First Amendment*, Haiman advances an argument similar to the one I have just advanced against Fish. Haiman argues that, if we attempt to censor speech *just because* it "incites" persons to do evil acts, then we are in fact treating the persons so incited as mere machines. Haiman does not make the point about responsibility that I made, but what he does say has interesting implications for his understanding of the self. He says,

> If one assumes that speech is like a match or a spark or a small fire that can burst into a bigger one, one commits the same mistake that is made when one presumes that speech is like the trigger of a gun. Fires come into being through a physical chain reaction, without mediation by a human mind or intervention by a human will. The problem with a speech-act perspective, whether explicitly based on contemporary linguistic

theories or unconsciously employing metaphors like triggers and fire, is that human beings get left out of the equation.

At this point a reader might be thinking, Wait a minute. Don't people sometimes act like robots? Is the author not giving them too much credit for rational decision making? But the reader should note that I have claimed nothing about people making *rational* decisions, only that they are *conscious* of what they are doing and, presumably, have the capacity to stop themselves from doing it, no matter how much anger a speaker may have awakened in them. My use of the term *awakened* is itself perhaps as unfortunate a metaphor as triggers and fire, because anger is not literally awakened by words alone. Those words must be followed by the listener's interpretation of their meaning, along with some preexisting hostility or other reason [interesting word choice—EMG] for a readiness to respond violently, plus the physical circumstances that make such a response feasible. Except for the noise they make, words are not like the sound of an alarm clock nor are they comparable to the shaking of someone to wake them up, where the awakening can be immediate and automatic.

To be sure, having the capacity to stop oneself from responding to a speaker's words may not be entirely true of listeners who are insane, drugged, hypnotized, seriously retarded, too young to understand the consequences of their actions, or somehow under the physical control of the speaker. In those unusual situations, I see less of a problem likening provocative or inciting utterances to triggers and fires or even calling them speech acts. But the First Amendment was not designed with the insane, the enslaved, or the mentally incapacitated in mind, and I reject the idea that we should build our normal law of communication around them.[23]

To my mind, the most interesting question raised by the preceding lengthy quotation concerns the relationship Haiman sees between rea-

---

23. Franklyn S. Haiman, *"Speech Acts" and the First Amendment* (Carbondale, Ill.: Southern Illinois University Press, 1990), 24–25, emphasis in original.

son and the self. One may reasonably ask, if a person's actions are not controlled by that person's reason, are those actions in any meaningful sense controlled by that person? It seems that Haiman's answer to this question must (alas) be yes and no. Notice that at the *beginning* of the passage, Haiman insists that his understanding of the First Amendment does *not* depend on an assumption that human action is motivated by reason, but only on the much weaker assumption that humans are generally conscious of their actions. In insisting only upon this weaker assumption, Haiman sounds very much like Rorty, who would surely want to avoid anything that might implicate us in a "metaphysical" discussion of reason. But now notice that, at the *conclusion* of the passage, Haiman insists that First Amendment law *not* be designed with the insane, enslaved, or mentally incapacitated in mind. But, it would seem to follow, *a fortiori*, that First Amendment law must then be designed around the assumption that humans are inherently rational, not just inherently conscious of their actions (for one can certainly be conscious of one's actions and not be rational).

Indeed, despite his *initial* remark that (with respect to free speech questions) he will *not* assume individuals are necessarily rational, it seems that Haiman is quite *reluctant* to abandon just this assumption—and with good reason. For (as we shall shortly see) one must assume human action is generally motivated by reason, in order to believe (with Justice Brandeis) that "the fitting remedy for evil counsels is good ones." I *know* that Haiman would agree with Brandeis, and so I take his remark about not assuming that individuals are necessarily rational as evidencing a bit of theoretical confusion on his part. The occurrence of this confusion in his book is somewhat odd, given that three years before the book was published Haiman seemed to focus on the *connection* between free speech and rationality. In his 1990 keynote address to the Speech Communication Association—an address that is critically entitled "Majorities Versus the First Amendment: *Rationality* on Trial"— Haiman contends that "[t]rue rationality is indeed on trial as we enter the third century of the First Amendment."[24] As he explains it,

> Although we are a long way from anything that might fairly be characterized as a tyranny of the majority, I would like to suggest

---

24. Haiman's address was delivered in Chicago, Illinois, on November 2, 1990. It is reprinted in *Communication Monographs* 58 (September 1991): 327–35. This quotation appears on page 335.

that we are heading too much in that direction. . . . Gathering under the banner of what is being called "communitarianism," and no doubt reacting against what is perceived as individualism run amok, we are seeing and hearing a flood of appeals in speeches, columns, books, and prestigious law journal articles for greater "civility" in our discourse, more deference to the sensibilities of the so-called "community," more rationality—*as these advocates define that term*—in public debate.[25]

If I understand him correctly, Haiman thinks of "communitarianism" the way many contemporary critics think of "political correctness"—a phrase that Haiman does not use. At any rate, on Haiman's account, communitarianism is undesirable precisely because it seeks to impose upon the individual the necessarily limited view of the community. In our contemporary political climate, such imposition often takes the form of things like "speech codes." But what *exactly* does all of this have to do with *reason*? This I must let Haiman attempt to explain. He says,

One of the ironies of the new communitarianism is the pride it takes in its reasonableness—reasonable in its deference to the standards of decency of the so-called community, reasonable in its recognition of the supposed limits of human tolerance, reasonable in its willingness to exclude from the marketplace of ideas the rhetoric of grunts and groans—such as flag burning, pornographic images, and racial slurs—a rhetoric which allegedly makes no contribution to rational discourse.

I say this is ironic because it is a corruption of rationality. What is a community if not a composite of *all* its members, not 51% nor two-thirds nor 95%, but everyone? What, therefore, is a so-called community standard of decency if 5%, one-third, or 49% of that community do not share it? It is a *majority* standard, perhaps even the standard of an overwhelming majority, but let us not pretend it is unanimous and try to pass it off as that of the entire community. The substitution in recent discourse of the word "communitarianism" for "majoritarianism" is a bit of verbal legerdemain, intentional

---

25. Ibid., 328, emphasis added.

or not, which masks the fact that a community and a majority
are not identical. Not that there is anything wrong with majority standards for some purposes, and that they cannot or
should not be used as a basis for the outlawing of murder,
rape, and robbery, even if the murderers, rapists, and robbers
do not agree. But we must not be taken in by the fallacy that
because such standards are justifiably invoked for murder,
rape, and robbery they are similarly justified as a basis for the
banning of words, pictures, or other symbols of which the
majority does not approve. Rather let us hold to the time-
tested premise of Thomas Jefferson that "It is time enough for
the rightful purposes of civil government for its officers to
interfere when principles break out into overt acts against
peace and good order."[26]

I can use this passage to help tie together a number of threads that
have been discussed so far. Notice first the distinction Haiman (a good
liberal) insists upon between persuasion and force. He insists that we *not*
view "murder, rape, and robbery" in *essentially* the same way that we
view "words, pictures, or other symbols of which the majority does not
approve." And he attempts to give this distinction some weight by quoting Thomas Jefferson's famous Bill for Establishing Religious Freedom—written one year after Jefferson penned the Declaration of
Independence, and one of only three acts for which he *explicitly* said he
wished to be remembered.[27]

Notice second the *connection* Haiman seems to make between liberalism and reason. To be sure, this connection is not made as clearly
and explicitly as it could be, but it is evidenced nonetheless in the opening sentences of the second paragraph of the aforementioned quotation.
These first few sentences constitute an unmistakable allusion to John
Stuart Mill's remark—quoted by Haiman earlier in the speech—that "If
all mankind minus one were of one opinion, mankind would be no more

---

26. Ibid., 333, emphasis in original.
27. The other two acts were the writing of the Declaration of Independence and the
    founding of the University of Virginia. Jefferson's Bill for Establishing Religious
    Freedom was not officially passed by the Virginia Assembly until 1786. For a rivet-
    ing discussion of Jefferson's Bill and other aspects of the American tradition of free-
    dom of religion, see William Lee Miller, *The First Liberty: Religion and the
    American Republic* (New York: Paragon, 1988).

justified in silencing that one person than he, if he had the power, would be justified in silencing mankind."[28] Mill gives the following reason for this prohibition against allowing a "tyranny of the majority" in the realm of speech—a reason with which I am once again sure Haiman would be in agreement.

> [T]he peculiar evil of silencing the expression of an opinion is that it is robbing the human race, posterity as well as the existing generation—those who dissent from the opinion, still more than those who hold it. If the opinion is right, they are deprived of the opportunity of exchanging error for truth; if wrong, they lose, what is almost as great a benefit, the clearer perception and livelier impression of truth produced by collision with error.[29]

In good liberal fashion, Mill believes that a "clearer perception and livelier impression of truth" is a benefit to humankind, *just because* such a clearer perception will *naturally* lead to a more just world. This is so, in Mill's view, even though humans are necessarily fallible beings. This faith—*yes*, let us call it that—in what I have called the unforced force of reason to bring about a minimally just society, even in the face of human fallibility, is *unique* to liberalism. It is a faith that is implicit in *all* of Haiman's arguments for freedom of speech. It is a faith that goes hand in hand with what Rorty calls our Western culture of hope. It is, I will argue, a faith that liberalism cannot do without. It is also, to be sure, a faith that is often severely tested by the experience of history, and perhaps even more so by the insights of literature.

To purse this last point, let me return to Stanley Fish, our representative antiliberal. It may just be the case that Fish, whose work on Milton's poetry is exemplary, cannot shake the feeling that our poets and novelists have more to tell us about ourselves than we may wish to admit. Certainly what they tell us is often disturbing, for in literature evil is frequently associated with a strong facility for the persuasive use of language—consider Milton's Satan, or Shakespeare's Iago, or Melville's John Claggart. To me, the climactic scene in Herman Melville's *Billy Budd* dramatizes this point perfectly. The year is 1791, and we are aboard

---

28. John Stuart Mill, *On Liberty* (New York: Macmillan/Library of Liberal Arts, 1965), 21.
29. Ibid.

the British naval ship *Belliponent*. In the presence of Captain Vere, the master-at-arms John Claggart, by cleverly manipulating purely circumstantial evidence, is proceeding falsely, though quite persuasively, to implicate the wholesome and innocent Billy Budd in a conspiracy to commit mutiny. Unable to answer Claggart's charges by speech, the physically powerful yet inarticulate Billy Budd does the only thing he can do: he *acts*, by striking Claggart once in the forehead, killing him instantly. The once innocent Billy Budd is now a killer. Yet we sympathize with him, because we feel that, when faced with someone like Claggart, perhaps counter-speech *is* ineffective, and thus force is the *only* response.

But this view of ourselves, and of the human condition, is far too pessimistic. It holds that in language—the very thing that makes us human—we can find no resources to defeat those who would use language inhumanly.[30] Liberalism says, whether this view be true or not, *at worst* we cannot know; therefore, we ought freely to choose to believe it is *not* so. This leads to our liberal faith in reason, which I have just sketched.

Over the centuries (even the millennia) this faith has been discussed in a number of ways. Often the discussion has turned "metaphysical" and the faith in reason has been connected to views about the natural superiority of Truth over Falsehood. These views locate this superiority precisely in the ability of Truth to transcend the localized, individuated, parochial world in which Falsehood finds a home, and instead to appeal to something common to all humans. Hence, after more than 2,000 years of continuing the conversation, we Western liberals now find ourselves heirs to a vocabulary that is largely (if not entirely) structured around what Thomas McCarthy calls "transcultural notions of validity."[31] Just such a notion is evidenced in this opening comment from Aristotle's treatise on *Rhetoric*: "Rhetoric is useful, because the true and the just are

---

30. I understand that my definition of language as "the very thing that makes us human" is certainly arguable. I am using the term *language* here to mean something like "logos." Obviously communication includes more than the use of "logos," and obviously being human involves more than simply being able to use logos or being able to communicate. But, if pressed, I would agree with Aristotle and others, that the human species' capacity to use logos (as distinct from any given individual's capacity) is what makes the species unique.
31. Thomas McCarthy, "Private Irony and Public Decency: Richard Rorty's New Pragmatism," *Critical Inquiry* 16 (winter 1990): 361.

naturally superior to their opposites, so that, if decisions are improperly made, they must owe their defeat to their own advocates."[32] The same notion is reflected in John Milton's *Areopagitica*. "And though all the winds of doctrine were let loose to play upon the earth, so Truth be in the field, we do injuriously by licensing and prohibiting to misdoubt her strength. Let her and Falsehood grapple; who ever knew Truth put to the worse, in a free and open encounter?"[33] Thomas Jefferson expressed this notion with characteristic eloquence in his Bill for Establishing Religious Freedom. "[T]ruth is great and will prevail if left to herself . . . she is the proper and sufficient antagonist to error, and has nothing to fear from the conflict unless by human interposition disarmed of her natural weapons, free argument and debate. . . ."[34] Finally, since I must stop somewhere, I will note that Justice Brandeis frames this notion concisely, in a remark I have repeated several times: "[T]he fitting remedy for evil counsels is good ones."

Whether or not we call such notions "metaphysical" or "transcultural," they are inextricably linked with other beliefs that we as liberals wish to hold on to. In particular, the faith expressed in the aforementioned quotations is strongly linked with our Western culture of hope. To abandon or deride the idea expressed in these quotations would bring us perilously close to abandoning or deriding our sense of liberal hope. Once again, Stanley Fish's writings on free speech are on point here, as reflective, I think, of the type of attitude and outlook we liberals should avoid.

Fish's apparent abandonment of liberal hope is most evident in his treatment of John Milton. Fish begins his essay on free speech by alluding to the earlier quotation by Milton, but he then proceeds to dismiss the larger principle embodied in the quotation, first, because in the course of counseling tolerance, Milton specifically excludes tolerance of Catholics (which to me proves not that the principle is wrong, but only that Milton did not heed his own counsel), and second, because Milton's whole approach simply "continues in a secular form the Puritan celebration of millenarian hopes. . . ."[35] This, I think, is Fish's *real*

---

32. Aristotle, *Rhetoric*, Loeb Classical Library, 11.
33. John Milton, *Areopagitica* (Santa Barbara: Bandanna Books, 1992), 41.
34. Thomas Jefferson, "Bill For Establishing Religious Freedom," in William Lee Miller, *The First Liberty: Religion and the American Republic*, 358.
35. Fish, *There's No Such Thing as Free Speech, and It's a Good Thing, Too*, 109.

objection. He rejects the idea that we should put any "faith" in a *vague* notion of Truth that only offers the *hope* of a better tomorrow, precisely because such faith may have the effect of preventing us from changing matters *right now*. As Fish says, "In a specifically religious vision like Milton's, this [faith] makes perfect sense (it is indeed the whole of Christianity), but in the context of a politics that puts its trust in the world and not in the Holy Spirit, it raises more questions than it answers. . . ."[36] Perhaps it does. But I tend to think that Fish may be over-focused on Milton's Puritanism, and on religion in general. If we replace the Puritan "celebration of millenarian hopes" with the standard liberal's *melioristic attitude toward life*, we can keep the notion of human progress and drop the idea that it must come about through the Holy Spirit.

This, in essence, was the project of the Enlightenment, with respect to *political* life. We should not soon forget that it is largely because of such faith—in progress and in reason—that our liberal culture of hope has managed to avoid the extreme cynicism about politics and about the human condition that is so clearly reflected in the concluding counsel that Fish offers his readers. "[S]o long as so-called free-speech principles have been fashioned by your enemy . . . contest their relevance to the issue at hand; but if you manage to refashion them in line with your purposes, urge them with a vengeance."[37]

Reading that last sentence, I cannot help thinking that in Stanley Fish's tragically configured moral universe, there is no place for human solidarity, no place for enlightened critique or moral progress; "ignorant armies clash by night," and the only political principle is: do it unto others, before they do it unto you. Now this is a strong claim indeed. And one may think that, in an effort to defend liberalism against its critics, I am here engaging in hyperbole, and thus being unfair to Fish. But this is not so. In all the pages, of all the essays, of all the books I have read by Stanley Fish, I have found no passage more disturbing and more demanding of rejection than the sentence I now quote. It appears in an essay, "You Can Only Fight Discrimination with Discrimination," the title of which seems perfectly to summarize Fish's dismal worldview.

---

36. Ibid., 110.
37. Ibid., 114.

The amount of unfairness in the world can *never* be eliminated *or even diminished*; it can *only* be *redistributed* as in the course of *political* struggle one angled formulation of what it means to be equitable gives way to another.[38]

In Fish's zero-sum society, the alleviation of suffering for one group (say blacks) must *always* be accompanied by the imposition of (at least) an equal degree of suffering on another group (say whites). This is (at best) the position we find ourselves in if we reject what I have called the standard liberal's melioristic attitude toward life. But since we liberals cannot reject this attitude and remain liberals, we must also embrace the beliefs that go along with this attitude. One such belief is embodied in Rorty's claim that a "liberal society is one whose ideals can be fulfilled by persuasion rather than force." This belief says, roughly, that if we keep the conversation going long enough, things will naturally get better without the need to resort to force. I have tried to show that this belief, in turn, entails a further belief about what I have called the capacity of the unforced force of reason to bring about a just society. I have argued that our liberal hope is naturally (or one might say, *narratively*) connected to our faith in reason. We have seen this connection made explicit in the writings of any number of liberals throughout the centuries. I think it fair to say that Western liberalism is permeated with a faith in reason.

But now, at the close of the twentieth century, with the fortunes of liberalism decidedly on the rise, Rorty advances an odd suggestion. He says that we should continue to celebrate the workings of liberal institutions, indeed we should attempt to expand the reach of these institutions to other cultures, but at the same time we should try to break the connection between liberalism and reason. Interestingly, Rorty provides a *reason* for his suggestion. He claims that Enlightenment rationality has become an "impediment" to the continuation of liberal institutions. In the remainder of this section I shall try to show why Rorty is incorrect to think that we *can* break the connection between liberal institutions and reason, and also incorrect to think that such a connection has become an *impediment* to the continuation of such institutions.

---

38. Fish, "You Can Only Fight Discrimination with Discrimination," in *There's No Such Thing as Free Speech, and It's a Good Thing, Too*, 73, emphasis added.

WHAT EXACTLY DO WE MEAN when we say that liberalism is grounded on reason? We mean that the political practices we undertake as liberals are, in the final analysis, nonsensical apart from specific ideas about the ultimate ability of reason to bring about a minimally just society. Certainly this is the case with our extended example of the First Amendment. There can be no better illustration of a central liberal political freedom that is so *directly* connected with reason. Francis Canavan makes this point very clearly when he writes

> The purposes of the First Amendment are ends that reason recognizes and approves. Those who think that asking, "Whose reason?" is a crushing reply that effectively disposes of that proposition should be prepared to explain *on what grounds* they defend the amendment. Since the question they ask implicitly denies that there is a commonly-shared human reason, they cannot present arguments that appeal to the reason of mankind. By their definition reason is always someone's reason, and therefore individual and private. The only grounds they can offer, therefore, are a private preference for freedom of expression and a corresponding distaste for limiting it. Justice Brennan spoke for them when he said: "A given word may have a unique capacity to capsule an idea, evoke an emotion, or conjure an image. Indeed, for those of us who place an appropriately high value on our cherished First Amendment rights, the word 'censor' is such a word." The sentiment, as sentiments go, is admirable. But does an emotional revulsion against "censorship" furnish a sufficient *explanation* of why we have *and should* maintain freedom of speech? One may reasonably doubt it and continue to believe that *the First Amendment stands upon our trust in reason or on nothing at all.*[39]

In response to the above passage, Rorty would try to make us comfortable with saying to ourselves that the First Amendment simply stands on nothing at all. In Rorty's view, we will be comfortable saying this just as soon as we bring about a culture in which we do not *need* to be prepared to *explain* on what *grounds* we defend the First Amendment. As

---

39. Francis Canavan, *Freedom of Expression: Purpose as Limit* (Durham, N.C.: Carolina Academic Press, 1984), 36–37, emphasis added, footnote omitted.

Rorty might put it, we do not need to *explain* the First Amendment, *we simply need to enact and defend it*. In other words, Rorty's ideal liberal culture would be thoroughly antifoundationalist. It would have no need for philosophical backups for its institutions. It would not attempt to *justify* the workings of those institutions on the basis of something that went beyond those institutions, something that pretended to be universal, or transcultural. It would be content simply to attempt to defend, extend, and perfect these institutions.

Some might object that this view would put the workings of liberal societies at risk. But, paradoxically, that objection is an example of the type of thinking Rorty wants us to discard. As Rorty puts it, his "ideally liberal polity" would "not assume that a form of cultural life is no stronger than its philosophical foundations. Instead, it would drop the idea of such foundations. It would regard the justification of liberal society simply as a matter of historical comparison with other attempts at social organization—those of the past and those envisaged by utopians."[40]

I can sum up Rorty's antifoundationalist position and provide a starting point for my own response to that position by noting (with Lynn Baker) that Rorty's political philosophy seems to amount to what "the Nike people say, 'Just do it.'"[41] In response, Rorty says that he prefers the phrase "Let's try it!" to the phrase "Just do it!" because the former phrase better reflects the spirit of "experimentation" that is central to the project of Rorty's favorite, pragmatic, antifoundationalist philosophers like John Dewey. Further, Rorty tries to show how his ideally liberal, antifoundationalist society is possible by telling what he calls (troping Booker T. Washington) an "'up from principles' story" that underscores "the steady decline [in Western culture] in requests for legitimation and for citation of authority over the last few hundred years, [and] the steady increase in willingness to experiment."[42]

Unlike Rorty, I would tell a different story about what has happened in liberal societies over the last few hundred years, a story that preserves a place for a minimalist, foundationalist rhetoric in such societies. My story would not try to point to a steady decline in requests for legitima-

---

40. Rorty, *Contingency, Irony, and Solidarity*, 53.
41. Lynn A. Baker, "'Just Do It': Pragmatism and Progressive Social Change," *Virginia Law Review* 78 (1992): 718.
42. Richard Rorty, "What Can You Expect From Anti-Foundationalist Philosophers?: A Reply to Lynn Baker," *Virginia Law Review* 78 (1992): 722.

tion over the last few hundred years, because the story I tell would contend that requests for legitimation *never* decline (or increase), they just *change their focus.* So my story would see liberal society's steady increase in a willingness to experiment *as the result of, and legitimated by,* a correspondingly steady increase in our political faith in the authority of reason. I think my story becomes more plausible than Rorty's once we see that, even in liberal societies, there are still some things we do not experiment with; there are some things about which we never say, "Let's try it!" One of those things is, of course, the substitution of *force* for *persuasion.* In other words, we cannot *experiment* with the principle of freedom of speech, because that principle is, in a sense, the laboratory in which we conduct our experiments. As liberals, we cannot say about censorship, "Let's try it!" because our willingness to say, "Let's try it" is nonsensical, apart from our willingness to abjure censorship. Rorty himself seems to recognize this point. Recall his remark, at the very beginning of this section, to the effect that, in desperate political circumstances, when revolutionaries are busy wildly (and necessarily) experimenting, what *always* remains relevant is, roughly, freedom of speech. So in the end my story would conclude by tying in this point about freedom of speech with a larger view of reason, as I have tried to do throughout this section. To repeat: the key aspect to see in all of this is that requests for legitimation never increase or decrease, they simply change their focus. Liberal societies do not differ from other societies in escaping the need for legitimation. They differ from other societies in taking *reason* as the source of *their* legitimation.

So much then for Rorty's claim that liberalism can be separated from reason. I now want to examine his more disturbing claim that the explicit recognition of this connection between liberalism and reason has become an impediment to the continuation of liberal institutions. Rorty advances this claim with a curious caveat. He writes, "[T]he vocabulary of Enlightenment rationalism, *although it was essential to the beginnings of liberal democracy*, has become an impediment to the preservation and progress of democratic societies."[43] As far as I can see, the *only* evidence Rorty adduces for this seemingly extraordinary claim is drawn from his own, more or less empirical, observations about liberal societies. In other words, Rorty is making a pragmatic, as opposed to a philosophical, argument. He is saying that, given the practical realities of our present-day

---

43. Rorty, *Contingency, Irony, and Solidarity,* 44, emphasis added.

liberal societies, continued appeals to reason will not help, and will actually hinder, our attempts to do what we as liberals want to do. In making this claim, Rorty may be falling victim to the same negative tendency he finds in Thomas McCarthy. Specifically, Rorty may be viewing society too much from the perspective of a *professional* philosopher.[44] He may be assuming that the specialized books and articles that professional philosophers read and find important are also, necessarily, what society at large finds important.

To see how Rorty might fall into this trap, I will examine the two (and only two) pieces of evidence I can find in *Contingency, Irony, and Solidarity*, which Rorty uses to support the claim that liberal practices are now endangered by a vocabulary of Enlightenment rationalism. The first piece of evidence is drawn from Rorty's reading of Max Horkheimer and Theodore W. Adorno's work *Dialectic of Enlightenment*. Rorty argues that Horkheimer and Adorno

> point out, correctly, I think, that the forces unleashed by the Enlightenment have undermined the Enlightenment's own convictions. What they called the "dissolvant rationality" of Enlightenment has, in the course of the triumph of Enlightenment ideas during the last two centuries, undercut the ideas of "rationality" and of "human nature" which the eighteenth century took for granted.[45]

Assuming *arguendo* that, say, Jürgen Habermas's work has *not* provided a convincing response to Horkheimer and Adorno's claim that Enlightenment rationality must necessarily undercut itself, I still think Rorty needs to provide some evidence that Horkheimer and Adorno's predictions have, indeed, come to pass. I think such evidence is hard to find in liberal society *at large*. Indeed, many of liberalism's "heroes" — individuals like Martin Luther King Jr., whose work Rorty lauds — have

---

44. In an exchange with Thomas McCarthy, Rorty has written:

> McCarthy thinks that the ideals of political and cultural freedom are linked, in our culture, to "transcultural notions of validity." He says that our culture is "everywhere structured around" such notions. Maybe so, but maybe the temptation to believe that it is so structured is just a professional deformation of us philosophy professors.

See Rorty, "Truth and Freedom: A Reply to Thomas McCarthy," 635.
45. Rorty, *Contingency, Irony, and Solidarity*, 56.

fairly consistently structured their own rhetoric around at least minimally
foundationalist appeals to rationality and a common human nature—in
part because they know that their audiences will respond to such
appeals.[46] In his 1963 "I Have a Dream" speech—perhaps the most
revered piece of American rhetoric in the last half century—King does
precisely this when he grounds his utopia in Jefferson's Enlightenment
vocabulary by saying, "I have a dream that one day this nation will rise
up and live out the true meaning of its creed: 'We hold these truth to be
self-evident; that all men are created equal.'"[47] It is interesting to note that
no one who opposed King's goals thought it would be at all persuasive to
respond to him by pointing out that Jefferson's enlightenment vocabulary of self-evident *truths,* and a common (equal) human nature, theoretically undercuts itself. Such responses would not work in *our*
foundationalist culture. To be sure, I am not claiming that *all* King
needed to do in the summer of 1963 was invoke Jefferson's Enlightenment vocabulary, and then simply wait for discrimination to end. While
that alone would not have been *un*persuasive, King knew that he needed
to draw on *all* the resources his culture had to offer. So he coupled Jefferson's Enlightenment vocabulary with a compelling description of
what was wrong with America, and a inspiring dream of how things
could get better. Still, let me be clear about where the "burden of proof"
lies here. *Rorty* is arguing that Jefferson's Enlightenment vocabulary is
actually an impediment to liberal causes. To prove this, Rorty would
need to show, for example, that King's invocation of Jefferson actually
made his "I Have a Dream" speech *less* persuasive than it would have
been without such a reference. This I do not think Rorty can prove. It
seems then to run counter to good, pragmatic thinking to urge us to drop
the vocabulary of Enlightenment rationalism because two German émi-

---

46. In a *New York Times* op–ed piece, Rorty says that Martin Luther King Jr. "is some-
    body every American can be proud of." On my reading of this very short article, it
    seems that Rorty locates King's persuasiveness *solely* in the fact that King relentlessly
    challenged us to live up to our American ideals. But I would agree with McCarthy.
    King, and most of his audience, undoubtedly thought these ideals transcended
    American culture. And that thought gave King's appeals an added degree of persua-
    siveness. See Richard Rorty, "The Unpatriotic Academy," *New York Times*, 13 Feb-
    ruary 1994, sec. 4, 15.
47. Martin Luther King Jr., "I Have a Dream," in James Andrews and David Zarefsky,
    *Contemporary American Voices: Significant Speeches in American History 1945–
    Present* (New York: Longman, 1992), 80.

gré philosophers have "point[ed] out, correctly" that such rationalism undercuts itself.

To drive this point home, let me quote John Lyne, who sums up a good deal of what I have been trying to argue in the previous paragraph.

> In the face of a complex history, our most eloquent orators and statecrafters have found it useful if not necessary to express themselves in terms of enduring principles and observations on the nature of the human condition—notions to which Rorty cannot seem to state his objections often enough, as though they were philosophical errors. Taking these objections seriously, we would seem obliged to say that Mr. Jefferson was surely engaging in the universalist tendency of Enlightenment philosophy in declaring that "all men are created equal," and that the Court at Nuremburg was engaging in clap-trap in speaking of "crimes against humanity," just as the United Nations was piping hot air in its declaration on the universal rights of human kind. Maybe. Yet these "universals" have a manifestly practical value, because they help to secure some stability in the application of values dearly held. They are not simply reflections of the philosophical realism Rorty is so at pains to avoid. Can we imagine the culture of liberalism without them? I, frankly, cannot. And even if I could, I do not see, as a contingent matter, why these expressions of ideals should be given up.[48]

The only point I would add (for emphasis) to Lyne's remarks is that Rorty's insistence that we abandon "universals" in our liberal political discourse is *not* based primarily (or perhaps at all) on his belief that these ideas represent "philosophical errors." To be sure, Rorty *does* see these ideas as "reflections of . . . philosophical realism," and he *is* "at pains to avoid" such reflections. But, to repeat, Rorty thinks that these universals have now become a *political* (not merely a philosophical) *impediment* to our liberal goals.

The second piece of evidence Rorty adduces to support this claim is more general in scope than the first, but ultimately no more persuasive. He writes

---

48. John Lyne, "The Culture of Inquiry," *Quarterly Journal of Speech* 76 (1990): 193.

The idea that [liberal culture] ought to have foundations was
a result of Enlightenment scientism, which was in turn a sur-
vival of the religious need to have human projects underwrit-
ten by a nonhuman authority. It was natural for liberal
political thought in the eighteenth century to try to associate
itself with the most promising cultural development of the
time, the natural sciences. But unfortunately the Enlightenment wove much of its political rhetoric around a picture of
the scientist as a sort of priest, someone who achieved contact
with nonhuman truth by being "logical," "methodical," and
"objective." This was a useful tactic in its day, but it is less useful nowadays. For, in the first place, the sciences are no longer
the most interesting or promising or exciting area of culture.
In the second place, historians of science have made clear
how little this picture of the scientist has to do with actual scientific achievement, how pointless it is to try to isolate something called "the scientific method." Although the sciences
have burgeoned a thousandfold since the end of the eighteenth century, and have thereby made possible the realiza-
tion of political goals which could never have been realized
without them, they have nevertheless receded into the background of cultural life. This recession is due largely to the
increasing difficulty of mastering the various languages in
which the various sciences are conducted. It is not something
to be deplored but, rather, something to be coped with. We
can do so by switching attention to the areas which are at the
forefront of culture, those which excite the imagination of the
young, namely, art and utopian politics.[49]

Here I think Rorty reasons invalidly from the incontrovertible
premise that the various languages of the various sciences have become
increasingly difficult to master, to the conclusion that this somehow
makes Enlightenment rationalism "less useful" to liberal societies.
(Notice how Rorty softens his claim here, something that is "less useful"
is not *necessarily* an "impediment.") Nonetheless, to paraphrase Rorty,
we should not assume that Enlightenment rationalism cannot survive
the cultural "recession" of those who were, *at first*, most closely associ-

49. Rorty, *Contingency, Irony, and Solidarity,* 52.

ated with it. Surely the sciences had become exceedingly complex by the early 1960s. And just as surely, Martin Luther King Jr. was no scientist. But I see no evidence that King's appeals to Enlightenment rationalism were any less useful in the 1960s, than very similar appeals to Enlightenment rationalism were to Jefferson in the late eighteenth century.

Additionally, Rorty's suggestion that we replace the apparently unexciting vocabulary of Enlightenment rationalism with the currently exciting vocabulary offered by "art and utopian politics" seems to be in serious tension with his overall project. For, as Rorty notes throughout *Contingency, Irony, and Solidarity*, the aesthetic impulse is often private, and necessarily irrational. As I noted in chapter 1, in Rorty's view, the artist, or strong poet, must create himself or herself by breaking free from the insipid metaphors of his or her culture. Rorty insists that this is a necessarily private act, and while it might be very exciting for the artist, I would argue that it is not something we want to make central to the shared vocabulary of liberal politics. Nancy Fraser perfectly sums up this problem with Rorty's approach when she notes that, "In a culture supposedly already organized around a metaphorics of liberation and social reform, to seek new, more vivid, less hackneyed metaphors is to court political disaster."[50] But perhaps Rorty has changed his mind about the desirability of structuring our political vocabulary around the exciting areas of art and utopian politics. In a 1992 article discussing the monumental political changes in Eastern Europe since 1989, and in particular the way in which these changes have seemed thoroughly to discredit the once captivating vocabulary of "socialism," Rorty claims that "Western leftists" like himself "can best acknowledge the revolutions of 1989 and 1991 by resolving to *banalize* our vocabulary of political deliberation."[51] So much for art and utopian politics.

I CONCLUDE FROM THIS entire discussion that, to be able to tell ourselves a coherent story about ourselves as liberals, we must maintain a strong distinction between persuasion and force (as Rorty wishes us to), *and* to do this we must maintain a minimalist foundationalist political rhetoric

---

50. Fraser, "Solidarity or Singularity? Richard Rorty between Romanticism and Technocracy," 99.
51. Richard Rorty, "The Intellectuals at the End of Socialism," *The Yale Review* 80 (April 1992): 5.

that centers on reason. This is how our beliefs as liberals "hang together." Having said that, the reader may be wondering what, exactly, I mean by the term *reason*. By expanding on what I mean by this term I will, of course, be expanding further on my understanding of liberalism. So I will now claim that, as liberals, we must understand reason to be 1) a species universal, and 2) transparent to itself. In the following section I shall examine closely these two aspects of reason.

Universality, Transparency, and Truth

Let me begin this section by juxtaposing two quotations from two liberals, past and present. The first quotation, from Thomas Jefferson's Bill for Establishing Religious Freedom, we have seen before. Recall Jefferson affirming that

> [T]ruth is great and will prevail if left to herself . . . she is the proper and sufficient antagonist to error, and has nothing to fear from the conflict unless by human interposition disarmed of her natural weapons, *free argument and debate.* . . .[52]

Now listen to Rorty affirming that

> A liberal society is one which is content to call "true" (or "right" or "just") whatever the outcome of undistorted communication happens to be, whatever view wins in a *free and open encounter.*[53]

At first glance, these quotations seem similar. Both Jefferson and Rorty want to connect political truth to free and open discussions. But Rorty would prefer that we liberals get out of the habit of asking *how* this connection works. He thinks we should simply be "content" to make the connection, and then leave it at that. In Rorty's view, anyone who believes there is such a connection (or at least anyone who acts as though he or she believes this) is to be called a liberal. And that, as Rorty might put it, is all we can profitably say about the connection.

Once again, I would argue that believing there is such a connection also entails having other beliefs. These other beliefs tell us some-

---

52. Thomas Jefferson's *Bill for Establishing Religious Freedom* (1777), in William Lee Miller, *The First Liberty: Religion and the American Republic*, 358, emphasis added.
53. Rorty, *Contingency, Irony, and Solidarity*, 67, emphasis added.

thing further about the way we see ourselves and our liberal *democratic* society. It is, I think, profitable to know this about ourselves.

So self-reflective liberals will ask, *how* does truth emerge from a free and open discussion? Presumably, if truth emerges from *any* free and open discussion, then truth is independent of any one individual in the discussion. Another way of putting this point is to say that truth is independent of anything *particular* to anyone in the discussion. This must mean that truth is discoverable by a faculty common to *all* individuals in the discussion. Call such a faculty reason, and say that reason is a truth-seeking faculty that is also a species universal.

This is what I meant, in section 1 of chapter 1, when I noted that, in the traditional view of philosophy, reason is assumed to be a faculty common to all humans. I suggested a computer analogy in which we think of reason as being "hardwired" into all (nonphysiologically defective) humans. One could go further with this analogy and say that the capacity to reason is linked with the capacity to use language—*any* language. When Kenneth Burke notes that, "Given the potentiality for speech, the child of any culture will speak the language which it hears. There is no mental equipment for speaking Chinese which is different from the mental equipment for speaking English. . . ." he is making a point with which Noam Chomsky would certainly agree, and a point that suggests that there is a certain type of hardware necessary for speech that is identical for all humans and that is independent of the particular "softwares" that constitute different languages.[54] The link between the capacity to use language and the capacity to reason can be made more clear by considering the following: Presumably, if the two statements, "All men are mortal" and "Socrates is a man" are translated into *any* language, the (nonmentally defective) user of that language will always be able to conclude (in his or her language), "Socrates is mortal." Since the time of Socrates, at least, it is precisely this ability to complete such a syllogism that philosophers have taken both as evidence of the ability to reason, and, correspondingly, as evidence of the human species' *specific difference* from other animals.

Of course, it will immediately be objected that, since the time of Socrates, at least, *recognition* of the capacity to reason has been denied to

---

54. See Kenneth Burke, *Counter-Statement* (Berkeley: University of California Press, 1968), 48–49; see also Noam Chomsky, *Aspects of the Theory of Syntax* (Cambridge: MIT Press, 1965).

certain groups (those out of power) by other groups (those in power). While this is certainly true, it seems to me no more than evidence of unreasonable behavior on the part of those in power. Still, it is instructive to digress for a moment and consider the two most flagrant examples in which a particular group's capacity to reason has not been recognized by another, more (socially) powerful group.

In her book *The Man of Reason: "Male" and "Female" in Western Philosophy*, Genevieve Lloyd points out the various ways in which Western thought throughout the ages (i.e., the thought of Western males) has tended to think of "reason" as the *exclusive* province of the "male." Lloyd persuasively argues that such exclusionary thinking has structured both Western philosophy, and Western society in general, to the disadvantage of women. In a *qualified* sense, then, "reason" has become "male" in Western thought. But in saying this, Lloyd is *not* adopting an essentialist position. She is not saying that reasoning is done differently by males and females. In fact, she reminds us that reason *is* gender neutral when she cautions that, "The claim that Reason is male need not at all involve sexual relativism about truth, or any suggestion that the principles of logical thought valid for men do not hold also for female reasoners."[55] What this claim does involve is a recognition of the (unreasonable) historical factors influencing Western thought. Lloyd again states, "The obstacles to female cultivation of Reason spring to a large extent from the fact that our ideals of Reason have historically incorporated an exclusion of the feminine, and that femininity itself has been partly constituted through such practices of exclusion."[56] But to repeat the point I made above: to the extent that such exclusions are *unreasonable*, they do not provide any evidence of the nonuniversality of reason.

Women, of course, have not been the only group to suffer from the unreasonable denial of reason. In his remarkable work *Black Athena: The Afroasiatic Roots of Classical Civilization*, Martin Bernal argues that during the eighteenth and nineteenth centuries, the very centuries in which the West was codifying the principles of liberal politics, a concerted effort was being made *not* to recognize the capacity to reason in non-Western peoples (including non-Western women, of course, and in particular African and Asian individuals). But what is so fascinating about these

---

55. Genevieve Lloyd, *The Man of Reason: "Male" and "Female" in Western Philosophy* (Minneapolis: University of Minnesota Press, 1984), 109.

56. Ibid., x.

attempts is that *previous to this time*, many non-Western cultures were considered equal, if not superior, to the West in their capacity to reason. With regard especially to African (Egyptian) and Chinese cultures, Bernal notes

> Both were seen as having *superior* writing systems representing ideas, not sounds; and both had profound and ancient philosophies. Their most attractive feature, however, seems to have been that they were ruled rationally, without superstition, by a corps of men recruited for their morality and required to undergo rigorous initiation and training.[57]

What might account then for the West's sudden and unreasonable shift in perspective toward non-Westerners in the eighteenth and nineteenth century? Bernal provides an easily generalizable answer when he notes that "after the rise of black slavery and racism, European thinkers were concerned to keep black Africans as far as possible from European civilization."[58] In other words, after the rise of slavery, Western thinkers were forced to deny that individuals of African descent had the capacity to reason. Slavery could not be justified within *our* post–Enlightenment liberal culture if it applied to persons, and persons were seen as beings who could reason. Of course, this denial was itself unreasonable. And just as we saw with the case of women, now that we understand its *historical* roots, we can see that such a denial does nothing to lessen our belief in the universality of reason.

Now to return from our digression, I can sum up what I have been trying to say so far about the *universality* of reason with this terse (and somewhat circular) assertion: *Anyone we can talk to, we can reason with.* This, in turn, raises two final questions.

First, *can* we talk with everyone? Is that *theoretically* possible, or might we find some untranslatable language used by individuals who might, nonetheless, be thought to be as reasonable as ourselves? Here I agree with Rorty, who argues that the idea of an untranslatable language is incoherent. He writes, "I do not see how we could tell when we had come against a human practice *which we knew to be linguistic* and also

---

57. Martin Bernal, *Black Athena: The Afroasiatic Roots of Classical Civilization*, vol. 1, *The Fabrication of Ancient Greece 1785–1985* (New Brunswick, N.J.: Rutgers University Press, 1987), 25, emphasis added.
58. Ibid., 30.

knew to be so foreign that we must give up hope of knowing what it would be like to engage in it."[59] The point is that the only way *we* can *know* that a language *is* a language, is to know that it can be translated *by us*. Hence, we must, theoretically, be able to speak the language of any community of individuals we might come across, for if we could not, we could not know this community of individuals as a community of individuals.

The second question raised by my aforementioned assertion might be put as follows: What does it mean to *talk* to someone? We can imagine "talking" either to a young child, or a mentally retarded individual, and not being convinced that either had the capacity to reason. In the case of the child, our judgment would simply be premature, if not altogether incorrect. Presumably, all normal children have the *capacity* to reason (again, they have this by membership in the species). But such a capacity surely needs time to develop. The case of the mentally retarded individual is, however, more difficult both from a theoretical, and a liberal political, perspective. Some mentally retarded individuals may actually be born without the *capacity* to reason; others may lose that capacity sometime in their life. From a liberal *political* perspective, we might reasonably ask whether all mentally retarded individuals should, for example, be allowed to vote. If the answer is no, we must ask where we draw the line. Again, one could imagine talking, in some rudimentary way, with a severely mentally retarded individual (for example, the character Benjy in William Faulkner's *The Sound and the Fury*) and yet not thinking for a moment that this person was in any way reasonable. On the other hand, one could imagine talking with a less severely mentally retarded individual (for example, the character Benny in the NBC television series *L.A. Law*) and believing this individual was capable of reasoning.

But, to repeat, where do we draw the line? Here I can only fall back on *essentially* what I said at the beginning of this section. We should say that an individual has the capacity to be reasonable if and only if he or she can use a language. To say that one is able to use a language we must at least be able to imagine engaging in a conversation with that individual. But we cannot imagine engaging in a conversation with someone who *cannot* perform the most rudimentary aspects of reasoning—that is, who cannot complete a syllogism. This method of "line drawing" will

---

59. Rorty, "Cosmopolitanism without Emancipation," in *Objectivity, Relativism, and Truth: Philosophical Papers, Volume I* (Cambridge: University Press, 1991), 215, emphasis added.

probably exclude, from the set of all reasonable individuals, the *severely* mentally retarded. But it may also tend to exclude the poetical genius who could *never* speak in a more "mundane" discourse, as well as the Zen master who *always* spoke in koans. Nonetheless, for the purposes of liberal politics, we may need to exclude these individuals *from political discussions*. Or, to put this last point more gently, for the purposes of liberal politics, much as we might wish to include these individuals in our political discussions, we cannot see how such discussions could continue to make sense if they *were* included. Having said all of that, I cannot leave this issue without addressing what I think are the two most obvious objections that will be raised against the mechanism for line drawing that I have just suggested, as well as the larger discussion of the universality of reason.

First, it might be argued that some animals may be capable of using a language; that we can, in some sense, "talk" with some other species. If this is so, then reason might not be *exclusive* to the human species. Reason might not represent the *specific difference* between us and other animals. Indeed, it has been argued that chimpanzees in particular can be taught American Sign Language.[60] Here I think Lord Zuckerman is most convincing. In a review of the literature on the subject, he has written, "[T]he only aspect of ASL [American Sign Language] which a handful of apes have been patiently taught to acquire is the semantic—the representational aspects of objects or actions. For example, a chimpanzee can be taught to sign for 'cup' or 'apple' [but it] cannot be trained to use or understand any *syntactic* rules."[61] The completion of any syllogism is, of course, impossible without some understanding of syntactic rules.

The second objection that may be raised to tying reason to language use may be said to be the converse of the first objection. It might be argued that if animals are not reasonable because they cannot use a language, and they cannot use a language because they cannot complete a syllogism, then certainly *computers*, which can complete syllogisms, can be said to use a language, and must therefore be thought of as being reasonable. While computers can certainly complete syllogisms, it is hard—though perhaps not *impossible*—to imagine carrying on a conver-

---

60. For an interesting discussion of this entire issue, see Derek Bickerton, *Language and Species* (Chicago: University of Chicago Press, 1991).

61. See Lord Zuckerman, "Apes 'R' not us," *The New York Review of Books*, May 30, 1991, 47, emphasis added.

sation with a computer. But what would it mean to "carry on a conversation" with a computer, and would doing so then allow us to say that the computer was reasonable? And would saying so then force us to see reason as, again, not *exclusively* human? Considerations like these get us into the whole area of artificial intelligence, and to the related question of whether computers can be taught "natural" languages. Here I think the British logician Alan Turing, who died in 1954, *still* has the last word on the subject.

Turing asked what many were asking in the 1950s: "Can machines think?" He proposed to explore this question through what he called an "Imitation Game." (Turing's game has since become known as the "Turing Test.") I can best explain how Turing helps us answer the questions I have just posed by quoting at length from his 1950 article, entitled "Computing Machinery and Intelligence," in which he describes the "Imitation Game." (Remember, the article was written in 1950, when the development of computers was in its infancy). About his game, Turing says this,

> It is played with three people: a man (A), a woman (B), and an interrogator (C) who may be of either sex. The interrogator stays in a room apart from the other two. The object of the game for the interrogator is to determine which of the other two is the man and which is the woman. He knows them by labels X and Y, and at the end of the game he says either "X is A and Y is B" or "X is B and Y is A." The interrogator is allowed to put questions to A and B, thus,
>
> C: Will X please tell me the length of his or her hair?
>
> Now suppose X is actually A, then A must answer. It is A's object in the game to try to cause C to make the wrong identification. His answer might therefore be
>
> "My hair is shingled, and the longest strands are about nine inches long."
>
> In order that tones of voice may not help the interrogator, the answers should be written, or better still, typewritten. The ideal arrangement is to have a teleprinter communicating between the two rooms. Alternatively the questions and answers can be repeated by an intermediary. The object of the

game for the third player (B) is to help the interrogator. The best strategy for her is probably to give truthful answers. She can add such things as "I am the woman, don't listen to him!" to her answers, but it will avail nothing as the man can make similar remarks. We now ask the question, "What will happen when a machine takes the part of A in this game?" Will the interrogator decide wrongly as often when the game is played like this as he does when the game is played between a man and a woman? These questions replace our original, "Can machines think?"[62]

Turing's last two questions also help us answer the question of what it would be like to "carry on a conversation" with a computer. To extend Turing's idea, suppose we replaced *either* player A or B in the imitation game with a computer and then slightly modified the game so that the new objective was for the interrogator to determine which "player" was the *human*. What would happen when the interrogator could decide correctly no more often than he or she decides incorrectly? This replaces the question, "What would it be like to carry on a conversation with a computer?" In short, I think the key insight of the Turing Test can be expressed as follows: When, *based strictly on "the conversation,"* we have no more certainty about whether we are conversing with a machine or with a human, then machines can think, and use language, and reason. Does this mean that when computers can pass this modified version of the Turing Test they should be given the status of citizens of a liberal polity? My thoroughly pragmatic (and admittedly evasive) answer to this question is: *Only* when *computers* can ask that question need *we* trouble ourselves about answering it.[63]

---

62. Alan Turing, "Computing Machinery and Intelligence," *Mind*, Vol. LIX, No. 236, 1950, 433–34.
63. In a crucial comment that applies equally to his own version of the Imitation Game, and my modified version of the game, Turing notes

> It may be urged that when playing the "imitation game" the best strategy for the machine may possibly be something other than imitation of the behavior of man. This may be, but I think it is unlikely that there is any great effect of this kind. In any case there is no intention to investigate here the theory of the game, and it will be assumed that the best strategy is to try to provide answers that would naturally be given by a man. (Turing, "Computing Machinery and Intelligence," 435)

So much, then, for my discussion of the universality of reason. I hope to have shown what it means to believe that reason is a species universal. Why this belief is important in a liberal polity should be obvious: The ideal, universal, liberal polity will include all and only those who have the capacity to reason.[64] But, since this capacity excludes *no one* on the basis of gender, race, or any other such classification, we can safely say that the ideal liberal polity could consist of the community of *all* reasonable individuals. Let me now turn to the second assumption liberals must make about reason, the assumption that reason is "transparent to itself."

TO SEE WHAT IS MEANT by this phrase—"transparent to itself"—we need to back up, slightly, to the beginning of this very sentence. I have said, "*To see* what is meant by this phrase . . ." There is nothing particularly remarkable about this phrase—I mean the phrase, "to see"—and its occurrence within the development of a discussion about reason and

---

Interestingly, although he says it is not his purpose to investigate the theory of the Imitation Game, Turing's article can easily (and, I think, persuasively) be interpreted as doing nothing else *but that* for twenty-eight pages. Clearly, when we investigate the theory of the game we are investigating what it means for humans to think, and for computers to think. But I would argue with Turing's assumption that the best strategy for the computer would be to try to "imitate the behavior of man." Turing seems to think that when asked a question, the computer should attempt to give the answer that a human would give when asked the same question. Perhaps this would be the approach of the *first* generation thinking machines. But, the *second* generation thinking machines would not attempt to give the answer that a human would give to a particular question. Rather, they would attempt to give the answer that the *questioner* would think the human would give to the particular question. Remember, the *ultimate* goal of the game is to fool the questioner. Now what happens when we design a computer that is *better* at making us think it is a human, than a human is at making us think he or she is a human? In such a case computers might be said to understand us better than we understand ourselves. For some further, fascinating thoughts on the Turing Test, see Douglas R. Hofstadter, *Gödel, Escher, Bach: An Eternal Golden Braid* (New York: Vintage Books, 1980), 595–99.

64. Critically, to be included in a liberal *polity* means only that one is included in discussions about self-government. As far as I can see, this in no way implies that liberal *societies* would *necessarily* treat individuals not included in discussions about self-government (i.e., the severely mentally retarded) any worse than any other society would treat such individuals. Indeed, liberal societies might treat such individuals better than nonliberal societies.

truth would probably go unnoticed. Dead metaphors do not generally get noticed. But the phrase "to see" is quite obviously a metaphor, perhaps *the* key metaphor in the text of Western philosophy. To see how this has come about, one might begin by noting that our word for "idea" comes from the Greek word meaning "to see," while our word for "theory" also comes from the Greek word meaning "to look at." Along these same lines we might wish to take a careful look at the opening lines of Aristotle's *Metaphysics*.

> All men by nature desire to know. An indication of this is the delight we take in our senses; for even apart from their usefulness they are loved for themselves; and above all others the sense of sight. For not only with a view to action, but even when we are not going to do anything, we prefer sight to almost everything else. The reason is that this, most of all the senses, makes us know and brings to light many differences between things.[65]

Saint Paul was clearly borrowing a metaphor from Greek philosophy when, with respect to this world and the next, he wrote, "For now we see through a glass, darkly; but then face to face: now I know in part; but then shall I know even as also I am known" (*First Corinthians* 13:12). Of course, as this passage implies, Christianity (and religion in general) understands reason as being not quite fully transparent to itself, a point that will become more clear shortly. For now, however, what is important is tracing the metaphor. The biblical passage just quoted is from the King James Version of the Bible, published in the seventeenth century. That same century saw the publication of Rene Descartes' *Discourse on the Method*, and John Locke's most important philosophical work, *Essay Concerning Human Understanding*. Our notion of the "eye of the mind" inspecting, reasoning, and thereby knowing comes directly from both of these philosophers. Understanding that, and noting also that in the seventeenth century the word "glass," as it is used in the aforementioned passage, would have referred to a "mirror," we are brought (more or less) directly to the vision of truth as something acquired by gazing into the *mirror* of nature within our own mind. Rorty wants us to reject this vision, just as Dewey wanted us to reject what he called the "spectator theory of

---

65. Aristotle, *Metaphysics* 980A, in *The Complete Works of Aristotle*, ed. Jonathan Barnes, trans. W. D. Ross (Princeton: University Press, 1984), 1552.

knowledge,"[66] and Heidegger wished us to reject the *entire metaphorics* of "seeing" and to replace it with "hearing," which "constitutes the primary and authentic way in which Dasein is open for its ownmost potentiality-for-Being."[67]

But dead metaphors die hard, so to speak. In an essay on "Rhetoric after Deconstruction," James Aune also suggests that we might consider abandoning the metaphor of "seeing" in Western philosophy. But in making this very suggestion, Aune becomes ensnared in the metaphor itself. He writes,

> If . . . deconstruction seems like a parody of the Socratic method, perhaps the best way of viewing [1] the implications of deconstruction for rhetoric is to see [2] deconstruction as refusing Athens in favor of Jerusalem. For if we conceive of language as reducible to *seeing* (consider the visual metaphors that underlie such Greek terms as "idea" and "theory") then philosophy from the beginning wishes to make language disappear. Rhetoric becomes simply the shadow-side of philosophy, the secret armory for philosophy's perennial war against religion and literature. If, on the other hand, we refuse to separate knowing, speaking, acting, and hearing, then we refuse, like the ancient Hebrews, the entire problematic that gives us "rhetoric" and "philosophy" in the first place. How little sense the first book of Genesis makes to the Greek mind, in that the Creator's speech and action are one! Perhaps the best we can do is remain in exile, reading endlessly, trying to see [3] where we got the text of the world wrong in the first place.[68]

I count three metaphors for seeing in a philosophical passage that attempts to convince us that we should drop our metaphors for seeing. And, since Aune is writing an essay on deconstruction, it might not be unfair to insist, with Derrida, that metaphors matter; they are, in a sense, all that we have. Derrida calls "writing"—and I think we could now sim-

66. See John Dewey, *The Quest for Certainty* (New York: Harper & Row, 1960), especially p. 23.

67. Martin Heidegger, *Being and Time*, trans. John Macquarrie and Edward Robinson (New York: Harper & Row, 1962), 206.

68. James Arnt Aune, "Rhetoric after Deconstruction," in *Rhetoric and Philosophy*, ed. Richard A. Cherwitz (Hillsdale, N.J.: Lawrence Erlbaum Associates, 1990), 272, emphasis in original, citation omitted.

ilarly call "seeing"—"a 'metaphor' philosophy will never . . . be able to do without, however uncritical its treatment might be."[69]

To say then that reason is transparent to itself is to work off an ingrained metaphor in Western thought, a metaphor that implicitly connects truth with the ability to see clearly (i.e., entirely and completely) how one has arrived at that truth. This is precisely what the reasonable individual claims as his or her unique ability as a reasonable individual. To put this point slightly more concretely (if again circularly), and to demonstrate the difference between claims to reasonableness and other claims, we could say the following: To the extent that poets, for example, are seized by the muse, and preachers by the voice of God, neither really *knows* what he or she is saying. Only reasonable individuals can give reasons for their statements. It is precisely the ability to provide such reasons, and the assumption (which we have just been over) that reason is a universal quality that all humans—simply by membership in the species—have in common, which uniquely differentiates the reasonable individual's persuasive speech from that of the poet or the preacher. The reasonable individual's speech is transparent to itself.

Again, if this sounds a bit too abstract, I can perhaps illustrate this *specific* point about reason's transparency to itself more clearly by examining an even more concrete example. The example I have in mind is a short story drawn from the genre of science fiction, certainly one of the most expansive literary genres ever created. It would, I think, be fair to say that there is probably a work of science fiction to illustrate *any* philosophical idea one can come up with. With that in mind, consider Isaac Asimov's 1957 short story entitled *The Feeling of Power*.

For our purposes, the plot of this piece of vintage-era science fiction can be quickly sketched. The scene is Earth, at least a thousand years in the future. Because Asimov is (at one level, at least) writing an allegory, important aspects of the human condition have remained unchanged over the course of the millennium. Granted, Asimov's Earth is apparently united under a democratic government. But, as was the case with the America of the fifties, this Earth of the future is also involved in a cold war of sorts with an evil adversary—in this case, the planet Deneb. Leaders on both sides feel the ultimate outcome of the war will be determined by whichever side has the superior technology. Now, in the matter of

---

69. Jacques Derrida, "Plato's Pharmacy," in *Dissemination*, trans. Barbara Johnson (Chicago: University of Chicago Press, 1981), 149.

technology, things *have* significantly changed. As in most science fiction stories of this era, Asimov has imagined a future Earth in which computers have taken over almost all aspects of life. This is a critical element of the story. Indeed, computers in this imaginary future have become so complex that they even design other computers. As programmer-first-class Jehan Shuman explains to the President of Earth (and to the reader, of course), "It seems that at one time computers were designed directly by human beings. Those were simple computers, of course, this being before the time of the rational use of computers to design more advanced computers had been established."[70] Asimov assumes (perhaps too pessimistically) that the hypertrophy of computer usage will necessarily lead to an atrophy of the knowledge of computation. Specifically, in programmer-first-class Shuman's world, no one knows how to do simple (and presumably more complex) mathematics. At the very least, no one can add, subtract, multiply, divide, or do anything else with numbers. Perhaps as both cause and consequence of this, pocket calculators are, of necessity, ubiquitous in this world.

Enter Myron Aub, "an aging low-grade Technician" (76). Aub was an otherwise undistinguished fellow, except that "[t]here was just this hobby of his that the great Programmer [Shuman] had found out about and was now making such a frightening fuss over" (76). The fuss was being made at a meeting in the New Pentagon attended by a high-ranking military officer named General Weider, an equally powerful civilian leader named Congressman Brant, Programmer Shuman, and Aub. It seems that after having discovered Aub's hobby, Shuman became convinced, and was now out to convince Weider and Brant, that this hobby could somehow make the difference in Earth's struggle with Deneb. Aub's hobby involved playing with numbers. All he had discovered, really, was how to multiply two numbers without a computer. But this ability was still very much a *mystery* to everyone else in Aub's world, including his immediate audience.

Aub is repeatedly asked to multiply various numbers. Alone in a corner of the room, patiently working with pencil and paper only, he

---

70. Isaac Asimov, *The Feeling of Power*, in *Nine Tomorrows: Tales of the Near Future* (New York: Doubleday & Company, 1959), 80, subsequent page numbers in the text will refer to this anthology. What one needs with a programmer-first-class in a world where computers design, and we would presume *program*, themselves is unclear. Let us just say that slightly more than the normal degree of suspension of disbelief is necessary when reading this story.

complies with every request and eventually produces the correct answer. Yet since neither Weider nor Brant *knows* how Aub does it, he is repeatedly labeled "an illusionist," a "magic-making Technician." His work is thought to be something like "trick manipulation." At one point, General Weider, who seems highly skeptical of the whole affair, assumes that Aub is really using a new type of computer, "a *paper* computer." Finally, Shuman has Aub come forward and *demonstrate* the way in which he comes up with these true answers. Weider and Brant are then able to see clearly how Aub has arrived at these "truths." The scene in which this takes place begins with Shuman asking,

> "General, would you be so kind as to suggest a number?"
> "Seventeen," said the general.
> "And you, Congressman?"
> "Twenty-three."
> "Good! Aub, multiply those numbers and please show the gentlemen your manner of doing it."
> "Yes, Programmer," said Aub, ducking his head . . . His forehead corrugated as he made painstaking marks on the paper.
> General Weider interrupted him sharply. "Let's see that."
> Aub passed him the paper, and Weider said, "Well, it looks like the figure seventeen."
> Congressman Brant nodded and said, "So it does, but I suppose anyone can copy figures off a computer. I think I could make a passable seventeen myself, even without practice."
> "If you will let Aub continue, gentleman," said Shuman . . .
> Aub continued, his hand trembling a little. Finally he said in a low voice, "The answer is three hundred and ninety-one."
> Congressman Brant took out his computer [i.e., pocket calculator] and flicked it, "By Godfrey, so it is. How did he guess?"
> "No guess, Congressman," said Shuman. "He computed that result. He did it on this sheet of paper."
> "Humbug," said the general impatiently. "A computer is one thing and marks on paper are another."

"*Explain*, Aub," said Shuman.

"Yes, Programmer. Well, gentleman, I write down seventeen and just underneath it, I write twenty-three. Next, I say to myself. . . . seven times three is twenty-one, so I write down twenty-one. Then one times three is three, so I write down a three under the two of twenty-one . . . Three plus two makes five, *you see*, so the twenty-one becomes a fifty-one. Now you let that go for a while and start fresh. You multiply seven and two, that's fourteen, and one and two, that's two. Put them down like this and it adds up to thirty four. Now if you put the thirty-four under the fifty-one in this way and add them, you get three hundred and ninety-one and that's the answer." (76–78, emphasis added)

Granted, one may not be fully able to understand Aub's explanation—it may not be fully transparent—unless one first sees, for example, that seven times three is twenty one. But that, in turn, could easily be made clear. One could be shown seven sets of three things and taught to count them. Similarly, one could be taught the notation in a base-ten number system, and then shown why, in the previous example, you "write down a three under the two of twenty-one." Again, all of this could be made fully transparent to anyone who could reason; anyone, in fact, who could complete a syllogism.

To my mind, Asimov's short story helps us get clear on the critical difference I alluded to earlier: the difference between the reasonable individual's persuasive speech and the speech of the poet or priest.[71] Only reasonable individuals can make their speech transparent to itself in something like the same way that Aub was able to make his reasoning with numbers transparent to itself. That is the difference between reason and art or religion. This difference means that reasonable claims must *always* be able to be made clear to—to be *communicable* to—any other reasonable individual. This requirement acts like something of a *check* on such reasonable claims. More than *simple* peer agreement is involved where reason is concerned. If we assume that reason is a species univer-

---

71. I use the terms *poet* and *priest* somewhat loosely and generally here to refer to individuals whose speech is not reasonable, because it is not transparent to itself. This does not mean, of course, that neither the poet nor the priest has the *capacity* to be a reasonable individual. It simply means that in speaking *as poet or priest*, they are not speaking reasonably.

sal, then there must always be *something* outside of every *particular* conversation, to which any member of that conversation can appeal. In the sense in which I have described it in this section, reason, a truth-seeking faculty that is both a species universal and transparent to itself, transcends any *localized* conversation.

This, of course, is a point Rorty simply refuses to see. But his refusal puts him in what I think is a difficult position. One could say that, having abandoned reason, Rorty has nothing left to fall back on but particular, localized conversations—even if those "local" conversations take place on a broad cultural level, as in the "conversation" of the West. One *could* say that. And I am sure Rorty would happily agree. For he is continuously urging us to abandon the attempt to adopt a "God's-eye" view of the human condition—a view which thinks it can finally get a perspective on all possible perspectives. But *I* would rather say, having forcefully *excluded* reason from the conversation, Rorty has nothing left to fall back on but a *poorer* conversation. For surely we lose nothing if we continue to include reason. But if we do exclude reason, we lose one more "spur" (perhaps sharp or perhaps dull) in the conversation—a spur that motivates us to continue searching for other perspectives and other voices, with the faith that whatever voices we hear can be accepted or *answered* within the conversation. To follow up on this point, and to bring the discussion back to a more explicit focus on persuasion and force, I want to conclude this chapter by examining what *may* be the most enduring legacy of the twentieth century.

Critical Coda: Answering Hitler

Sooner or later, and often quite a bit sooner than later, *any* discussion of persuasion and force will come around to the matter of Hitler and Nazism. When the discussion does make this turn, we demand answers. On one level, we demand an answer to the question of how Hitler could have been so persuasive—how he could have managed to dupe millions of seemingly intelligent, literate, educated individuals. In response to this type of question, sociologists and cultural critics of various schools can point to the effects of economic depression on a country's population, or to the power of mass communication technology, or to a combination of these and a hundred other factors. But, on a second, deeper level, we also tend to demand an answer not just to the question of how Hitler was so persuasive, but *to that persuasion itself*. In other words, we demand an answer to Hitler that "proves" we are right, and he was wrong. And we often demand *this* type of answer from our philosophers. Rorty thinks this is quite unfortunate. In an exchange with Thomas McCarthy, he laments, "[W]e philosophers are still called on to 'answer Hitler,' and abused if we confess our inability to do so."[72]

Although Rorty declines to answer *Hitler* directly, he does take up the challenge of answering a somewhat related question: How should we liberals attempt to persuade a Nazi to change his or her ways? Rorty's answer to this question is extensive and sophisticated. Indeed, it embodies a redescription of his *entire* perspective on the relationship between persuasion and force. In order, then, to do him justice, I need to quote Rorty at some length. He starts off by confessing,

> I have always (well, not always, but for the last twenty years or so) been puzzled about what was supposed to count as a knockdown answer to Hitler. Would it answer him to tell him that there was a God in Heaven who was on our side? How do we reply to him when he asks for evidence for this claim? Would it answer him to say that his views are incompatible with the construction of a society in which communication is undistorted, and that his refusal of a voice to his opponents contradicts the presupposition of his own communicative acts? What if Hitler rejoins that to interpret truth as a product of free and open encounters rather than as what emerges from the genius of a destined leader begs the question against him? (What if, in other words, he goes Heideggerian on us?) Richard Hare's view that there is no way to "refute" a sophisticated, consistent, passionate, psychopath—for example, a Nazi who would favor his own elimination if he himself turned out to be a Jew—seems to me right, but to show more about the idea of "refutation" than about Nazism.
>
> If I were assigned the task not of refuting or answering but of *converting* a Nazi (one a bit more sane and conversable than Hitler himself), I would have some idea of how to set to work. I could show him how nice things can be in free societies, how horrible things are in the Nazi camps, how the Führer can plausibly be redescribed as an ignorant paranoid

---

72. Rorty, "Truth and Freedom: A Reply to Thomas McCarthy," 637.

rather than as an inspired prophet, how the Treaty of Versailles can be redescribed as a reasonable compromise rather than a vendetta, and so on. These tactics might or might not work, but at least they would not be an intellectual exercise in what [Karl–Otto] Apel calls *Letzbegründung*. They would be the sort of thing that sometimes actually changes people's minds. By contrast, attempts at showing the philosophically sophisticated Nazi that he is caught in a logical or pragmatic self-contradiction will simply impel him to construct invidious redescriptions of the presuppositions of the charge of contradiction (the sort of redescriptions Heidegger put at the Nazis' disposal).[73]

Would it be unfair to say that the persuasiveness of Rorty's views on persuasion stand or fall on the persuasiveness of these two paragraphs? Probably. Nonetheless, the gravity of the issues he is addressing suggests we assign that kind of weight to these remarks. It also *demands* that we examine them very closely.

To begin with, notice that Rorty has set himself a slightly more manageable task than we might have supposed. He is not going to attempt to convert *any* Nazi, just one "a bit more sane and conversable than Hitler himself." But what can this requirement possibly mean? Presumably, a Nazi who was convinced that truth emerged from the genius of the destined leader (Hitler) would not be conversable—unless he or she were conversing with Hitler. But such a Nazi probably would not wish even to converse with Hitler, *for conversation implies some degree of equality*. So this particular Nazi would simply *listen*, and listen only to Hitler. In a case like this, it does not seem that a conversational encounter could ever get started.

Rorty *clearly* understands this, and so he will *only* take up the task of attempting to convert a conversable Nazi. So far, so good. We would be at least somewhat justified in seeing a Nazi's willingness to engage in conversation as *prima facie* evidence of his or her openness to persuasion. On this point I think Rorty would agree. But if we were engaging in a conversation as important as this one, it would only make sense to draw on *all* of the linguistic and symbolic resources at our disposal. Now

---

73. Rorty, "Truth and Freedom: A Reply to Thomas McCarthy," 636–37, emphasis in original, footnotes omitted.

notice: Just as soon as the conversation begins, *Rorty* excludes reason. He is not going to attempt to *answer*, but rather to *convert*. Very curiously, on Rorty's account it seems that an answer can *never* facilitate a conversion. But why is this so?

One might *initially* assume this is so because, even if we were to "answer" the Nazi by *demonstrating* to him or her that some of his or her beliefs logically contradict other beliefs he or she has, he or she would simply *ignore the contradiction*. But remember, we are conversing with a "sane" Nazi. Hence, he or she *cannot* ignore large contradictions in his or her belief system and remain sane. So we liberals now seem to have the upper hand. If we can just produce enough "cognitive dissonance" in the Nazi, he or she will be forced to convert. And it seems that producing such cognitive dissonance should not be that difficult. As Thomas McCarthy points out, Nazism "drew on the resources of the wider [Western] culture," and so *it opened itself up* to criticisms that demonstrated that it contradicted the assumptions of that wider culture. So, as McCarthy continues, "It is not surprising that those organizations that spawned [Nazism] went to such lengths to suppress the 'free and open encounters' that, according to Rorty, are needed to get at the truth."[74] In other words, Nazism practiced censorship because it had to—because it could not defend its principles in a consistent way in a free and open encounter. But since we are imagining that we are, right now, in just such a free and open encounter with a conservable Nazi, why can we not answer him or her, and thus convert him or her, by demonstrating that he or she adheres to a self-contradictory view?

Because, Rorty would respond, "attempts at showing the philosophically sophisticated Nazi that he is caught in a logical or pragmatic self-contradiction will simply impel him to construct invidious redescriptions of the presuppositions of the charge of contradiction. . . ." This a Nazi could do, for example, by going "Heideggerian on us," and arguing that truth emerges from the genius of a destined leader, *not* from free and open encounters. Of course, that is only one of a number of dialectical moves the Nazi can use to get out of any contradiction into which we forced him or her. After all, as Rorty says, "Any fool thing can be made to seem rational by being set in an appropriate context, surrounded by a set of beliefs and desires with which it coheres."[75] In other words, any par-

---

74. Thomas McCarthy, "Ironist Theory as a Vocation: A Response to Rorty's Reply," 647.
75. Rorty, "Truth and Freedom: A Reply to Thomas McCarthy," 640.

ticular belief can be made to appear rational, if by "rational" one means "able to be derived in a 'logical' way from a set of prior beliefs." Of course, these "prior beliefs" will themselves need to be made to appear rational in the same way—that is, by being derived from a set of still prior beliefs. But it now seems that if our philosophically sophisticated Nazi does attempt to escape the charge of self-contradiction made against him or her by redescribing "the presuppositions of the charge of contradiction," he or she will be exceedingly busy. For what are these "presuppositions of the charge of contradiction" but the very *suppositions* of Western culture? Hence, our philosopher Nazi will need to redescribe Western culture almost from the start—from Plato onward. Unfortunately, the very type of redescription our philosopher Nazi is looking for was (on Rorty's account) put at his or her disposal by Heidegger. But even if Heidegger had not existed, there is no theoretical reason why such a vast redescription could not be undertaken and perhaps be successful. Hence, there does not seem to be any rational way of limiting the dialectal moves our reasonable Nazi could make. He or she could, therefore, always be at least theoretically capable of escaping any charge of contradiction we lodged against him or her.

So much then for reason. At this point, I think we are justified in posing the following question: If Rorty insists that we abandon reason when conversing with our imaginary Nazi, what *better* idea does he have for converting him or her?

Rorty suggests that he would engage in redescriptions of his own. This initially sounds somewhat promising. But one would still think that these redescriptions must draw on something *other* than themselves to be effective. What could this "other" be? Rorty does not say—*explicitly*. But there are very interesting *implications* in some of his redescriptions. Consider, for example, Rorty's claim that he would show his conversational partner "how horrible things are in the Nazi camps." It is not clear how much *re*description is involved here, but let us assume that Rorty were to do this. What good would come of it? More to the point, why does Rorty suggest that we choose this approach *over* reason? As far as I can see, in order to believe that we should attempt this redescription, one needs to assume that the Nazi has at least some compassion left in him or her. But where does this assumption come from? Are we to assume that our philosophically sophisticated Nazi is also a tenderhearted soul? Does compassion now replace reason as a species universal? This indeed is what Jean-Jacques Rousseau thought. In his *Discourse on the Origin and Foun-*

dations of the Inequality Among Men, Rousseau insists that man is born with "an *innate* repugnance to see his fellow man suffer." And he goes on to assert,

> I do not believe I have any contradiction to fear in granting man the *sole natural virtue* that the most excessive detractor of human virtues was forced to recognize. I speak of pity, a disposition that is appropriate to beings as weak and subject to as many ills as we are; a virtue all the more *universal* and useful to man because it precedes in him the use of all reflection; and so natural that even beasts sometimes give perceptible signs of it.[76]

But surely Rousseau's optimism, *grounded* as it is in the belief that humans have an innate capacity to feel pity, is simply unavailable to Rorty. Remember, for Rorty, socialization "goes all the way down."[77] Rorty would probably respond to the aforementioned quotation by arguing that the "innate repugnance to see his fellow man suffer" of which Rousseau speaks is not really innate at all. It has merely been socialized into inhabitants of a Western culture permeated with Christian ideals.[78] There are, presumably, other cultures that do not socialize this particular attribute into their members. So we have no reason for believing that a redescription that drew on feelings of compassion would work. Of course, as Rorty would quickly point out, we have no reason for believing it would *not* work either. Granted. This leaves Rorty in the following odd predicament: He apparently has no reason for believing that anything *other* than appeals to reason will work to convert a conversable Nazi, but he nonetheless *insists* that appeals to reason itself will *not* work.

But where does this insistence about the impotence of reason come from? It is certainly not grounded in some philosophical argument about the nature of language or truth. Rorty emphatically does not want to paint himself into the corner of arguing against argument, or reasoning

---

76. Jean-Jacques Rousseau, *Discourse on the Origin and Foundations of Inequality Among Men*, in *The First and Second Discourses*, trans. Roger D. and Judith R. Master (New York: St. Martin's Press, 1964), 130, emphasis added.

77. Rorty, *Contingency, Irony, and Solidarity*, xiii.

78. In *Contingency, Irony, and Solidarity*, Rorty writes, "Christianity did not know that its purpose was the alleviation of cruelty. . . . But *we* now know [this], for we latecomers can tell the kind of story of progress which those who are actually making progress cannot" (55, emphasis in original).

against reason. So he insists, "I am *not* saying that the idea of truth is 'invalid' or 'untenable,' nor that it 'deconstructs itself'. . . ."[79]

Perhaps then this insistence on the impotence of reason is a pragmatic gesture. Apparently Rorty believes that, when faced with philosophically sophisticated Nazis, we liberals are better served by redescriptive endeavors than by reason. Is this because liberal redescriptions can "activate" some species universal other than reason—something like compassion? No, we have already seen that *no* universals exist. Is it then because liberals can *redescribe* better than Nazis, so that, to trope Jefferson, liberal redescriptions are great and will prevail? Apparently *this* is not the case either. On Rorty's account, we liberals do not have *any* redescriptive powers available to us that are not also *equally* available to the Nazi. In other words, anything we can redescribe as looking bad (like the Nazi camps), he or she can equally well redescribe as looking good. *Anything?* Yes, anything. Consider the case of Hitler himself. Rorty writes,

> Someday somebody will write a novel about Hitler that will portray [i.e., redescribe] him as he saw himself, one that will momentarily [but why *only* momentarily!—EMG] make its readers feel that the poor man was much misunderstood. . . . Someday somebody will write a novel about Stalin as Good Old Uncle Joe. I hope nobody writes either novel very soon, because reading such a novel seems too much for the remaining victims of either murderer to have to bear. But such novels will someday be written. If we are to be faithful to the wisdom of the novel, they *must* be written.[80]

So, to recapitulate: We are attempting to convert a conversable Nazi. We know that appeals to reason will fail to convert him or her. We know that we cannot appeal to emotions like compassion either, because these are merely products of socialization, and hence we cannot be sure that our conversable Nazi has any *particular* emotions.[81] But, *crucially*, even if he or she did (accidentally) have the capacity to feel compassion, we would

---

79. Rorty, "Truth and Freedom: A Reply to Thomas McCarthy," 641, emphasis added.
80. Ibid., 639, emphasis in original.
81. Apparently, however, he or she can be humiliated. Could we then *shame* the Nazi into behaving humanely? Obviously, Rorty would disagree. Nonetheless, I cannot think of any noncontradictory way for him to do so.

still need to redescribe his or her situation in such a way as to bring that emotion to work on him or her in the way *we* desired. But remember, he or she can redescribe everything just as well as we can. Hence, while we are busy redescribing the world in order to convert our Nazi interlocutor, he or she is (presumably) busy redescribing the world in order to convert us. This is, after all, exactly what it means to engage in a *conversation*.

But now consider the position in which we suddenly find ourselves. We are in a conversation with our *exact* conversational equal. At stake is a view of truth as either that which emerges from a free and open encounter, or that which emerges from the genius of a destined leader. In short, liberalism or antiliberalism. If we leave it entirely up to redescriptive *chance*, we have no more reason for believing we will finally end up a liberal society than for believing that we will finally end up a Nazi society. But we liberals know one thing *right now*: We know we *never* want to become a Nazi society. If this is the case, however, we *liberals* would never attempt to *converse* with a Nazi, for if we did so we *might* be persuaded to become a Nazi *ourselves*. But the situation is even more dire than that. If Rorty is correct in what he says, then we liberals should act now to eliminate forcefully the possibility that antiliberals could engage in conversation *with us*. We must deny Nazis freedom of speech within *our* society. And we would have to do this using *physical* force, since it would be too dangerous to attempt to *talk* Nazis into keeping silent, or changing their views. We could not risk attempts at engaging in counter-speech, since, once again, *we* might get converted. So I conclude that if Rorty really means what he says about the impotence of reason and the power and *neutrality* of redescription, he should advocate the forceful and complete suppression of all antiliberal speech. It simply would not be *pragmatic* of him to suggest we do otherwise.

Of course, Rorty does not advocate this. Indeed, to bring this discussion around to where we began, Rorty believes that a "liberal society is one whose ideals can be fulfilled by persuasion rather than force." I take it that one of the "ideals" of liberal society would be its own preservation. So I conclude that to have the beliefs about liberal society that someone like Rorty has—in particular, to believe that liberal societies can fulfill their ideals and maintain themselves against nonforceful challenges to these ideals (i.e., challenges in the form of speech) *without themselves resorting to force*—one must have *some* faith in Jefferson's claim that "Truth is . . . the proper *and sufficient* antagonist to error" and has nothing to fear in a free and open encounter. In the end, it is only such faith that keeps us liberals, *liberal*.

4

Characters and Citizenship

A *Literary Redescription*

A liberal society asks relatively little of its citizens because—its critics say—it thinks they are capable of relatively little. Beyond the requirement that citizens abjure the use of force in settling disputes, liberal societies are content to let their citizens do pretty much as they please. On this, Rorty is correct: Liberal societies do not (and should not) seek to *perfect* their citizens. They should be content (as I put it in chapter 2) to remain on the surface, and attempt only (as I put it in chapter 3) to maximize tolerance, minimize suffering, and secure individual liberty. In this light, the title of the present chapter will seem quixotic. For it is generally communitarians, rather than liberals, who want to draw our attention to the connection between character and citizenship.[1] I must emphasize, therefore, that I have not now turned around and joined the communitarians in their criticism of liberalism. My intention in what follows is not to add my voice to the standard communitarian criticism of liberalism—the criticism that liberalism produces citizens that are unworthy of our admiration. Liberals should not (and I will not) worry too much about the type of citizens that form liberal polities. Still, I will concede to the communitarians a minimal point: there is some

---

1. I am using the term *communitarian* as Michael Sandel uses it, not as Franklyn Haiman used it in the quotation in chapter 3.

connection between the laws of a given society and the type of individual who must live according to those laws. I will argue that *Rorty's* ideal liberal society is most comfortably inhabited by a certain type of liberal individual—an individual with certain specific characteristics. But perhaps "argue" is, after all, not the right word to use here. My purpose in the following chapter is simply to provide a literary resdecription of Rorty's recent political philosophy. I begin with a short justification for this endeavor—a justification with which I think Rorty would agree.

Philosophy versus Literature

At least since the publication of *Contingency, Irony, and Solidarity,* and *arguably* well before that, Rorty has seemed to display what can only be called an unabashed reverence for imaginary literature—and, in particular, the modern novel. This reverence comes out of Rorty's firm conviction that the genre of philosophy (and, in particular, "constructive philosophy" of the Habermasian type) has simply played itself out. To put it loosely, in Rorty's view, what we seem to need now is more fiction and less philosophy. Hence, in an article published in 1990, Rorty announced, "I happily join Milan Kundera in appealing to the novel against philosophy."[2] What Rorty, following Kundera, finds so appealing about imaginative literature (and, again, in particular the modern novel) is its "unboundedness," its "unconditionality." For both Rorty and Kundera, imaginative literature provides us finite humans with an infinite source of redescriptions from which we can select in order to help us get through life.[3] This is in direct contrast to philosophy which attempts to "bound," or to "ground," us in a *particular* worldview by way of argumentation and demonstration. Rorty puts the point this way: "The novel does not offer an argument within the same dialectical space we have previously been occupying, but rather the glimpse of other such spaces. The urge to redescribe, cultivated by reading novels, is different from the urge to demonstrate, cultivated by reading metaphysics."[4]

---

2. Richard Rorty, "Truth and Freedom: A Reply to Thomas McCarthy," *Critical Inquiry* 16 (spring 1990): 638.
3. Put in just this way, there is a suggestive connection here between Rorty's "pragmatic" approach to literature and Kenneth Burke's understanding of literature "as equipment for living." See Kenneth Burke, "Literature As Equipment for Living," in *The Philosophy of Literary Form: Studies in Symbolic Action* (Berkeley: University of California Press, 1941), 293–304.
4. Rorty, "Truth and Freedom: A Reply to Thomas McCarthy," 638.

At first glance, the division Rorty makes between philosophy and the novel might seem to mirror the division between the public and the private, as well as the division between what he calls "constructive philosophy" (practiced by those like Habermas) and "ironist theory" (practiced by those like Derrida). But, with a second glance, the situation becomes more complex. Rorty does not seem content to leave both sides in this division on equal footing. He does not seem content to treat the demands of each as "equally valid, yet forever incommensurable." Indeed, he seeks to privilege one side over the other. In particular, it seems Rorty simply lines up with the Derridians in claiming that there really is no such thing as constructive philosophy since, in reality, it's all just writing. This view has invited a strong rebuttal from the same constructive philosopher who took Rorty to task in chapter 1. In an essay entitled "On Leveling the Genre Distinction between Philosophy and Literature," Jürgen Habermas has argued against the attempts of post–structuralists, especially Jacques Derrida, to "equate philosophy with literature and criticism."[5] Habermas argues that such "leveling" as the post–structuralists advocate does damage both to philosophy and to literature. But Habermas is not content merely to stamp out this practice on the Continent. He next turns a philosophical eye on America and observes that,

> Richard Rorty proposes a similar leveling; unlike Derrida, however, he does not remain idealistically fixated upon the history of metaphysics as a transcendent happening that determines everything intramundane. According to Rorty, science and morality, economics and politics, are delivered up to a process of language-creating protuberances *in just the same way* as art and philosophy. Like Kuhnian history of science, the flux of interpretations beats rhythmically between revolutions and normalizations of language. He observes this back-and-forth between two situations in all fields of cultural life: "One is the sort of situation encountered when people pretty much agree on what is wanted, and are talking about how best to get it. In such a situation there is no need to say anything terribly unfamiliar, for argument is typically about the truth of

---

5. Jürgen Habermas, "On Leveling the Genre Distinction between Philosophy and Literature," in *The Philosophical Discourse of Modernity: Twelve Lectures*, trans. Frederick Lawrence (Cambridge: MIT Press, 1978), 207.

assertions rather than about the utility of vocabularies. The contrasting situation is one in which everything is up for grabs at once—in which the motives and terms of discussions are a central subject of argument. . . . In such periods people begin to toss around old words in new senses, to throw in the occasional neologism, and thus to hammer out a new idiom which initially attracts attention to itself and only after gets put to work." One notices how the Nietzschean pathos of a *Lebensphilosophie* that has made the linguistic turn beclouds the sober insights of pragmatism; in the picture painted by Rorty, the renovative process of linguistic world-disclosure no longer has a *counterpoise* in the testing processes of intramundane practice. The "Yes" and "No" of communicatively acting agents is so prejudiced and rhetorically overdetermined by their linguistic contexts that the anomalies that start to arise during the phases of exhaustion are taken to represent only symptoms of waning vitality, or aging process analogous to processes of nature—and are not seen as the result of *deficient* solutions to problems and *invalid* answers.[6]

Whether beclouded by Nietzsche or not, it does seem clear that Rorty has simply decided to cast his lot with the novelists as opposed to the philosophers; with persons like Kundera, who believe not only that the novel addresses the same issues as philosophy but, indeed, that it addresses these issues *better* than philosophy. As Kundera writes in *The Art of the Novel*, "The *sole raison d'étre* of a novel is to discover what *only the novel can discover*. A novel that does not discover a hitherto unknown segment of existence is immoral. Knowledge is the novel's only morality." This is surely a provocative claim, to which Kundera adds,

[A]ll the great existential themes Heidegger analyzes in *Being and Time*—considering these to have been neglected by all earlier European philosophy—had been unveiled, displayed, illuminated by four centuries of the novel (four centuries of European reincarnation of the novel). In its own way, through its own logic, the novel discovered the various dimensions of existence one by one: with Cervantes and his contemporaries, it inquires into the nature of adventure; with Richardson, it

---

6. Ibid., 206, emphasis in original, footnote omitted.

begins to examine "what happens inside," to unmask the secret life of the feelings; with Balzac, it discovers man's rootedness in history; with Flaubert, it explores the *terra* previously *incognita* of the everyday; with Tolstoy, it focuses on the intrusion of the irrational in human behavior and decisions. It probes time: the elusive past with Proust, the elusive present with Joyce. With Thomas Mann, it examines the role of the myths from the remote past that control our present actions. Et cetera, et cetera.[7]

Without getting too far into the particulars, it seems that for Kundera (and also for Rorty) "the wisdom of the novel," the "truths" of imaginary literature, are represented in and by the *characters* that inhabit the work. Apparently, it takes a certain amount of strength to identify with literary characters and thereby "realize" the wisdom of the novel. The romantic poet John Keats defined this special strength as "negative capability," that rare quality in which "a man is capable of being in uncertainties, Mysteries, doubts, without an irritable reaching after fact and reason."[8] This, then, is Kundera, once again and finally, sounding very much like his nineteenth-century predecessor.

> To take, with Descartes, the *thinking self* as the basis of everything, and thus to face the universe alone, is to adopt an attitude that Hegel was right to call heroic.
> To take, with Cervantes, the world as ambiguity, to be obliged to face not a single absolute truth but a welter of contradictory truths (truths embodied in *imaginary selves* called characters), to have as one's only certainty the *wisdom of uncertainty*, requires no less courage.[9]

Following Kundera, I now want to redescribe the "character" (in the literary sense of that word) of the liberal ironist, and then to redescribe some alternatives. But so as not to move too far away from Rorty's own ground, the *terms* in which I shall redescribe the liberal iro-

---

7. Milan Kundera, *The Art of the Novel*, trans. Linda Asher (New York: 1988), 5–6, emphasis in original.
8. The definition is from a letter written by Keats in 1817. The letter is quoted in Roger Shattuck, "The Innocent Eye and the Armed Vision," in *The Innocent Eye: On Modern Literature & The Arts* (New York: Farrar Strauss Giroux, 1984), 346.
9. Kundera, *The Art of the Novel*, 6–7, emphasis added.

nist are *exclusively* Rorty's own terms. They are the terms that I have been using throughout this book. They are also, in a general sense, what Kenneth Burke would call "dialectical terms"—terms that must be paired with their "opposites" in order to be understood.[10]

For my *present* purposes, I want to focus on three sets of "key" dialectical pairs that emerge from Rorty's recent work: the ironists versus the metaphysicians, the liberals versus the nonliberals, and those who believe that one can separate the public from the private versus those who believe one cannot separate the public from the private. (This last pair might be described as the noncommunitarians versus the communitarians, or the individualists versus the communitarians, or even the Jeffersonians versus the Aristotelians. But since Rorty does not invoke terms like *communitarian* or *individualist* in the same way that he speaks of ironists, metaphysicians, liberals, and nonliberals, I have decided to spell out the aspects of the last pair in more detail.) Plotting each one of these three pairs of terms against the other two, we are left with eight distinct combinations of "worldviews" represented by: (A) the nonliberal metaphysician, who sees a split between the public and the private realms; (B) the nonliberal metaphysician, who does not see a split between the public and the private realms; (C) the liberal metaphysician, who sees a split between the public and private realms; (D) the liberal metaphysician, who does not see a split between the public and private realms; (E) the nonliberal ironist, who sees a split between the public and private realms; (F) the nonliberal ironist, who does not see a split between the public and private realms; (G) the liberal ironist, who sees a split between the public and private realms; and (H) the liberal ironist, who does not see a split between the public and private realms.

Now in an effort to make these worldviews "concrete," and in keeping with my attempt (when possible) to meet Rorty on his own ground, I have tried to pair off these eight worldviews with examples of individual *literary* characters who seem (to me at least) to embody these outlooks or attitudes. Where possible, I have drawn these characters specifically from the genre of the modern novel. Were my own knowledge of this particular literary genre more complete, I have absolutely no doubt that I would have been able to find all eight character types for which I was searching within the collective pages of the modern novel. Indeed, if one read

---

10. For a discussion of the concept of "dialectical" terms, see Kenneth Burke, *A Rhetoric of Motives* (Berkeley: University of California Press, 1969), 183–89.

closely and cleverly enough, it is not inconceivable that one could find all eight character types within one sufficiently "grand" modern novel—say Rorty's own apparent favorite, *Remembrance of Things Past*. Unfortunately, I have on occasion needed to move beyond the specific boundaries of the modern novel in order to come up with the required characters. I have not strayed too far, however. All of the characters I use can be found within the pages of modern American and European prose fiction. It is left for the reader to decide how well the various characters I have chosen actually "fit" the worldviews that they are designed to characterize.

I would be less than honest with the reader if I did not admit that one of the aims of the following exercise is simply to have a little fun with Rorty's recent philosophical writings. While what I have in mind is not exactly a literary lark, it is certainly not "serious" philosophical analysis of the type that I hope to have provided in the previous two chapters. Still, what I shall be doing is precisely the type of "criticism" to which Rorty seems most amenable. In an exchange with Thomas McCarthy, Rorty has written, "I *am* opened up to criticism by critics like Habermas, McCarthy, Nancy Fraser, and others, because they are able to redescribe my own position in terms that make me say, 'Gee, there might be something to that; when so described, I *do* look pretty bad.'"[11] My own effort at redescription does not represent an attempt to make Rorty look "bad." Instead, it simply represents an attempt to provide a literary characterization of Rorty's recent philosophy.

To sum up, then: In the next section I shall examine the political philosophies (broadly speaking) represented by each of the eight worldviews that Rorty's own terminology generates and match those philosophies with literary characters in order to put a poetical twist on the whole scheme. We will then have eight different worldviews and eight different characters, all generated by Rorty's own philosophical terminology and all *potential* candidates for how we could choose to view our world and our own "self." Which worldview should we adopt? If all the world's a stage, which *character* should we choose to be? Rorty's own choice is inscribed in the pages of *Contingency, Irony, and Solidarity*. The ideal citizen of his utopia matches one of these eight characters *perfectly*. But is this the character *we* should wish to be? Is this *really* the character Rorty would wish us—and himself—to be? How does this character compare to the alternatives? These are the questions I shall explore in the

---

11. Richard Rorty, "Truth and Freedom: A Reply to Thomas McCarthy," 635.

final section of this chapter. Remember, this redescriptive endeavor represents precisely the type of criticism toward which Rorty feels most receptive. I am playing *his* language game now.

Two final points: First, for the purposes of this entire exercise, I am assuming—as I think Rorty must also—that it is at least possible to find enough characters to represent each one of the eight worldviews I have sketched, even though some of these worldviews seem flatly *self*-contradictory. Internal consistency, it should be noted, is only *really* on point where "rigorous" analytic philosophy is involved. Literary musings, on the other hand, represent the very province of ambiguity, creative tension, multidimensional characters, and so forth. In this "figurative" domain, consistency and a certain straightforwardness of presentation are to be shunned. Perhaps that is why Rorty appears to feel most comfortable in this environment.

Second, to do justice to this redescriptive project, it will be necessary for me to sketch, at some length, each one of the eight worldviews involved and each one of the characters that corresponds to it. I do this even though Rorty would insist (and I would agree) that only liberal worldviews should be considered possible candidates for the type of citizen we should wish to be. This, of course, would automatically eliminate the four *non*liberal worldviews from consideration as alternatives. These nonliberal worldviews are sketched, nonetheless, precisely because they can provide us with further insight into what it means to be a liberal. Beyond the elementary appeal of thoroughness, then, there is also a holistic logic to this lengthy process. One gains the fullest perspective on any single character by comparing it to *all* of the other characters. Call this a perspective by multiple incongruity.[12] Such a *complete* perspective is necessary if my own redescription of a master redescriber is to be persuasive. Consider, then, the diagram on the following page.

Characters and Their Worldviews

Let us look first at the box labeled A. Here we find the convergence of one who is a metaphysician, one who is nonliberal, and, finally, one who believes that the public and private realms can be separated. Since this is the first worldview we will be examining, it might be helpful to take

---

12. See Kenneth Burke, *Permanence and Change: An Anatomy of Purpose* (Berkeley: University of California Press, 1984), 71–163.

A RORTYIAN TYPOLOGY
with *Character Sketches*

		One who *does* see a split between the public and the private realms.	One who does *not* see a split between the public and the private realms.
METAPHYSICIAN	NONLIBERAL	**A** A Troubled Metaphysician *Hadji Murad*	**B** A Dangerous Metaphysician *Jorge*
METAPHYSICIAN	LIBERAL	**C** A "Good" Citizen *Unnamed*	**D** The "Ideal" Citizen *Atticus Finch*
IRONIST	NONLIBERAL	**E** A Survivor *Sabina*	**F** A Dangerous Ironist *O'Brien*
IRONIST	LIBERAL	**G** Rorty's "Ideal" Citizen *Walter Mitty*	**H** Rorty Himself *Julius McAdoo*

these three "character traits"—metaphysician, nonliberal, split between public and private—one at a time in order to see exactly how I am using these traits within the context of the present exercise, and more generally to see where I am attempting to go with this entire typology.

In chapter 1 I noted that, "The metaphysician is one who believes that humans are ultimately accountable to some higher, nonhuman reality—God, or Reason, or Natural Law, or some analogous 'Truth.'" I mentioned, as examples of metaphysicians, both Jürgen Habermas and Loyola. These are also two of the examples Rorty uses. But notice: although Habermas and Loyola share one character trait—they are both metaphysicians—they do not necessarily share any other character traits. That is one of the key aspects of this typology. I need to insist that each one of these pairs of "dialectical terms" is *independent* of the other two pairs. Although such insistence is bound to generate character types who hold seemingly *internally inconsistent* worldviews, I need to stress once again that consistency is not on point in this exercise.

Notice, then, that while Habermas and Loyola are both metaphysicians, they differ on the matter of liberalism. Simply put, Habermas is a liberal while Loyola is a nonliberal. This raises the important question: What precisely is the difference between a liberal and a nonliberal? Again, in chapter 2 I sought to answer this question by, somewhat rhetorically, asking another question. "If a liberal is one who believes that it is the case that 'cruelty is the worst thing we do,' then is a nonliberal one who believes that it is not the case that 'cruelty is the worst thing we do?'" We saw that, following Rorty's definition of liberalism, and speaking strictly, the answer to this question was yes. But we also saw that this answer did not really get us very far, since Rorty's definition of liberalism, as it is offered in *Contingency, Irony, and Solidarity*, fails to *define* (that is, to *exclude*). I have been over this ground before, and it is not my intention to revisit any of the *arguments* made in the previous chapters. Rather, for my present purposes, I want to put aside these arguments (however persuasive I think they are) and instead just accept what I think is, from Rorty's perspective, the best (i.e., most defensible) definition of liberalism. As I see it, for Rorty, a liberal is *basically* someone who desires to avoid cruelty (including the cruelty of humiliation); someone who adheres to the standard democratic principles of free speech, equality under the law, due process of law, and so forth; and someone who is in relatively close accord with the economic arrangements that follow from Rawlsian, welfare-state capitalism. Of course, there may be serious theoretical problems with the basic sketch of liberalism I have just provided. But remember, my intention in the present section is to *redescribe*, not to *argue*. So whatever else we might say about Habermas, it is clear that he is, in Rorty's view, *basically* a liberal. This liberalism is reflected in Habermas's basic desire (as Rorty sees it) to defend and extend the fundamental precepts of liberal democracy *as such*.[13] Similarly, whatever

---

13. Thomas McCarthy has pointed out how thoroughly Rorty misreads Habermas on the matter of liberalism, in particular, on the indissovlable tension Habermas sees between capitalism and democracy. See McCarthy, "Ironist Theory as a Vocation: A Response to Rorty's Reply," *Critical Inquiry* 16 (spring 1990): 644–55. McCarthy wants to claim that this misreading means that Habermas is, in fact, not the kind of liberal Rorty thinks he is—that is, Habermas is not just a good, Rawlsian, welfare-

else we might say about Loyola, it is clear that he is, in Rorty's view, *basically* a nonliberal. Habermas and Loyola, then, serve as paradigm cases of the liberal and the nonliberal, respectively. Throughout the remainder of this section, when I use the terms *liberal* and *nonliberal* I shall be applying these broad definitions.

All of which brings us to the last of the three dialectical pairs: those who see a split between the public and private realms, and those who do not. On one level this opposition seems relatively easy to understand, hence unproblematic. But, in its *relationship* to the other dialectical pairs, this particular pair might give us some problems. Specifically, it might be difficult to see how a metaphysician, for example, could also believe there to be a legitimate separation between the public and the private realms. A metaphysician, as I said, believes that humans are ultimately responsible to some nonhuman "Truth"—God, reason, or whatever. But surely, for any given metaphysician, there cannot ultimately be more than one Truth. Such is the nature of Truth. Hence, there appears to be a totalizing impulse to metaphysics. Yet would not such a totalizing impulse necessarily preclude a metaphysician from being able to separate the public and private realms? How could a true metaphysician apply one set of principles in public and another in private? Ultimately, as a metaphysician, would he or she not need to synthesize these two sets of principles into one larger set, or simply subordinate one set to the other? To take a concrete example, how completely could a member of one of the major religions in American believe in the separation of church and state? In the final analysis, would not such an individual either need to see the demands of the state as being subordinate to the demands of his or her church, or, as fundamentalists fear is more likely, to see the demands of his or her church as being subordinate to the demands of the state?

I want to get around this general dilemma regarding the tension between specific elements within a given dialectic pair and specific elements in *other* dialectal pairs in much the same way Rorty gets around

state capitalist with a few modifications. Rorty would of course reply that this misreading of which he is accused exists—if it exists at all—only on a "philosophical" level. In other words, Rorty would argue that, regardless of the theoretical machinations (which, when dealing with Habermas, can be quite complex), *in practice* Habermas's defense of progressive European-style socialism with modifications amounts to pretty much the same thing as Rawlsian welfare-state capitalism with modifications.

similar dilemmas: by simply ignoring it. Or rather, I want to get around this dilemma by claiming that the tension that may exist within the portrait of a metaphysician who sees the public and the private realms as separate is no greater than the tension that may exist within many (perhaps most) other combinations in this typology. Consider, for example, the liberal ironist himself or herself. Even Rorty admits there is a "prima facie" tension between ironism and liberalism. He concedes that, at first glance, "there is something about being an ironist which unsuits one for being a liberal."[14] As I noted at the end of chapter 2, the tension is apparent at several levels. To now restate my previous point using the language of liberalism sketched a few paragraphs back, we can say that the liberal wishes the desire to act democratically to be an invariant part of everyone's final vocabulary, while the ironist still rebels against the suggestion that any part of anyone's final vocabulary should be seen as invariant. Rorty, of course, suggests that in addressing this tension we might wish to split up the liberal ironist self into a public liberal part and a private ironic part. But this "suggestion" does not exactly constitute a *theoretical* argument that such a split is possible. Indeed, it is not clear that there are any good theoretical arguments to be made in regard to this issue. Rather, it is more a matter of redescription. Rorty would probably insist, then, that we should not argue about the theoretical consistency of any one of the eight worldviews. Rather, we should simply describe the types of persons who might embody each of these worldviews, and then compare these descriptions.

So the question is, what type of character best "fits" the worldview represented in box A, the worldview whose terminology I have just sought to explain at some length? We can approach an answer to this question by first noticing that any given metaphysician would need to see a split between the public and the private realms *only* if his or her own private metaphysical system were in conflict with the culture in which he or she lived. In other words, a Muslim living in an Islamic culture would simply feel no need to *create* a split between the public and private realms. Now assuming that all liberal (i.e., democratic) cultures are *fundamentally* the same, there are only two possible *types* of conflicts that can arise among cultures: the type of conflict that arises between liberal and nonliberal cultures, or the type of conflict that arises between two different nonliberal cultures. Since the character for whom we are searching is (by

---

14. Rorty, *Contingency, Irony, and Solidarity*, 88.

definition) a *nonliberal* metaphysician, and since, further, he or she must (by definition) see a split between the public and the private realms, he or she must be a nonliberal metaphysician embedded within a nonliberal culture not his or her own.

Actually, this is all quite a bit *less* complex than it sounds. Given the abundance of nonliberal cultures throughout human history, it is not difficult to find real-life examples of the type of character who might fit in box A. For example, any devout, but also law-abiding (i.e., nonrebellious) Muslim attempting to exist within the former Soviet Union, or even pre-Soviet czarist Russia, would be a concrete illustration of a nonliberal metaphysician who saw, or was forced to see, a split between the public and the private realms. Such an individual would need to negotiate, at least on an unconscious level, some balance between what I would say are the nonliberal demands of Islam and the nonliberal demands of Soviet-style communism, or the Christian orthodoxy of czarist Russia. *Exactly* how this balance might be achieved would obviously depend upon the individual. The fact that such a balance needed to be struck would, equally obviously, be a strong source of tension within the individual. But, as I said earlier, many if not most of the worldviews we are examining manifest significant tensions.

The portrait I have just sketched is reflected in the life of the title character of Leo Tolstoy's 1904 historical novella *Hadji Murad*.[15] Although not nearly as well known as Tolstoy's longer works, the literary critic Harold Bloom offers this assessment of *Hadji Murad*: "It is my personal touchstone for the sublime of prose fiction, to me the best story in the world, or at least the best that I have ever read."[16] Tolstoy's novella dramatizes the heroic life and death of Murad, a Muslim leader and tribal chieftain who lived in the Caucasus region of Asia. During the early part of the last century, that region was in severe turmoil. After having annexed the kingdom of Georgia in 1801, Alexander I and his successor Nicholas I both faced severe difficulties in their attempts to, as we might say today, "pacify" the region. By the middle of the nineteenth century,

---

15. The work was published in 1912, two years after Tolstoy's death. As usual, Tolstoy, who was himself personally involved in the Causaian campaign in his early twenties, and who undoubtedly drew on this experience, did a tremendous amount of background research for his novella. One of Tolstoy's biographers asserts that Tolstoy read and thoroughly digested over eighty books on the topic while writing *Hadji Murad*.

16. Harold Bloom, *The Western Canon: The Books and School of the Ages* (New York: Riverhead Books, 1994), 313.

Shamil, another Muslim leader, had emerged as the central figure lead-
ing the opposition against Russian occupation. By appealing directly to
religious differences, Shamil managed to convince a significant number
of Muslims that they should enlist in a holy war against the occupying
Christian army of czar Nicholas. For some reason, perhaps simple pride
or a lust for power, Hadji Murad, who at one point was a trusted follower
of Shamil, defected to the Russian side in 1851. But his defection was *not*
also the occasion for a religious conversion. It is important to emphasize
that Murad, who probably entertained visions of serving as the czar's
commander general of the Caucasus after Shamil was defeated,
remained a devout Muslim. This was undoubtedly a concern to the
Russian command. In his novella, Tolstoy has Officer Voronstov, the
Russian army officer to whom Murad surrendered himself, write the following line in a letter to the Minister of War shortly after Murad's defection: "The only thing Tarkhanov [a mutual fried of Voronstov and
Murad] has noticed in his intercourse with Hadji Murad that might
cause any anxiety, is his attachment to his religion."[17] Indeed, as Tolstoy
characterizes him, Murad remains a strict adherent to the Muslim law,
praying regularly and avoiding any interaction with the bare-shouldered
women he is forced to encounter at the governor's ball while he is a guest
of Russian nobility. Unfortunately Murad's life ends tragically when he is
shot by Russian soldiers for attempting to return, against orders, to his
home village to rescue his wives and children from Shamil.

On one level, then, Tolstoy's novella can be read as the story of
Murad's struggle to negotiate the demands of Muslim and Russian (Christian) culture. There are, undoubtedly, a great many novels (whether historical or entirely fictional) that dramatize conflicts of this nature—that is,
internal conflicts within a self caught between two opposing worldviews.
To my mind, Tolstoy's novella stands out partly due to its ability to sketch
this conflict in such vivid detail. Murad's ultimate failure to reconcile
these views (if, indeed, the end of the novella is read as evidencing such a
failure) may be suggestive of the difficulties inherent in being the type of
character one would put in box A But I do not think this novella provides
definitive proof that such a character could not exist, and even thrive.

Having taken the time to explain the construction of the previous
worldview in detail, I shall now move through the next five worldviews,

---

17. Leo Tolstoy, *Hadji Murad*, in *Great Short Works of Leo Tolstoy* (New York: Harper
& Row, 1967), 612.

B through *F*, and the characterizations that correspond to them, with somewhat greater dispatch. However, the last two worldviews to be discussed in this section, *G* and *H*, represent, respectively, the worldview held by the type of individual Rorty says he wants to populate his liberal utopia and what I believe to be an appropriate characterization of Rorty himself. Hence, I shall spend a considerable amount of time on them.

Let us next consider box *B*: the nonliberal metaphysician, who sees no split between the public and the private. The individual who fits this worldview would simply be a nonliberal who lived in a nonliberal culture with which he or she fully identified. Again, there are many real-life examples of such an individual. We have already encountered one in the person of Saint Ignatius Loyola. The historical figure Loyola, a devout Christian, lived within a culture fully dominated by a Christian worldview, and hence had no need to create a split between the public and the private realms.

There are, once again, a vast number of literary characters who would fit this worldview. I have chosen one from what I believe to be one of the most superbly written novels to have appeared in the last two decades: Umberto Eco's *The Name of the Rose*. One could do worse than describe this novel as a historical, postmodern, deconstructionist, murder mystery evidencing obvious stylistic affinities with the work of Edgar Allan Poe and Jorge Luis Borges. *The Name of the Rose* purports to be the more or less faithful English (well, Italian really) translation of a fourteenth-century Latin manuscript written by Adso of the monastery of Melk, and more or less faithfully reprinted in a nineteenth-century volume of French translations by a certain Abbé Vallet. Eco's "manuscript," as he calls it—the third in chronological order— claims to reproduce the first person narrative of Adso, as he and his master, William of Baskerville, a learned Fransican, travel to another monastery (whose name is never revealed) and, over a seven-day period, involve themselves in intrigue and murder that culminates in the startling discovery of the lost second volume of Aristotle's *Poetics*. As I said, *The Name of the Rose* is a superb novel. But is it relevant? Does it have anything to say to us today? Is this novel the type of work that Kundera and Rorty would hold up as being perhaps superior to philosophy in its ability to reveal to us something important about ourselves? On this point, Eco, writing in the 1980 "preface" to this simple "translation," indulges in a bit of satirical bravura equal to anything in Swift or Voltaire. Eco writes,

I transcribe my text with no concern for timeliness. In the years when I discovered the Abbé Vallet volume [1968], there was a widespread conviction that one should write only out of a commitment to the present, in order to change the world. Now, after ten years or more, the man of letters (restored to his loftiest dignity) can happily write out of pure love of writing. And so I now feel free to tell, for sheer narrative pleasure, the story of Adso of Melk, and I am comforted and consoled in finding it immeasurably remote in time (now that the waking of reason has dispelled all the monsters that its sleep had generated), gloriously lacking in any relevance for our day, atemporally alien to our hopes and our certainties.[18]

Clearly, Eco *is* attempting to say something in this novel. One of the most important messages Eco intends involves a warning not to listen to or become like Jorge of Burgos, a central character in the novel, and also the character whom I have chosen to occupy box B. Jorge is one of the oldest monks at the monastery and hence very much an authority figure, perhaps more so than the Abbot himself. Jorge is also completely rigid when it comes to "the Law," deadly serious about everything, morbid almost beyond imagination, and in all respects the "perfect" metaphysician. There are, to be sure, obvious parallels here between Jorge and the historical figure of Loyola, as well as between Jorge and Dostoesky's portrait of the Grand Inquisitor. The distinguishing feature of these fictional and nonfictional characters adheres in their unyielding belief, common to all metaphysicians, that the knowledge of Truth exists, and that we humans must be *responsible to that knowledge*. As Jorge himself says in a terrifyingly eloquent speech to his fellow monks, "[T]he property of knowledge, as a divine thing, is that it is complete and has been defined since the beginning, in the perfection of the Word which expresses itself to itself."[19] It is significant that this remark is uttered in the context of a very serious speech about the apocalypse. Seriousness and Truth seem strongly connected. When one is speaking the Truth, one should naturally be serious. Conversely, when one is serious, it is hoped that one is speaking the Truth. In neither case is there room for playfulness, frivolity, or a *comic* attitude. This last point may help draw out

18. Umberto Eco, *The Name of the Rose*, trans. William Weaver (New York: Harcourt Brace Jovanovich, 1980), 5.
19. Ibid., 399.

another important connection. Employing Kenneth Burke's terminology, I think it would be fair to say that the metaphysical impulse locates itself within the "tragic" frame, while the ironic impulse locates itself within the "comic" frame.[20] This in turn helps explain why Jorge feels compelled to kill several of his fellow monks, and ultimately to take his own life, all in a desperate attempt to prevent the *second* book of Aristotle's *Poetics* from being discovered. For Jorge, it is a matter of seeing to it that the correct one of these two — in his mind, mutually exclusive — frames of reference wins out in the end. These frames are illustrated and explained in books one and two of the *Poetics*, respectively. Book one, of course, deals with tragedy. Book two either dealt with, or would have dealt with, comedy. Jorge's attempt to suppress book two is not so much an attempt to eliminate entirely the comic frame, or laughter. As William of Baskerville, the one who finally uncovers Jorge's sinister plot, says, "You cannot eliminate laughter by eliminating the [second] book [of the *Poetics*]."[21] Rather, Jorge's twisted plan of indefinite censorship represents a somewhat paradoxical attempt to ensure that the comic frame is not taken seriously. In Jorge's view, laughter and comedy are permissible as long as they are properly subordinated within a tragic frame. Presumably,

---

20. For a discussion of the "tragic" and "comic" frames, see Kenneth Burke, *Attitudes Toward History* (Berkeley: University of California Press, 1984), especially pp. 37–44. Now, if we follow the "logic" of my suggestion that we associate the metaphysician with the tragic frame and the ironist with the comic frame, and if we further assume that Jorge is an evil, indeed a *satanic* figure in *The Name of the Rose*, all this would imply that we should "locate" Jorge within the tragic frame. Generalizing, it would imply that we should locate Satan himself within the tragic frame. But, as "The Lord" himself repeatedly says, in a dialogue sketched by Burke, "It's more complicated than that" (see Burke, *The Rhetoric of Religion: Studies in Logology* [Berkeley: University of California Press, 1970], 273–316). In an imaginary dialogue between The Lord and Satan, Burke sketches the character of Satan as "an agile youth, [who] wears fool's cap with devil's horns, and a harlequin costume of two colors, dividing him down the middle" (276). The harlequin costume of two colors, *divided down the middle*, is perhaps an allusion to the Yoruba trickster figure in African mythology who wears a cap of two colors divided down the middle. The trickster, so the myth has it, rides his horse directly *between* two humans, who are facing one another, and then delights in the argument that ensues as to the color of his cap. Each human is, of course, seeing the cap from only *one* perspective. For a fuller discussion of the trickster figure, see my subsequent discussion of Julius McAdoo. So to say we should locate "evil" in the comic frame, or in the tragic frame, may be premature. It's more complicated than that.
21. Eco, *The Name of the Rose*, 473.

Jorge feels that the study of book two of the *Poetics* could put comedy on the same footing as tragedy, and that is what must remain impermissible. Perhaps in the final analysis, Eco is suggesting the need for a *balance* between the comic and tragic frames. On this reading, Jorge is a dangerous metaphysician, precisely because he is taken too seriously by his fellow monks. In this regard, Jorge's exceptional skill at public speaking is *suggestive*. On one level, history seems to show that seriousness of purpose, whether for good or ill, translates into persuasive power. We are moved (at least *en masse*) by tragedy, not comedy.

But for a number of reasons Jorge is a relatively uncommon type. Fortunately, perhaps, it is difficult to maintain the level of seriousness he embodies. Instead, the more common character type—indeed, to my mind, the *most* common type—is represented by the figure found in box C. Here we find the liberal metaphysician who sees a split between the public and the private. The type of character we are looking for here is embodied in the good citizen *living in a democratic culture* who goes to work faithfully every weekday (that's the liberal part), who then, say, goes to church faithfully every Sunday (that's the metaphysical part), and who sees no connection between weekdays and weekends (that's the bit about the split).

At least at first glance, there is some resemblance between this figure and the character of The Common Man in Robert Bolt's play *A Man For All Seasons*. The Common Man has a number of roles in this drama. To take only the most important cases: he is Matthew, Thomas More's (relatively) faithful stewart; he is, later in the play, More's jailer; still later, he is John Dauncey, the foreman of the jury that wrongfully convicts More of treason; and, finally, he is More's executioner. What any character who might show up in box C and The Common Man seem to have in common is the relative *ease* with which each could make the split between his public and private life. Both of these characters would be good citizens who do their jobs well, and don't let their consciences bother them in the process. For example, The Common Man, in his character as the jailer, has this to say to the audience: "The pay scale being what it is they have to take a rather common type of man into the prison service. But it's a job. Bit nearer the knuckle than most perhaps, but it's a job like any other job. . . ."[22] When, to absolutely no avail,

---

22. Robert Bolt, "A Man For All Seasons: A Play in Two Acts" (New York: Vintage Books, 1962), 73.

Thomas More pleads with his jailer (this Common Man) for just a few additional seconds beyond the allotted time he is given to see his wife, he gets this reply from the jailer: "You understand my position, sir, there's nothing I can do! I'm a plain, simple man and just want to keep out of trouble." To which More replies, passionately, "Oh, Sweet Jesus! These plain, simple men!"[23] More's rebuke is stinging, and it contributes to our vision of The Common Man as a contemptible character. But, apparently, Robert Bolt did not intend to leave this impression. Instead, he wanted his audience to see The Common Man as a sympathetic, even admirable, fellow. In the preface to *A Man For All Seasons*, Bolt says the following about The Common Man:

> He is intended to draw the audience into the play, not thrust them off it. In this respect he largely fails, and for a reason I had not foreseen. He is called "The Common Man" (just as there is a character called "The King") and the word "common" was intended primarily to indicate "that which is common to us all." But he was taken instead as a portrayal of that mythical beast, The Man in the Street. This in itself was not so bad; after all he was intended to be something with which everyone would be able to identify. But once he was identified as common in that sense, my character was by one party accepted as a properly belittling account of that vulgar person, and by another party bitterly resented on his behalf. (Myself, I had meant him to be attractive, and his philosophy impregnable.) What both these parties had in common—if I may use the word—is that they thought of him as somebody else. Wherever he might have been, this Common Man, he was certainly not in the theatre. He is harder to find than a unicorn. But I must modify that. He was not in the stalls, among his fashionable detractors and defenders. But in the laughter this character drew down from the gallery, that laughter which is the most heartening sound our Theatre knows, I thought I heard once or twice a rueful note of recognition.[24]

As Bolt correctly points out, even among common men The Common Man is often bitterly resented. Among that specific group of

---

23. Ibid., 85.
24. Ibid., xvii.

"uncommon" men who are wont to call themselves "philosophers"—and (here I agree somewhat with Rorty), in particular, among ironist philosophers—The Common Man is an odious figure indeed. For Heidegger, The Common Man is, of course, das Man. Enough said. For Nietzsche, The Common Man is that figure in whose presence Zarathustra, after having come down from the mountain, is made physically ill. And finally, it should be noted that Ralph Waldo Emerson, in a way a kind of heroic figure for Rorty, has no use for the conformity of The Common Man either. "Whoso would be a man must be a nonconformist."[25]

But notice, the key difference between The Common Man and any character who would fit in box C is that the former is definitely not a *liberal* metaphysician, while the latter must be. (Obviously I do not take Henry VIII's England to be a *liberal* society.) Yet I am sure some will argue that this difference—the society in which a common man happens accidentally to reside—is but a trifle. It will be said, with Thoreau, that common men are the same everywhere; and that, inasmuch as such men make no moral distinctions in their public acts, "They are as likely to serve the devil, without intending it, as God."[26] Common men, it will be argued, are just "good citizens." On this view, there is no great difference *in character* between the "good citizen" of Hitler's Germany and the "good citizen" of Churchill's England.

But Rorty wants to make sure that we do maintain a clear distinction, *in political fact,* if not in personal character, between these two historical models. For Rorty, an individual is a *good* citizen *if and only if* he or she is a law-abiding member of a democratic (i.e., liberal) society. Notice that, on this definition, the word "good" has something to do *both* with the way in which an individual carries out his or her duties of citizenship (i.e., he or she must be law abiding) *and* with the type of society in which an individual claims citizenship. Hence, a law-abiding Nazi would not be a good citizen, since he or she would not be a member of a democratic society. Of course, this is a plainly ethnocentric definition. But this is quite consistent with Rorty's overall view of liberalism and community.

It should be clear by now that The Common Man does not fit in box C, because he is a law-abiding member of a nonliberal society.

---

25. Ralph Waldo Emerson, "Self-Reliance," in *Emerson: Essays and Lectures* (New York: The Library of America, 1983), 261.
26. Henry David Thoreau, *Resistance to Civil Government* in *The Norton Anthology of American Literature,* vol. 1 (New York: W. W. Norton & Company, 1979), 1,515.

Indeed, it is not clear that the character of The Common Man would really "fit" anywhere within this Rortyian typology. But this is not a problem. Although we do need to find a character for every box, we should not expect that, in this limited typology, we have here generated a box for every type of character. The Common Man has served an explanatory purpose, however. The type of character who *will* fit in box C resembles The Common Man, but is a liberal as opposed to a nonliberal. Happily, there are numerous examples of a *liberal* Common Man throughout the pages of the modern novel. They are, in a sense, all around us, though often unnamed. In Stephen Crane's *The Red Badge of Courage* they are the "good" soldiers, Henry Flemming's comrades who, in between battles, speak gently and read the Bible—not for inspiration or self-reflection, but simply for solace. In Ralph Ellison's *Invisible Man* they are the "good" police officers who are simply following orders as they *lawfully* evict an elderly black woman from her apartment, and yet, who strangely empathize with her as she clutches her Bible. One of these officers, identified only as "the marshal," "standing with his blue steel pistol and his blue serge suit" says to the black woman, "Look lady . . . I don't want to do this, I *have* to do it. They sent me up here to do it. If it was left to me, you could stay here till hell freezes over. . . ."[27] Unmistakably, these are the common men. And it is perhaps appropriate that they should remain unnamed, for, as common men, they do not stand out. So in box *C* I will simply put the liberal common man.

As I have said, these common men, when they find themselves within liberal societies, make good citizens. In a sense, we need them simply to keep the machinery going. It will immediately be objected, however, that a serious wrong was done to this black woman, even if these officers were operating "strictly" within the "law." Of course, Rorty would agree. But he would also point out, I think, that *short of violent revolution*, liberal societies offer the best—indeed the *only*—hope we have of changing the laws that allow evictions like this to happen. And yet, who will change these laws? Certainly not the common men. For just as surely as they are good citizens, they are not *ideal* citizens. They cannot change society for the better. It takes a different kind of character to do that, the kind of character we find in box *D*.

---

27. Ralph Ellison, *Invisible Man* (New York: Vintage Books, 1980), 270, emphasis in original.

Here we are looking for a liberal metaphysician who sees no split between the public and the private. In other words, we are looking for someone who sees no *essential* difference between the liberal society in which he or she lives, and his or her private metaphysical system. Such an individual would, of course, need to adopt a metaphysical system that is liberal. There is only one metaphysical system that meets this requirement: Enlightenment rationalism, the metaphysical system upon which liberalism is theoretically based. So the character we are looking for is *something* like a Kantian moral philosopher. Or, to update this image somewhat, we are looking for a fictional character who more or less embodies Jürgen Habermas's philosophical outlook. Habermas's entire project, of course, is centered around defending Enlightenment reason from its philosophical enemies. Habermas sees this philosophical task as being *politically* vital as well. As Rorty correctly points out, "Habermas thinks it *essential* to a democratic society that its self-image embody the universalism, and some form of the rationalism, of the Enlightenment."[28] Habermas thinks that without such a self-image, liberal societies could not survive. The character we are looking for must also think this.

I have suggested that such a character would amount to the "ideal" citizen. He or she would differ from the merely "good" citizen in one critical respect: he or she would not see an *essential* difference between his or her public and private responsibilities. If such an ideal citizen were ordered to carry out some action that was against the letter of law, he or she would, of course, refuse. As long as our laws were well written, this would make him or her imperious to graft, corruption, abuse of authority, and the like. Certainly we would expect nothing less of an ideal citizen. If this individual were ordered to carry out some action that was, strictly speaking, legal, but that was nonetheless unjust—an action like evicting an elderly black woman in the middle of winter because she could not pay her rent—I imagine that our ideal citizen might carry out the law, but *simultaneously* work to see the law changed. To be more precise on this last point, our ideal citizen would work to change the *law* that allowed this injustice to take place, but he or she would not work to change the rule of law itself. Indeed, our ideal citizen would always work justly to *uphold* the rule of law in liberal societies. He or she could do so in good conscience, and even optimistically, since he or she must believe that unjust laws could not be an *essential* element of the liberal society.

---

28. Rorty, *Contingency, Irony, and Solidarity*, 67, emphasis added.

Such unjust laws, in the eyes of our ideal citizen, could only be *mistakes* that need to be, and that always could be, remedied *by passing additional just laws*. Notice the critical connection in the mind of our ideal citizen between justice and the written law. Notice also that, since our ideal citizen fully identifies his or her personal good with the good of the community, he or she would see it *in his or her own best interest* to work to change laws that allow elderly black women to be evicted from their apartments in the middle of winter.

Once again, at least at first glance, there appears to be more than just a surface resemblance between the figure of the ideal citizen and Robert Bolt's characterization of Sir Thomas More. Indeed, *Bolt's* Sir Thomas looks quite a bit more like an Enlightenment deist than a Catholic saint. At the very least, More is clearly a lawyer and a rationalist first, and a Catholic saint second. This point comes out very clearly in what is probably the most often-quoted scene in the play. Sir Thomas, in the company of his wife Alice, his daughter Margaret,[29] and her fiancé Roper, has just suffered a visit from Richard Rich, the man who will eventually perjure himself and thus directly cause More's execution. Everyone, including More, knows that Rich is basically a weak and evil person. Everyone, including More, believes that Rich will eventually do something wicked and corrupt. Everyone, *except* More, wants to see Richard Rich arrested immediately. This is the exchange:

Alice:　　Arrest him!

Margaret: Father, that man's bad.

More:　　There is no law against that.

Roper:　　There is! God's law!

More:　　Then God can arrest him.

Roper:　　Sophistication upon sophistication!

More:　　No, sheer simplicity. The law, Roper, the law. I know what's legal and not what's right. And I'll stick to what's legal.

Roper:　　Then you set man's law above God's!

More:　　No, far below; but let me draw your attention to a fact—I'm not God. The currents and eddies of right

---

29. She is referred to by Thomas as "Meg."

	and wrong, which you find such plain sailing, I can't navigate. I'm no voyager. But in the thickets of the law, oh, there I'm a forester. I doubt if there's a man alive who could follow me there, thank God . . .
Alice:	While you talk, he's gone!
More:	And go he should, if he was the Devil himself, until he broke the law!
Roper:	So now you'd give the Devil benefit of law!
More:	Yes. What would you do? Cut a great road through the law to get after the Devil!
Roper:	I'd cut down every law in England to do that.
More:	Oh? And when the last law was down, and the Devil turned round on you—where would you hide, Roper, the laws all being flat? This country's planted thick with laws from coast to coast—man's laws, not God's—and if you cut them down—and you're just the man to do it—d'you really think you could stand upright in the winds that would blow then. Yes, I'd give the Devil benefit of law, for my own safety's sake.
Roper:	I have long suspected this; this is the golden calf; the law's your god.
More:	Oh, Roper, you're a fool. God's my god. But I find him rather too subtle . . . I don't know where he is nor what he wants.[30]

What is most striking about this scene, perhaps, is the poverty of Roper's response to More. Roper should have pointed out more clearly that Sir Thomas's vision of the law, and its uses, causes him to commit the sin of intellectual pride. Sir Thomas seems to believe that he—a mere mortal—could use man's laws to hide or keep himself safe from the Devil. Of course, this is precisely what a clever Devil would want him to think. Surely More's human intellect could be no match for the infinite sophistication of the Devil. (". . . the serpent was more subtil than any beast of the field which the Lord God had made" *Genesis* 3:1.) Had this

---

30. Bolt, "A Man For All Seasons," 37–38.

been another play, Roper might have argued that, contrary to More's view, what keeps us safe from the Devil is not what is in our heads, but what is in our hearts. From this it follows that man's laws can have nothing to do with salvation, nor, perhaps, even with justice among men.

But to return to the matter of what literary character could fit in box *D*, it should be clear that Bolt's Sir Thomas More is not a possibility. Like Bolt's character, The Common Man, More is living in a nonliberal society. He cannot, therefore, affect change through the process of democratic politics. Hence he does not have the ability to fall back on the quintessential liberal "faith" that everything will eventually work out if we simply keep the conversation going long enough. The best More can do in his society is stand firmly for his principles, hope that such a stand provides an example to others, and be willing to die (as he does) for those principles. We are now looking for a character who fully embodies Thomas More's proto-Enlightenment philosophy and strong moral character, but who happens to reside in a democratic society. There is indeed just such a figure within the pages of the modern novel. I refer to Atticus Finch, the quiet hero of Harper Lee's Pulitzer Prize-winning novel *To Kill a Mockingbird*.

Set in a small, rural, segregated town in Alabama, sometime in the mid 1930s, *To Kill a Mockingbird* tells the story of bigotry and prejudice, and the struggle of one man—Atticus Finch—to overcome these evils using *only* his reason and intellect, and the force of character these qualities generate. Atticus Finch (who is white) is a quiet man, a single parent trying to raise a son and a very precious eight-year-old daughter. He is also one of the most respected men in the community; he is reelected every term to the state legislature without opposition. Atticus is the very embodiment of an individual who sees no split between the public and the private. As Miss Maudie, one of his neighbors, says, "Atticus Finch is the same in his house as he is on the public streets."[31] And finally, Mr. Finch is a lawyer—a very good lawyer. As it happens, Atticus is appointed by the local judge to defend Tom Robinson, a young black man falsely accused of raping a white woman. Atticus has no illusions about the trial. He knows it will be extraordinarily difficult to convince a jury of Southern white men that a black man did not commit what would be to them the most heinous crime imaginable. But Atticus must try his best to see that justice is done. When others think there is no hope for justice, Atti-

---

31. Harper Lee, *To Kill a Mockingbird* (New York: J.B. Lippincott Company, 1960), 53.

cus perseveres, gaining strength from his unshakable faith in the court system, in the rule of law, in the universality of reason, and, ultimately, in the promise of liberal society. There is no question, Atticus Finch is the quintessential liberal metaphysician. His closing argument to the jury reads like a page of Enlightenment philosophy. It could easily have been written by an Enlightenment philosopher like Thomas Jefferson, whom Atticus references, or by another lawyer, Sir Thomas More, who (at least on Bolt's account) anticipates the Enlightenment by a few centuries. The following remarks represent Atticus's closing comments, the last thing he says to the jury. Notice the emphasis on reason over passion. Notice also the thinly veiled swipe at communism—at the time, not an insignificant challenger to liberalism.

> One more thing, gentlemen, before I quit. Thomas Jefferson once said that all men are created equal. . . . There is a tendency in this year of grace, 1935, for certain people to use this phrase out of context, to satisfy all conditions. . . . We know all men are not created equal in the sense some people would have us believe—some people are smarter than others, some people have more opportunity because they're born with it, some men make more money than others, some ladies make better cakes than others—some people are born gifted beyond the normal scope of most men.
>
> But there is one way in this country in which all men are created equal—there is one human institution that makes a pauper the equal of a Rockefeller, the stupid man the equal of an Einstein, and the ignorant man the equal of any college president. That institution, gentlemen, is a court. It can be the Supreme Court of the United States or the humblest J.P. court in the land, or this honorable court which you serve. Our courts have their faults, as does any human institution, but in this country our courts are the great levelers, and in our courts all men are created equal.
>
> I'm no idealist to believe firmly in the integrity of our courts and in the jury system—that is no ideal to me, it is a living, working reality. Gentlemen, a court is no better than each man of you sitting before me on this jury. A court is only as sound as its jury, and a jury is only as sound as the men who make it up. I am confident that you gentlemen will review

without passion the evidence you have heard, come to a decision, and restore this defendant to his family. In the name of God, *do your duty.*[32]

Of course, Atticus loses the case. But he does not lose his faith in the court system, in the law, in reason, or in liberalism. As Atticus explains to his son Jem, who has been made cynical by the outcome of the case, "If you had been on that jury, son, and eleven other boys like you, Tom would be a free man. . . . So far nothing in your life has interfered with your reasoning process. Those are twelve reasonable men in everyday life, Tom's jury, but you saw something come between them and reason."[33] A liberal metaphysician to the end, Atticus tries to explain to his children that, in time, liberal society will overcome all of its prejudices and reason will prevail.

I have said that the type of character we see in Atticus Finch would represent the ideal citizen. But, upon closer inspection, this claim needs to be modified. Certainly there are qualities we must admire in Atticus. He is every bit the good liberal Rorty is looking for—in all senses of the term liberal. And despite the fact that he lost the Robinson case, he is still quite a persuasive character. After waiting, with the rest of the town, well into the night for the inevitable guilty verdict in the Robinson case, Miss Maudie sums up Atticus's singular achievement in this way: "I thought, Atticus Finch won't win, he can't win, but he's the only man in these parts who can keep a jury out so long in a case like that. And I thought to myself, well, we're making a step—it's just a baby step, but it's a step."[34] Miss Maudie's evaluation raises an interesting question: From whence did Atticus's persuasive power come? The only answer, I think, is that it came simply from the elemental force of ideas, presented (*as they would have been perceived by his audience*) in straightforward, unadorned language. Atticus Finch was a persuasive speaker because he was exactly the same on the inside as he was on the outside; he was a reasonable, uncomplicated man who knew his mind and was able to express the reasonableness of his thoughts. He had a great deal of *ethos* in his community. In this sense, Atticus was a very good citizen indeed. Still, something is missing here. But it is not the case that this deficiency could be remedied merely by "supplementing" Atticus's character, for to supplement is (ulti-

---

32. Ibid., 217–18, emphasis added.
33. Ibid., 233.
34. Ibid., 228.

mately) to change essentially. In the final analysis, it may be an either/or proposition. To put this point more concretely, Atticus Finch made an excellent lawyer; he would have made a lousy poet. Not because he was in any way deficient in his depth of feeling, but rather because he seemed to lack the poetical turn—the gift of self-reflectivity—necessary to express feelings *and* ideas in *art*. Art in general, at least art during and after modernism, is nothing if not self-reflective. *This is why philosophy and art, the metaphysical attitude and the ironic attitude, may be eternal and irreconcilable opposites.*

I want to keep this idea in mind as I turn from a discussion of metaphysicians to a discussion of ironists. In box *E* we find the conjunction of the nonliberal ironist who sees a split between the public and the private. To start us off on the right track with the discussion of ironism, I want to use a character to fill this box who appears in Milan Kundera's thoroughly postmodern and delightfully entertaining novel *The Unbearable Lightness of Being*. Set in Prague immediately before, during, and immediately after the fateful spring of 1968, *The Unbearable Lightness of Being* is probably most often described as Tomas's narrative.

What can be said about the character Tomas? He is a doctor. That much is not in dispute. If one is charitable, one might say that he is a man who takes his pleasures in women seriously and often, but also a man who allows these women to adopt the same attitude toward him. He has, of course, several mistresses. Early in the novel, Tomas comes to this conclusion: "Making love with a woman and sleeping with a woman are two separate passions, not merely different but opposite. Love does not make itself felt in the desire for copulation (a desire that extends to an infinite number of women) but in the desire for shared sleep (a desire limited to one woman)."[35] This somewhat premature conclusion, placed, as it is, at the beginning of the novel, is perhaps designed to dramatize the "lightness" of Tomas's private life. He makes it a point of never actually falling asleep with any of his mistresses. This personal "lightness" is, however, "burdened" with the arrival of Tereza, who insists upon monogamy. Importantly, Tereza's arrival is the result of an unintended consequence of Tomas's actions. He was visiting a small town some distance from Prague. He chanced to stop at a particular restaurant and strike up a conversation with a particular waitress and issue a somewhat open-ended invi-

---

35. Milan Kundera, *The Unbearable Lightness of Being: A Lovers' Story*, trans. Michael Henry Heim (New York: Harper & Row, 1984), 15.

tation. Seeing nothing better to do with her life, Tereza decided to take him up on the invitation. The private burden this places on Tomas parallels a public burden that he is under, also as a result of an unintended consequence of his actions. It seems that during the heady days of the spring of 1968, Tomas was asked, somewhat by accident, to write an editorial in a relatively autonomous newspaper published by the Union of Czech writers and read primarily by the intelligentsia. In his editorial, Tomas addressed the question of whether the hard-line communists of the recent past—the "true believers" who claimed they were innocent of any wronging because they were ignorant, because they like everyone else were merely dupes of the system—were, in fact, innocent. Tomas somewhat fancifully compares them to Oedipus, who "did not know he was sleeping with his own mother, yet when he realized what had happened, he did not feel innocent. Unable to stand the sight of the misfortunes he had wrought by 'not knowing,' he put out his eyes and wandered blind away from Thebes."[36] Needless to say, when a few months later the hardliners, with the help of Soviet tanks, reasserted absolute control of the country, they were not pleased that Tomas had written the article. The solution, as they said, was simple. Tomas would write a retraction. Or rather, he would put his name to the retraction they had written. But for some reason Tomas could not do this. As a result, he loses his apartment, his money, and, ultimately, his practice as a doctor. In the end, he chooses to live monogamously in a small village with his wife Tereza.

From this it should be obvious that Tomas *cannot* be the character to fill box *E.* He does the one thing an ironist would never do: he ends up adopting one final vocabulary with which to describe himself. But there is another character in the novel, a character who, in many ways, parallels the *early* Tomas, yet who never seems *not* to feel the lightness of being. She is the character who should fill box *E.* Her name is Sabina, and she is Tomas's most intriguing mistress. She is also an artist, and as such she is a creature of infinitely many final vocabularies. But, importantly, she never takes any of these vocabularies very seriously. She never feels the desire to affiliate with any system; indeed, she feels a desire not to affiliate. This is illustrated by her approach toward parades.

When [as a young girl in Prague, Sabina] marched in the obligatory May Day parades, she could never keep in step,

36. Ibid., 177.

and the girl behind her would shout at her and purposely tread on her heals. When the time came to sing, she never knew the words of the songs and would merely open and close her mouth. But the other girls would notice and report her. From her youth on, she hated parades.[37]

This, I think, makes her an exemplary ironist. She is also a nonliberal due to her place of residence, Prague, and due to the fact that she is not drawn to the reform movement. As I said, she is not drawn to *any* movement.

Sabina is the nonliberal ironist who finds it possible to make a split between her public, nonliberal life and her private, artistic life in all of its guises. In this sense, she is a "survivor." Sabina does not run afoul of the secret police because of an article she wrote. Nor is it clear that she would not have signed a retraction if she found herself in Tomas's situation. If she did sign such a retraction, it is clear that she would not have thought of herself as betraying her *self*. Interestingly, this raises a question we examined more thoroughly in section 3 of chapter 2: Do the qualities of an ironist or the qualities of a metaphysician equip one to survive better in nonliberal cultures? In one of the most interesting passages of the novel, Kundera has this to say on the subject:

> It is a tragicomic fact that our proper upbringing has become an ally of the secret police. We do not know how to lie. The 'Tell the truth!' imperative drummed into us by our mamas and papas functions so automatically that we feel ashamed of lying even to a secret policeman during an interrogation. It is simpler for us to argue with him or insult him (which makes no sense whatever) than to lie to his face (which is the only thing to do).[38]

Tomas, it should be pointed out, does have a difficult time lying during his interrogation by the secret police. As I said, it is not clear that Sabina would. But then, it is not clear why the secret police would be interested in Sabina in the first place. Precisely because she sees a split between the public and the private she is no threat, and also no help, to anyone. She did, after all, march in the parades. This is not to condemn Sabina. Although she is no threat to the secret police, she is no threat to the reformers either. She is, as I said, a survivor.

---

37. Ibid., 99.
38. Ibid., 187–88.

The real *ironist* threat comes from characters like George Orwell's O'Brien: nonliberal ironists who see *no* split between the public and the private. I therefore think O'Brien fits quite well in box *F.* Having said that, I need to argue that Rorty is incorrect to assert that, in the end, O'Brien is *not* an ironist. Rorty asks and answers the question about O'Brien's status as an ironist in this way:

> . . . can one call O'Brien an ironist? Orwell gives him all the standard traits of the British intellectual of Orwell's youth. Indeed, my (unverifiable) hunch is that O'Brien is partially modeled on George Bernard Shaw, an important Socratic figure for Orwell's generation. But unlike Shaw, who shared Nietzsche's taste for the historical sublime, O'Brien has come to terms with the fact that the future will exactly resemble the recent past—not as a matter of metaphysical necessity but because the Party has worked out the techniques necessary to prevent change. *O'Brien has mastered doublethink, and is not troubled by doubts about himself or the Party* [my emphasis]. So he is *not,* in my sense, an ironist. But he still has the *gifts* which, in a time when doublethink had not yet been invented, would have made him an ironist. He does the only possible thing he can with those gifts: He uses them to form the sort of relationship he has with Winston. Presumably Winston is only one of a long series of people, each with a mind like O'Brien's own, whom O'Brien has searched out, studied from afar, and eventually learned enough about to enjoy torturing. With each he has entered into a long, close, intensely felt relationship, in order at the end to feel the pleasure of twisting and breaking the special, hidden, tender parts of a mind with the same gifts as his own—those parts which only he, and perhaps a few of his Minitru colleagues, know how to discover and torment. In this qualified sense, we can think of O'Brien as the last ironist in Europe—someone who is employed in the only way in which the end of liberal hope permits irony to be employed.[39]

Rorty obviously likes ironists quite a bit. Indeed, he himself is one. I strongly suspect that this is part of the reason why Rorty does not wish to

---

39. Rorty, *Contingency, Irony, and Solidarity,* 187, emphasis in original.

see O'Brien as an ironist. Who would wish to have O'Brien associated with any aspect of himself or herself? To avoid this association, Rorty focuses on this notion of doubt and insists that an ironist must have *radical* doubts about his or her final vocabulary. But as Shakespeare might say, "Rorty doth protest too much." Might we not suspect, in fact, that an apparent ironist who had radical, *existential* doubts about his or her final vocabulary was really a metaphysician in disguise? To take one's doubts too seriously is to take oneself too seriously. If I am correct on this point, then it follows that, in many ways, O'Brien is the perfect ironist. For, as Rorty correctly points out, while O'Brien *may* believe that history has come to an end with the Party, he does not believe this for any "metaphysical" reason. I emphasize the word "may" here. Is it possible that Rorty is actually taking O'Brien too seriously? Is it possible that O'Brien's insistence that history is a boot stamping in our face forever might just be one more mind game he plays to break Winston? The question is: Does O'Brien *need* to believe in the Party (or, indeed, in anything) to enjoy torturing Winston? Obviously not, for O'Brien surely does not torture Winston for the benefit of the Party. O'Brien tortures people only for his benefit. And in his own, twisted way, *while* torturing his victims, O'Brien enters into a type of *self-identification* with them, even though — in fact, *just because* — their final vocabularies are radically different from his. O'Brien, we may say, is a torture "artist" whose "medium" is the mind of the "other" and whose patron is the Party. But what if the Party *were* defeated sometime during O'Brien's life? Would he feel a really deep — *metaphysical* — sense of loss? I think this highly unlikely. Again, O'Brien *may* believe that the Party has all of the details worked out, but it is not clear that he really cares, as long as he gets to torture Winston. In this sense, he is like Humbert Humbert, the central character in Nabokov's *Lolita*, a work that Rorty also discusses extensively in *Contingency, Irony, and Solidarity*. Both characters, O'Brien and Humbert, are supremely incurious to anything that does not *directly* relate to their "artistic" enjoyment.

Finally, add to all of this the fact that Orwell repeatedly describes O'Brien as an ironic character — even using the word "irony" at several critical points in the novel. When we are first introduced to O'Brien, the "intrigu[ing]" — Orwell might easily have said "ironic" — contrast between his "urbane manner and his prize-fighter's physique" is highlighted, as is the *possibility* that his "political orthodoxy was not perfect."[40] Later in the

---

40. George Orwell, *1984* (New York: Harcourt Brace Jovaovich, 1977), 13.

novel, when Winston and O'Brien are talking of revolution in the relatively comfortable surroundings of O'Brien's apartment, it seemed to Winston that "more even than of strength, [O'Brien] gave an impression of confidence and of an understanding tinged by irony."[41] And lastly, there is the most ironic scene in the novel. It occurs shortly after Winston is arrested and taken to a holding cell in the Ministry of Love. At this point, Winston does not yet know that O'Brien has betrayed him and is, in fact, a member of the thought police. When, presently, Winston learns this, the scene abounds with dramatic and verbal irony. Orwell depicts the encounter in the following way:

> The boots were approaching again. The door opened. O'Brien came in [to the holding cell].
>
> Winston started to his feet. The shock of the sight had driven all caution out of him. For the first time in many years he forgot the presence of the telescreen.
>
> "They got you too!" he cried.
>
> "They got me a long time ago," said O'Brien with mild, almost regretful irony. He stepped aside. From behind him there emerged a broad-chested guard with a long black truncheon in his hand.
>
> "You knew this, Winston," said O'Brien. "Don't deceive yourself. You did know it—you have always known it."
>
> Yes, he saw now, he had always known it.[42]

Rorty should not deceive himself either. O'Brien has all of the *relevant* characteristics of a nonliberal ironist who sees no split between the public and the private realms. So in the end I *would* put "Rorty's O'Brien" in box *F*.

This leaves only boxes *G* and *H* to be filled. Consider, first, box *G*. Here we find a representation of the type of figure Rorty wants to populate his liberal utopia: the liberal ironist who sees a split between the public and private realms. As it happens, after reading *Contingency, Irony, and Solidarity*, and after speculating about the possible politics of a liberal ironist who sees a split between the public and the private, James Thurber's endearing little short story "The Secret Life of Walter Mitty" came almost immediately to my mind. Walter Mitty is, of course, the

---

41. Ibid., 144.
42. Ibid., 197.

middle-aged, henpecked husband who harmlessly, though continuously, daydreams about (let us say) "alternative realities." He is clearly a liberal, inasmuch as he is obviously a law-abiding member of a liberal society. This much I am sure Rorty would grant. But is there *any* way of describing (or redescribing) him as an ironist? Rorty, I think, would surely insist that there is not, for Mitty clearly lacks at least one of the essential ingredients of an ironist self: "radical and continuing doubts about the final vocabulary [he] uses. . . ."[43] Mitty's secret lives—his fantasies about being a famous surgeon, or a war hero, or even (most interestingly) a debonair murder suspect—would not, in Rorty's view, constitute radical doubts about a final vocabulary. Indeed, such fantasies might not even count as part of a final vocabulary. In the end I can imagine Rorty insisting that to see a comical character who first appeared in a *New Yorker* short story in 1939 as a serious candidate for an ironist self is not to take the concept of ironism seriously.

Let me begin my rebuttal with this last point. It seems to me at least problematic to insist that we should take ironism that seriously. There is, it strikes me, something inherently nonserious about ironism. As I said in regard to O'Brien, to take one's doubts too seriously is to take oneself too seriously. The simple fact that Mitty's fantasies appear comical to us does not imply that these fantasies are *unimportant* to him. Just imagine what Mitty would look like if, say, through some sort of operation, we eliminated only his ability to fantasize. Obviously he would not be the same character. And, I would argue, the prospect that we would do such a thing to him would frighten him. To my mind, on the *relevant* point of redescription, Mitty at least resembles a miniature (a *very* miniature) version of Rorty's candidate for exemplary ironist, Marcel Proust. Rorty argues that Proust wrote *Remembrance of Things Past*, and thereby redescribed himself for a very important reason. Proust wrote "to free himself from the descriptions of himself offered by the people he had met. He wanted not to be merely the person these other people thought they knew him to be, not to be frozen in the frame of a photograph shot from another person's perspective. He dreaded being, in Sartre's phrase, turned into a thing by the eye of the other. . . ."[44]

I think Mitty fantasizes for *very* similar reasons. Indeed, it is worth asking just how different Walter Mitty's "fantasy" lives are from Marcel

43. Rorty, *Contingency, Irony, and Solidarity*, 73.
44. Ibid., 102.

Proust's "fantasy" life. Granted, Proust was describing, *in retrospect,* actual events that took place in his life. Mitty, on the other hand, was imagining (or *describing to himself*) possible events in either the future or in some "timeless" present. (Notice, by the way, that none of Mitty's fantasies are, strictly speaking, impossible. None of his fantasies involve the "supernatural.") But I take the *relevant* point that Rorty is making in his analysis of Proust to be something quite different from all of this. On my reading of Rorty's reading of Proust, Proust was not writing primarily to offer an account of his past life that was factually different from that account which others might have had; nor, really, was he even writing to get clear on *exactly* what events did happen to him. Rather, Proust was writing for the purpose of convincing himself (*and others*) that he was *essentially* different—that his final vocabulary was different—from that person, or final vocabulary, which other people thought him to be, or to have. As Rorty argues, Proust "had written a book, and thus created a self—the author of that book—which these people [those who sought to describe Proust] could not have predicted or even envisaged."[45]

Mitty does something similar, on a much smaller scale. Mitty creates fantasies, descriptions of himself, which call into question, or at least differ from, the final vocabulary everyone else attributes to him. Rorty insists a final vocabulary can—and indeed, its most important parts *will*—contain descriptive terms like *progressive, rigorous,* and *creative.*[46] There seems to be no reason why such a vocabulary could not also include descriptive terms like *brave, intelligent, daring,* and so forth. Notice then that Mitty's fantasies often amount to descriptions of himself operating with a final vocabulary that employs these (how might one describe them, "heroic"?) terms. But it might be argued that these descriptive terms—brave, intelligent, daring—are not *fundamentally* different from those which Mitty can *probably* be expected to include in his normal, everyday, nonfantasy vocabulary. At least these terms are not *inconsistent with* other terms we strongly expect to be in Mitty's "normal" final vocabulary—terms like *loving, law abiding, decent,* and so forth. These are ways others probably see Mitty, hence he would have no "doubt" about who he was. And the concept of doubt seems key for Rorty. The ironist must entertain visions of himself or herself living (fantasizing) within at least two essentially different vocabularies.

45. Ibid.
46. Ibid., 73.

But look again at Mitty's secret lives. There is one fantasy in which Mitty imagines himself as a murder suspect. Indeed, in Mitty's fantasy he *physically assaults* an authority figure—in this case a district attorney. Mitty the murder suspect can certainly be expected to possess a final vocabulary that might include descriptive terms like *cunning, deceptive, crooked, dishonest,* and so forth. Surely this vocabulary *would* be at odds with the one previously described. Think about it. Walter Mitty, a banal, middle-age, law-abiding, seemingly decent guy describes himself to himself as a possible murderer, *and derives pleasure from doing so.* I would suggest that for a law-abiding citizen to be able to do this is to some degree at least evidence of an ironic nature. Granted, Mitty never *acts* on this "crooked" final vocabulary, but that is only because he really does know the difference between the public and private realm. Maybe there is more to Walter Mitty than meets the eye.

To drive home the point that there may in fact be something of a similarity between Proust and Mitty, consider that both engage in their various descriptions, or redescriptions, for *precisely* the same reason. Recall that Proust "dreaded" being described by, and therefore understood by, others. Now consider that Walter Mitty is described as—no, rather *describes himself* as—"Walter Mitty the Undefeated, *inscrutable* to the last."[47] Who is it that Mitty is worried about being defeated by if not society in general, those who describe him in *their* terms? This is why he must remain inscrutable to the last. It is as if Mitty were to say (to himself), you people out there think that I am just Walter Mitty, a "decent," "hardworking," "honest" guy, but I am really Walter Mitty the sometimes "brave," sometimes "crooked" *character* whom you will never truly capture with your banal descriptions.

In fact, I think Mitty actually has *more* of a claim to represent that type of character who belongs in box G than does Proust, *or* Proust's character, the narrator of *Remembrance of Things Past.* All three may be liberal ironists, but *only* Walter Mitty knows what it means to separate the public from the private sphere. Clearly, Marcel Proust the author writes, and Marcel Proust the narrator narrates, for an audience. As Thomas McCarthy notes in an essay on Rorty, "The alienating thrust of ironist intellectual life *requires* that it be kept private. I noted in my [previous]

---

47. James Thurber, "The Secret Life of Walter Mitty," in *A Treasury of Short Stories,* ed. Bernardine Kielty (New York: Simon and Schuster, 1947), 727, emphasis in original.

paper [on Rorty] that writing is not a private matter. Will Rorty then prevent his ironist intellectual from publishing?"[48] It seems that, ideally, this is exactly what Rorty must want. But only Walter Mitty meets this criteria, only his ironic redescriptions are "secret."

Of course, the fact that he can firmly separate the public from the private does not mean Walter Mitty is precluded from being socially productive, even socially progressive. Remember, Mitty, like Atticus Finch and *unlike* Thomas More, lives within a *liberal* society. Mitty, therefore, has the ability to affect positive (i.e., liberal) change simply by working within the vocabulary of his society. *He* does not need to challenge the "theory" behind "the system" in order to do good. If, for example, Mitty were a journalist, we could imagine him working diligently to track down and write good, progressive stories about, say, the evils of racism and sexism within his own culture. We could even imagine an updated version of Walter Mitty producing television "docudramas"—say, *The Ryan White Story*—that "educate" his culture about the ways in which AIDS victims are just like the rest of us. We could imagine a Walter Mitty character working at either of these occupations, and then, during his time off, fantasizing in vocabularies that *do* challenge the liberalism of his culture. But picking up on and extending McCarthy's insight about the public nature of writing, we could *not* imagine a Walter Mitty character writing a "radical" political dystopia that challenged the liberalism of his culture—a novel like Marge Percy's *Woman on the Edge of Time*. Writing (and publishing) such a novel might be a liberal act—in the sense that it might help alleviate the suffering of some individuals—but it would also, necessarily, involve an act of ironism in the public domain. And this is something Rorty could not allow. Simply put, because newspaper reports, ethnographies, and docudramas are basically nonironic and nonradical (in a theoretical sense), they represent that type of undertaking in which Rorty's liberal ironist could safely involve himself or herself. On the other hand, and despite what I imagine would be his strong protests to the contrary, Rorty's own view of the liberal ironist would preclude such a person from remaining a good liberal ironist while publishing a novel like the one just mentioned. To generalize this point, Rorty's ideal character, the liberal ironist who sees a split between the public and the private, could only be one type of writer: a "realist," or at best,

48. Thomas McCarthy, "Ironist Theory as a Vocation: A Response to Rorty's Reply," 652.

an "old journalism" style journalist. He or she could not be a novelist, in Kundera's sense of the term.

In the final analysis, then, the character best suited to be a citizen of Rorty's liberal utopia would seem to be Walter Mitty. Following this through to its conclusion, it would seem that if *we* wish to be ideal citizens of Rorty's utopia, we will become our own Walter Mitty. We will be careful, and indeed *content*, always to remain straightforward, unoriginal, pretty much uninteresting liberals in public, while fantasizing in private about being *oh so much more*.

But it might still be objected that Mitty could be more than he is, and he could be so in public while still remaining a liberal. Perhaps the only reason Mitty is not a famous surgeon, so it will be argued, is simply because he does not have it in him to be one. But that is *his* failing, not ours. And it is certainly not a failing that is inherent in Rorty's view of the liberal ironist. So perhaps it might just be the case that Mitty's fantasies about being "oh so much more" than he is come not from the Rortyian injunction that he keep his fantasies strictly private (notice that he does not even share them with his wife), but instead from the fact that he is not really much to begin with.

If the above line of argumentation were correct, it would suggest that Walter Mitty may not be the only character type we could label an "ideal" citizen of Rorty's liberal utopia. There may be even better character types available. But I think the above line of argumentation is flawed for at least two reasons.

First, as I have said, Mitty clearly could *not* "be" the individual "protagonists" in *all* of his fantasies *and remain a liberal*. Specifically, he could not be the murder suspect he fantasies about since that illiberal character physically assaults an officer of the law (the district attorney) *while that officer is lawfully performing his duty*. The point is, even if he wished to, *society* would not let Mitty carry out all of his fantasies. And that is surely not Mitty's fault.

Second, and perhaps more important, Mitty could never, *in reality*, be the protagonists in his *liberal* fantasies and remain an ironist. The reason is simple: Mitty could not be, for example, the famous surgeon he fantasizes about because *no one could*. Regardless of how hard Mitty worked or how brilliant he was, he could never be the "ideal" surgeon of his fantasy. Ideals do not exist in the real world. They only exist in fantasies, or in what may be the same thing, in *art*. With characteristic concision, Oscar Wilde expressed the insight I am trying to get at when he said, "Life imitates art."[49] I strongly suspect that there isn't a practicing attorney in this country who doesn't, somewhere deep within the well-springs of his or her litigious unconscious, secretly wish to be Perry Mason.[50] Similarly, I doubt there's a single member of the British intelligence service who hasn't secretly fantasized about being able to say, "The name's Bond, James Bond." The point is that only our fantasies can be perfect. And they can be perfect only to the extent that they exist for us alone, in private, in a world that is not "real." This is a point with which Rorty would surely agree. Hence, I conclude that he wants to commend to us the lifestyle of a Walter Mitty, a liberal ironist who sees a split between the public and the private.

In fairness to Rorty, there is nothing *terribly* wrong with this lifestyle. Mitty is, after all, a relatively well-adjusted, law-abiding, productive member of his community. He may even be socially progressive for all we know. Oddly, although this is the figure Rorty wishes to recommend to us, I now want to argue that it is *not* the type of figure represented by Rorty himself—or at least by the author of Rorty's books. Rorty—political philosopher, ironist theorist against ironist theory, and redescriber *par excellence*—is better represented by the figure of the liberal ironist who sees *no* split between the public and the private. This, finally, would be the character to be placed in box *H*.

There is, I think, an extraordinarily interesting example of just such a character in the figure of Uncle Julius McAdoo, the central character in a group of short stories written by the late nineteenth/early twentieth century American author Charles Chestnutt—himself a person of mixed racial ancestry, who was (according to one literary critic) "black by choice."[51] The first of Chestnutt's "Uncle Julius" stories, "The Goophered Grapevine," was published in *The Atlantic Monthly* in 1887. The remaining six stories in the set were later collected, and all seven were published in 1899 in book form under the title *The Conjure Woman*. Like the works of Eco and Kundera, Chestnutt's *The Conjure Woman* is a literary *tour de force* and a masterpiece of ironic fiction. What can be said to do these stories justice?

---

49. Oscar Wilde, *The Picture of Dorian Gray* (New York: Signet, 1962), 17.
50. And Perry Mason, mind you. Not just Clarence Darrow. For although Darrow was good, he was not perfect. After all, he *lost* his most famous case. Who do you think would have won if Mason had been defending Scopes?
51. See Robert M. Farnsworth's Introduction in Charles Chestnutt, *The Conjure Woman* (Ridgewood, N.J.: The Gregg Press, 1968), xviii.

Ostensively, the stories that comprise *The Conjure Woman* present the reader with the first person narrative of John, a white Northerner from Ohio who travels to North Carolina not too late after the Civil War, partly in hopes of finding a better physical climate for his frail wife Annie, and partly in hopes of finding a better business climate in the reconstruction era South. In the first story, John and Annie chance to meet Uncle Julius in the midst of an old, decrepit southern mansion.

> We drove between a pair of decayed gateposts—the gate itself had long since disappeared—and up a straight sandy lane, between two lines of rotting rail fence, partly concealed by jimpson-weeds and briers, to the open space where a dwelling-house had once stood, evidently a spacious mansion, if we might judge from the ruined chimneys that were still standing, and the brick pillars on which the sills rested. The house itself, we had been informed, had fallen victim to the fortunes of war.[52]

Uncle Julius, "a venerable-looking colored man," was sitting on a pine log. "He held on his knees a hat full of grapes, over which he was smacking his lips with great gusto, and a pile of grapeskins near him indicated that the performance was no new thing" (8). But, as John observes a few seconds later, "There was a shrewdness in his eyes, too, which was not altogether African, and which, as we afterwards learned from experience, was indicative of a corresponding shrewdness in his character" (10). John and Uncle Julius strike up a conversation, and John learns the mansion and the entire vineyard surrounding it are "goophered—conju'd, bewitch'" (11). John, of course, is incredulous. He ends up buying the land, very cheaply, from Uncle Julius, and then restoring the mansion and the vineyard. Naturally, John makes out quite well on the deal. But as a way of sharing the wealth, he hires Uncle Julius as a coachman. On the surface, the remaining six stories of *The Conjure Woman* all revolve around the vineyard or the surrounding land. In each of the stories, Uncle Julius has a tale to tell the new landowners about the history of the property or the surrounding area; a tale that seems to have a strange, but not adverse, effect on them. Just on this level, consider the strange effect *The Conjure Woman* itself was likely to have on its white audience.

---

52. Charles Chestnutt, *The Conjure Woman*, 8. Subsequent page numbers will be to the Gregg Press edition.

Charles Chestnutt, an author of mixed racial ancestry, is telling a story from the perspective of a white man who listens to a black man telling stories. As Lorne Fienberg notes,

> The subversive intent of *The Conjure Woman* has been remarked upon by several readers, but several aspects of Chestnutt's masking deserve elaboration. The collection does not even need to be opened before the duplicity begins. The cover of the first edition in 1899 baits a cunning trap for the unsuspecting white reader. Above the title, a reader confronts the jovial countenance of a smiling old darke framed by two mischievous white rabbits. The comfortable reader may immediately identify old friends in Uncle Remus, and Br'er Rabbit and approach Chestnutt's stories as accounts of the gracious life of the Old South cast in the mode of the popular plantation tales of Joel Chandler Harris and Thomas Nelson Page. There is a superficial resemblance between *The Conjure Woman* and the works of Harris and Page and between Chestnutt's narrator, Uncles Julius, and the garrulous uncles who tell nostalgic tales of the ante-bellum South in the works by the white authors. But Chestnutt uses the similarities to subvert both the familiar conventions of those popular works and the unsuspecting white reader's acquiescence in the slave system and the racial inequality those works affirm.[53]

The reference to Joel Chandler Harris's Uncle Remus Tales is critical here. The most intriguing character in Chandler's tales is, of course, Br'er rabbit—whose direct descendant we are all familiar with in the figure of Bugs Bunny. Like his cartoon counterpart, Br'er rabbit is the quintessential "trickster" figure, a being who is *spontaneously* at home in irony.[54] The trickster figure is the consummate ironist—a "figure" (in the literary sense of the word) who operates from within and between several language games and several final vocabularies—a figure who may always be in "doubt" about his final vocabulary, but who is not in *distress* about

---

53. Lorne Fienberg, "Charles W. Chestnutt and Uncle Julius: Black Storytellers at the Crossroads," *Studies in American Fiction*, vol. 15 (autumn 1987): 163.
54. For an excellent discussion of the whole connection between the trickster figure and the trope of irony, see Henry Louis Gates Jr., *The Signifying Monkey: A Theory of Afro–American Literary Criticism* (Oxford: University Press, 1988), especially, 64–88.

that doubt. (Recall here Keat's definition of "negative capability.") We have already seen how Charles Chestnutt ironically tropes the genre of the plantation tale for his own purposes. It is worth examining closely exactly how Uncle Julius embodies the elements of the trickster figure in his tales told to John and Annie. To do this, I want to consider very closely the third story in *The Conjure Woman*, entitled "Mars Jeems's Nightmare."

The story—as I said, narrated by John—begins somewhat problematically, as John is "forced" to fire Tom, a young, black, stable hand who is introduced as Uncle Julius's grandson. (Whether Tom is actually Uncle Julius's grandson is very much in doubt. But then, everything in the story is very much in doubt.) At any rate, as John says at the beginning of the tale, "My first impression of Tom proved to be correct. He turned out to be very trifling and I was much annoyed by his laziness, his carelessness, and his apparent lack of any sense of responsibility. I kept him longer than I should, on Julius's account, hoping that he might improve; but he seemed to grow worse instead of better, and when I finally reached the limit of my patience, I discharged him" (66). Of course, this just won't do for Uncle Julius. One day, shortly thereafter, as Uncle Julius was taking John and Annie on a ride down by the stream, all three happen to see a white man charging by. Again, as John reports it, "He was driving a horse, apparently a high-spirited creature, possessing, so far as I could see at a glance, the marks of good temper and good breeding; the gentleman, I had heard it suggested, was slightly deficient in both. The horse was rearing and plunging, and the man was beating him furiously with a buggy-whip" (69). Upon seeing this, Uncle Julius remarks that if the white man isn't careful, he'll end up having a dream like that of Mars Jeems McLean. Intrigued, John and Annie ask Uncle Julius to tell them about Mars Jeems's dream. And so he does.

It seems that before the war and just a piece up the road from where their coach was now sitting, Mars Jeems "had a big plantation en a heap er niggers. Mars Jeems wuz a ha'd man, en monst'us stric' wid his han's . . . Mars Jeems did n' make no 'lowance fer nachul bawn laz'ness, ner sickness, ner trouble in de min', ne nuffin. . . ." (70, 72). Things got so bad that one day one of the black field hands named Solomon went to see "Aun' Peggy, de free-nigger cunjuh'oman down by de Wim'l'ton Road" (76). Aun' Peggy gave Solomon a potion made of roots and herbs, which she called a "monst'us pow'ful kin' er goopher," and told him to slip it into Mars Jeems's soup that afternoon. But Solomon was a "good nigger" and was therefore concerned not to harm his master. "It ain' gwineter p'isen 'im, is it?" he asked (77). To which Aun' Peggy replied, "Oh, no . . . *it's gwine ter do 'im good*, but he'll hab a monst'us bad dream fus" (77 emphasis added). But Aun' Peggy cautions Solomon that extreme care must be exercised in the entire operation. As she says, one "has ter be kinder keerful 'bout cunj'in w'ite folks . . ." (77). Thus warned, Solomon takes the potion and does as he is told. A few days later, Mars Jeems decides he needs to go away on business for a few weeks.

Mars Jeems's absence meant that Mars Johnson, the overseer, was now in charge. Unfortunately for Solomon and his friends, Mars Johnson was even harsher and more cruel than Mars Jeems. As Uncle Julius explains, "Mars Jeems's oberseah wus a po' w'ite man name' Nick Johnson—de niggers called 'im Mars Johnson ter his face, but behin' his back dye useter call 'im Ole Nick, en de name suited 'im ter a T. He wuz wusser 'n Mars Jeems ever da'ed ter be" (75). Predictably, things go from bad to worse on the plantation. Then a seemingly insignificant, but nonetheless out of the ordinary, event occurs. Uncle Julius recalls it this way:

> About th'ee er fo' days atter Mars Jeems went erway, young Mars Dunkin McSwayne rode up ter de big house one day wid a nigger settin' behin' 'im in de buggy, tied ter de seat, en ax' ef Mars Jeems wuz home. Mars Johnson wuz at de house, and he say no.
>
> 'Well,' sez Mars Dunkin, sezee, 'I fotch dis nigger ober ter Mistah McLean fer ter pay a bet I made wid 'im las' week w'en we wuz playin' kya'ds te'gedder. I bet 'im a nigger man, en heah's one I reckon 'll fill de bill. He wuz tuk up de yuther day fer a stray nigger, en he could n' gib no 'count er hisse'f, en so he wuz sol' at oction, en I bought 'im. He's kinder brash, but I knows yo' powers, Mistah Johnson, en I reckon ef any-body kin make 'im toe de ma'k you is de man.' (80)

Mars Johnson wastes no time asserting his authority. He begins by asking the new arrival for his name, and receives this reply: "I dunno my name . . . en I doan 'member whar I come fum. My head is all kin' er mix' up" (82). At which point, and for no apparent reason

> Mars Johnson haul' off wid his rawhide en hit de noo nigger once. De noo man look' at Mars Johnson fer a minute ez ef he

did n' know w'at ter make er dis yer kin' er l'arnin'. But w'en de oberseah raise' his w'ip ter hit him ag'in, de noo nigger des haul' off en made fer Mars Johnson, en ef some er de yuther niggers had n' stop' 'im, it 'peared ez ef he mought 'a' made it wa'm fer Ole Nick dere fer a w'ile. But de oberseah made de yuther niggers he'p tie de noo nigger up, en den gun 'im fo'ty, wid a dozen er so th'owed in fer good measure, fer Ole Nick wuz nebber stingy wid dem kin'er rashuns. De nigger went on at a tarrable rate, des lack a wil'man, but co'se he wuz bleedzd ter take his med'cine, fer he wuz tied up en could n' he'p hisse'f. (82–83).

After this episode in gratuitous cruelty, Mars Johnson puts the new arrival to work in the fields. Unfortunately, "De nigger 'lowed he wa'n't useter wukkin', en would n' wuk, en Mars Johnson gun 'im anudder fo'ty fer laziness en impidence, en let 'im fas' a day er so mo', en den put 'im ter wuk ag'in. De nigger [still] could n' 'pear ter git it th'oo his min' dat he wuz a slabe en had ter wuk en min' de w'ite folks, spite er de fac' dat Ole Nick gun 'im a lesson eve'y day" (83–84). After a few days, however, Mars Johnson realized that he could do nothing productive with the recalcitrant stranger, "So he tied 'im up en sont 'im back ter Mars Dunkin" (84).

To, as they say, make a long story short: very shortly after the stranger is sent back to Mars Dunkin, Mars Jeems returns, somewhat unexpectedly, to the plantation. But "returns" is not quite the right word. Solomon finds Mars Jeems standing aimlessly below a tree near the edge of the plantation. Mars Jeems clearly looks shaken. "[H]e wuz dress' lack a po' w'ite man, en wuz barefooted, en look' monst'us pale en peaked, ez ef he'd des come th'oo a ha'd spell er sickness" (91). When Solomon asks about his appearance, Mars Jeems replies, "I ain' be'n sick, but I's had a monst'us bad dream—fac', a reg'lar, nach'ul nightmare" (91).

What actually happened to Mars Jeems is, of course, a matter of pure conjecture. But one thing is certain. After Mars Jeems returns to the main house and reassumes his position as head of the plantation, life becomes much easier for Solomon, his friends, and even for the white masters. All of this is due to a sudden change in character that has come over Mars Jeems. Commenting on the change in Mars Jeems, Uncle Julius explains that,

Anu' Peggy's goopher had made a noo man un 'im enti'ely. De nex' day atter he come back, he tol' de han's dey neenter wuk on'y fum sun ter sun, en he cut dey tasks down so dey did n' nobody hab ter stan' ober 'em wid a rawhide er a hick'ry. En he 'lowed ef de niggers want ter hab a dance in de big ba'n any Dad'day night, dey mought hab it. En bimeby . . . eve'ybody 'mence' ter say Mars Jeems McLean got a finer plantation, en slicker-lookin' niggers, en dat he 'uz makin' mo' cotton en co'n, dan any yuther gent'eman in de county. (98–99)

As any good storyteller would, Uncle Julius concludes his brief plantation narrative with a moral. "Dis yer tale goes ter show," he says, "dat w'ite folks w'at is so ha'd en stric', en doan make no 'lowance fer po' ign'ant niggers w'at ain' had no chanst ter l'arn, is li'ble ter hab bad dreams, ter say de leas', en dat dem w'at is kin' en good ter po' people is sho' ter prosper en git 'long en de worl'" (100).

After hearing Uncle Julius's tale, both John and Annie appear somewhat incredulous. Neither knows quite what to make of Uncle Julius's story. Nonetheless, the very next day Tom is rehired. Indeed, a marked change in attitude has come over John and Annie.

But exactly how is this change in attitude affected? Certainly Uncle Julius is no Atticus Finch. Which is to say, Uncle Julius does not *reason* with John or Annie about the plight of Tom. Clearly, that is not his style. Rather, Uncle Julius is "signifying"—sometimes written signifyin(g)— throughout his tale, just as Charles Chestnutt is signifying throughout *The Conjure Woman*. I have already suggested that Uncle Julius is the quin-tessential trickster figure. To draw an important connection, I would now assert that signifying is the trickster's sole *modus operandi*. Unfortunately, but certainly not unexpectedly, a suitable definition of the term *signifying* is as illusive as the practice itself is complex. Henry Louis Gates Jr. starts us off on our quest for a fitting definition by suggesting that

> [W]e might think of . . . signifying as the slave's trope, the trope of tropes, as Bloom characterizes metalepsis, "a trope-reversing trope, a figure of a figure." Signifying is a trope that subsumes other rhetorical tropes, including metaphor, metonymy, synec-doche, and irony (the "master" tropes), and also hyperbole, litotes, and metalepsis (Bloom's supplement to Burke.) To this list, we could easily add aporia, chiasmus and catachresis, all of which are used in the ritual of signifying.[55]

---

55. Henry Louis Gates Jr., "The blackness of blackness: a critique of the sign and the Signifying Monkey," in *Black Literature and Literary Theory*, ed. Henry Louis Gates Jr. (New York: Methuen, 1984), 286.

This definition helps us see how signifying works, but it does not tell us much about the way in which this practice is used. Roger D. Abrahams addresses this latter point when he argues that signifying is a "*technique* of indirect argument or persuasion."[56] Gates provides one example of the form this indirection might take by noting that "signifying can . . . be employed to *reverse* or *undermine* pretense or even one's opinion about one's own status."[57]

This, of course, is *precisely* what Uncle Julius, a former slave, does in "Mars Jeems's Nightmare." Julius, the trickster, describes a kind of reversal—Mars Jeems learns what it is like to be a slave—which, in turn, seems (at least unconsciously) to undermine John and Annie's opinion of their own privileged status. Consequently, Tom is rehired. Similarly, Charles Chestnutt, a literary trickster, works from within the genre of the plantation narrative in order to *subvert* the traditional role expectations his white audience would be likely to have of "black" literature. Consequently, white audiences achieve a higher level of empathy for black culture.

But, as I said earlier, all of this is, of course, pure conjecture. Or is it pure conjure? Perhaps I am reading too much into this whole idea of signifying. Uncle Julius himself insists that he is merely repeating a tale his mother told him. What evidence do we have that he is not doing precisely this? Why *not* take him at his word? For that matter, what evidence do we have that Charles Chestnutt envisioned himself as being anything more than a modestly talented writer who sought to achieve a small literary niche for himself by imitating the styles of such Southern luminaries as Joel Chandler Harris? The answers to these questions seem, at best, indeterminate. And that is the problem—if, again, "problem" is the right word—with signifying. It's not always clear who's fooling who. Indeed, this can never be made *perfectly* clear. Surely only a fool would believe Uncle Julius's tale. Yet he *appears* to believe it. Does this make Uncle Julius the fool? Perhaps. But surely only a fool would believe that anyone would believe Uncle Julius's tale. Does this make John or Annie the fool? Contemplating the infinitely self-recursive nature of this "problem" may have been what led Kimberly W. Benston to remark that by signifying

---

56. Quoted in Gates, "The Blackness of Blackness: A Critique of the Sign and the Signifying Monkey," 288, emphasis in original.
57. Gates, "The Blackness of Blackness: A Critique of the Sign and the Signifying Monkey," 289, emphasis in original.

one "tropes-a-dope."[58] While this characterization may be a bit harsh, it nevertheless draws our attention to the fact that when one signifies one is necessarily being more than a bit tricky. Put another way, when one signifies one refuses to play by the rules of a predetermined language game. For example, in the presence of good constructive philosophers, one who delights in signifying would refuse to make straightforward arguments—precisely the type of arguments upon which constructive philosophers insist. This insight might help explain contemporary philosophy's finest trickster figure Jacques Derrida. And it might also help explain Rorty's reaction to Derrida. Rorty, after all, is nobody's fool. Think of the Rorty of *Contingency, Irony, and Solidarity* as saying something like this: "Only a fool would believe that Derrida really believes deconstruction has any practical use at all. Of course, I get the (private) joke, so I don't really believe he believes it does."[59] Naturally, this is the kind of thing that causes good constructive philosophers to throw up their hands in disgust. Signifying, like deconstruction, appears to displace argumentation and reason in favor of what looks like mere literary showmanship or sophisticated storytelling.

By putting this last point in just those terms I hope to emphasize the connection between signifying and what Rorty calls "redescription." Following Rorty, might we say that signifying is redescription *par excellence*?

---

58. Quoted in Gates, "The Blackness of Blackness: A Critique of the Sign and the Signifying Monkey," 286.

59. In fact, what Rorty *does* say in *Contingency, Irony, and Solidarity*, is this:

> I suggest that we read Derrida's later writings as turning such systematic projects of undercutting into *private jokes*. In my view, Derrida's eventual solution to the problem of how to avoid the Heideggerian "we," and, more generally, avoid the trap into which Heidegger fell by attempting to affiliate with or incarnate something larger than himself, consists in what [Rodolphe] Gasché refers to disdainfully as "wild and private lucubrations." The later Derrida privatizes his philosophical thinking, and thereby breaks down the tension between ironism and theorizing. He simply drops theory—the attempt to see his predecessors steadily and whole—in favor of fantasizing about those predecessors, playing with them, giving free rein to the trains of associations they produce. *There is no moral to these fantasies, nor any public (pedagogic or political) use to be made of them*; but, for Derrida's readers, they may nevertheless be exemplary—suggestions of the sort of thing one might do, a sort of thing rarely done before. (125, emphasis added, footnote omitted)

Or following Rorty and Kundera, might we say that signifying is the art of the novelist and ironist theorist? To say either would, I think, amount to an admission that, in the proper hands, signifying can be a most—perhaps *the* most—powerful means of persuasion. After all, in the final analysis, Uncle Julius's Tom fairs much better than Atticus's.

On that provocative (and probably unfair) note, I want to conclude my examination of the character who could best fill box *H*. By now it should be clear that Uncle Julius is indeed an ironist who sees no split between the public and the private. Uncle Julius, as we have seen, does not keep his redescriptions to himself. Instead, he—very much in the manner of Rorty's ideal novelist—turns these redescriptions outward toward the public domain, and for a reason: *He wants to change things.* Finally, I would argue that Uncle Julius is also a liberal. His liberalism derives first from the simple fact that he lives within a liberal culture and seems to follow its laws. But on a second and much deeper level, we might also say that Uncle Julius is a liberal because he appears to use his ability at redescription to advance liberal causes—that is, he appears to use his abilities to sensitize people to various forms of cruelty and suffering.

That completes my Rortyian typology. As I said at the outset, I have undertaken this exercise both to sketch the various worldviews that are generated by Rorty's recent political philosophy and to make those world-views concrete by finding literary characters who embody them. It is now left for the reader to decide whether the fit between character and world-view is always as tight as it could be. In most cases, I think it is. Having said that, there is only one thing left to decide: Whom should we be? Or put otherwise: Which type of character, among those I have sketched, would constitute the *ideal* citizen of a true political utopia?

Conclusion: Richard Rorty—Inscrutable to the Last

The question I have just posed calls on us to make comparisons among the characters in our typology. But, as I said at the beginning of this chapter, we can narrow the field by half and therefore make these comparisons more manageable by eliminating (as Rorty would) all nonliberal characters. Such characters could only constitute *non*liberal societies in which no liberal would wish to live. Since we (Rorty's audience) are all good liberals, we can disregard all nonliberal worldviews. This, in turn, allows us to eliminate from consideration the characters who occupy boxes *A, B, E,* and *F.*

This leaves only the liberal characters. I have already suggested that the character who occupies box *C*, while a good citizen, is certainly not an *ideal* citizen. My central criticism against the character in box *C* was that he or she is basically inert matter, through and through. There is nothing, either in the public or private realms, to recommend this character as a candidate for a prospective citizen of a utopia. Indeed, there is really nothing to recommend this character as an *individual* character at all. We could think of this character as, in the words of T.S. Eliot, "an attendant lord, one that will do/ To swell a progress, start a scene or two/ Advise the prince; no doubt, an easy tool/ Deferential, glad to be of use. . . ."[60] Hence, we can eliminate from consideration the character in box *C*.

We are now left with only three possible choices: Atticus Finch, Walter Mitty, or Julius McAdoo. At first glance, it might appear that Atticus Finch is the obvious choice among these three. He is certainly the most reasonable, surely the most scrupulous and sincere in his dealings with his fellows, and therefore probably the most trustworthy. A community constituted by characters like Atticus Finch would be reasonable, open, impartial, just, courageous (without being foolhardy), optimistic (but not giddy about life), manly (in a quiet sort of way), and seemingly incorruptible. What more could one want from a citizen of a political utopia? More important, what possible arguments could Rorty make against preferring Atticus over his two other rivals?

The answer is that Rorty would need to find some *imperfection* in Atticus's character. Rorty would need to argue, as I did in section 2, that while Atticus is indeed reasonable, scrupulous, sincere, and trustworthy, he is all of these things to a fault. More important, he is also relatively — that is, relative to Mitty and Julius — boring and unimaginative. On this point, it *is* significant, I think, that Atticus is never shown reading, much less writing, poetry, unless one considers his closing arguments to the jury a form of poetry. But surely *he* would not consider them as such. Indeed, as far as I can see, Atticus is never shown appreciating art of *any* type. Atticus Finch is clearly much more a Philosopher than an Artist. And, as Igor Stravinsky is reported once to have said, "To be deprived of art and left alone with philosophy is to be close to hell."

Stravinsky's rather dramatic comment brings to mind a similar sentiment by Nietzsche, which I discussed in section 2 of chapter 1. Nietzsche

---

60. T.S. Eliot, "The Love Song of J. Alfred Prufrock," in *The Norton Anthology of American Literature*, vol. 2 (New York: W.W. Norton & Company, 1979), 1,222.

thought that individuals who did not create themselves—individuals who did not treat their own life as art—were worthy of no more than the status of a dying animal. As we saw, Rorty seems to agree with this sentiment. But he seeks to make it easier for the average person to create himself or herself by turning from Nietzsche to Freud and psychoanalysis. My particular criticism of that turn is not relevant here. What does seem relevant is the fact that we could scarcely imagine Atticus Finch in analysis. My point is *not* simply that Atticus is untroubled by his life. After all, Mitty also seems *relatively* untroubled. My point is that Atticus is *too* satisfied with his life— at least with the intellectual aspects of that life. Atticus has no fantasies, because he needs none. For Atticus, the universe is already ideal (in a moral sense), and his only concern seems to be how he can help realize that ideal in the material world. So, as shocking as this may seem, in Rorty's view, Atticus Finch is reduced to the status of a dying animal. Hence, we must also exclude him from consideration.

This, finally, leaves only Walter Mitty, a henpecked husband with (private) delusions of grandeur, or Julius McAdoo, an affable but uneducated chauffeur who delights in telling suspicious stories. They are, to put it mildly, two quite unlikely finalists for the title of "ideal citizen of a true political utopia." Nonetheless, if forced to choose, as choose he must, there is no doubt, based upon all he has said in *Contingency, Irony, and Solidarity*, that Rorty would prefer a society of Mittys to a society of Juliuses. The reason is simple: In Rorty's view, we risk much less in a society of Mittys. Remember, as I have sketched him, Walter Mitty is in no sense a "radical." He is certainly not the type of character who would *publicly* surprise us with revolutionary, or even odd, ideas. We can, however, imagine him working diligently within the present system. As long as that system is not in need of "radical" change, as long as there are no significant *theoretical* (as opposed to merely *practical*) problems with the system, we will wish for a society of only those who are practically, nontheoretically minded, *in the public realm*. Surely Mitty meets this requirement. Just as surely, Julius does not.

Remember, Julius is a trickster figure. He is a dissembler by nature, a figure of consummate irony. He has, as I have said, a very substantial persuasive power that is not tied—indeed, could not be tied—to any *universal* rule or ethic. Julius uses his power as he wills. He is a Nietzschean figure exercising his will to power. Granted, in "Mars Jeems's Nightmare," Julius does use this power for liberal ends. He gets Tom rehired. But surely he could do otherwise—if he wished to. Those who truly appreciate the complex character of the trickster figure will understand that his power cannot be limited through the simple *rule of law*. Just as some legal scholars have asserted that the interpretation of a given law is circumscribed *only* by the cleverness of the interpreter, so too it seems that Julius's power is circumscribed *only* by his ability to tell clever stories.[61] Those stories might be told for liberal ends, nonliberal ends, radical ends, or any purpose at all. And it seems there is no external way to control the process, just as, again, there is no external way to control the process of legal interpretation. Oddly enough, we seem then to be at the mercy of the Juliuses of the world. Yet we have no guarantee that they will remain liberal minded.

That is clearly what scares Rorty. He is concerned that the Juliuses of the world cannot be counted on to police themselves—to keep their "ironic" power *liberal*. But notice: the Walter Mittys of society must also be required to "police themselves," in the sense of keeping their own ironic power *private*. Rorty appears relatively sanguine about the prospects of *this* requirement actually working. On the other hand, Rorty does not seem at all sanguine about the success of the very similar requirement that the Juliuses of society keep their ironic power liberal. But this is curious. Why is it the case that ironic power can more easily be privatized than liberalized? As I attempted to demonstrate in section 2 of chapter 1, and throughout chapter 2, on a strictly *theoretical* level, neither the concept of a private ironism nor the concept of a liberal ironism is tenable. Yet the wisdom of the novel shows us that both of these concepts can be instantiated in the characters of Mitty and Julius, respectively. So we are led back to our earlier question: Why does Rorty prefer a society of Mittys to a society of Juliuses? We can now rephrase this question by asking: Why does Rorty prefer to insist that we liberals keep our ironic visions private? Why does he not prefer instead to insist that we keep our public ironism liberal?

Again, the answers to these questions seem to be related to Rorty's understanding of the risks involved. Notice that Mitty's public sense of justice (the phrase is something of a redundancy perhaps, for what would a nonpublic sense of justice look like?) is, as far as we can tell, fully cir-

---

61. For an example of the type of legal scholarship to which I refer, see Stanley Fish, *Doing What Comes Naturally: Change, Rhetoric, and the Practice of Theory in Literary and Legal Studies* (Durham, N.C.: Duke University Press, 1898), especially pp. 37–160.

cumscribed by the letter of the law. In this way, Mitty is very much like the figure in box C. His public actions are fully predictable. As long as liberalism can be "written" into law, the Mittys of the world can be counted on to remain liberal. If we understand the term *liberalism* as being roughly synonymous with the term justice, there is a certain unmistakably Habermasian quality to this formulation. As long as we can say *beforehand* what justice is, as long as we can express a *telos* of justice, a society of Mittys might indeed be utopian. The members of such a society would understand, on a theoretical level, what constituted justice. They would then work, on a practical level, to bring it about.

Such would not be the case with a society of Juliuses. I have suggested that Julius is, in a sense, beyond good and evil. That suggestion may, however, be a bit extreme, and hence in need of modification. Surely Julius is beyond being constrained by the dictates of the written law. But it is important to remember that, although he is not "legally" bound to do so, Julius does use his powers to pursue liberal ends. Indeed, in his unironic moods (assuming he had any), one can well imagine Julius saying something like the following: "Although I can't tell you what justice is, I can tell you that when John, a wealthy white man who seems to display no empathy at all, terminates the employment of Tom, a poor black man to whom society has given none of the same opportunities, that's *not* justice." Phrased in just this way, there is a certain unmistakably postmodern quality to Julius's conception of justice. While Julius cannot say what justice is—indeed, his very ability at ironic redescription demonstrates that it is impossible to fix the concept of justice *within language*—he nonetheless feels an obligation to the Other. In a sense, this attitude mirrors the recent political "philosophy" of such postmodern thinkers as Jacques Derrida, Jean-François Lyotard, and Immanuel Levinas. To select but one representative example, in *Au Juste* Lyotard asserts that

> any attempt to state the law . . . to place oneself in the position of enunciator of the *universal* prescription is obviously infatuation itself and absolute injustice, in point of fact.
>
> And so, when the question of what justice consists in is raised, the answer is: "It remains to be seen in each case," and always in *humor,* but also in worry, because one is never certain that one has been just; or that one can ever be just.[62]

---

62. Jean-François Lyotard and Jean-Loup Thebaud, *Au Juste,* trans. as *Just Gaming* by Wlad Godzich (Minneapolis: University of Minnesota Press, 1985), 99, emphasis added.

As Samuel Weber has correctly pointed out, this remark, as well as much of what constitutes postmodern thinking on the question of justice, suffers from the now all-too-familiar paradox of self-referentiality.[63] If we cannot speak of "absolutes" where justice is concerned, how can we speak of absolutes where injustice is concerned? (Notice, by the way, that Julius's imaginary remark that I presented earlier does *not* seem to suffer from the self-referential paradox. Julius is claiming that in the singular case of John firing Tom an injustice has been done. But he is not claiming that this case can be generalized to create a theory of justice.) Having noted the paradox of self-referentiality, I now want to try to move beyond it and focus on another, equally important aspect of Lyotard's remark: its heavily theological overtones. Lyotard seems to be saying, in the aforementioned passage, that regardless of how long we have, we can never know for certain if we are acting justly. It is *not* a question of *time*, in other words. Rather, it is a question of knowledge *as such*. In Lyotard's view, for some reason (original sin perhaps?) we can never have perfect knowledge of justice, *even theoretically*. Nonetheless, we are still commanded to do justice. But, I would hasten to add, these commands cannot themselves be justified by recourse to theoretical knowledge—or, I would argue, by recourse to any form of knowledge whatsoever (including revelation). The situation is one of radical singularity. As Derrida, focusing on Walter Benjamin's "Critique of Violence," asserts,

> "Thou shalt not kill" remains an absolute imperative once the principle of the most destructive divine violence commands the respect of the living being, beyond *droit*, beyond judgment. It is not a "criterion for judgment" but a "guideline for actions" of persons or communities who have to wrestle with it *in solitude* and *in exceptional cases*. That for Benjamin is the essence of Judaism which forbids all murder, except in the *singular* cases of legitimate self-defense. . . .[64]

---

63. Weber writes, "We are now beginning to understand why laughter must arise at this point as the articulation of the inarticulable, as the presentation of the unpresentable. By prescribing that no game, especially not that of prescription, should dominate the others, one is doing exactly what it is simultaneously claimed is being avoided: one is dominating the other games in order to protect them from domination" see "Literature—Just Making It," afterward to *Au Juste*, 105.

64. Jacques Derrida, "Force of Law: The 'Mystical Foundation of Authority,'" *Cardozo Law Review* (July/August 1990): 1,029, emphasis added.

But, again, no one can say beforehand, or in a generalizable sense, what "legitimate" would mean in the aforementioned remark. It is always an individual, irreducible question. To some this will appear as simply a nonsensical position. Even to those who do not agree it is nonsensical, this position will surely appear quite frustrating. It *commands* us, but it does not seem to provide the means to understand the *basis* of those commands. One is, therefore, always in doubt about *questions* of justice and liberalism.

Now notice: If, as it appears, Julius buys into something of a post-modern approach to justice, we can never say for certain what his next move will be—indeed, he can never say this for certain. Julius, unlike Mitty, is not constrained by the written law; his decisions are always based on the individual case. But I think we can still refer to Julius as a liberal, for there is a (*quite* paradoxical) way in which he reflects Rorty's own attitude toward liberalism, perhaps better than Rorty himself realizes. Notice that like "Thou shalt not kill," Rorty's liberal command, "Thou shalt not be cruel" is, as he repeatedly points outs, *ultimately ungroundable in theory.* (Rorty's liberal command also raises exactly the same unanswerable theoretical paradoxes, as does the proscription against killing: Can we be cruel in order to prevent cruelty to ourselves, or greater cruelty to others?)

To sum up, then: *In Rorty's mind*, a preference for Mitty over Julius seems to amount to a preference for a view of justice as (in some sense) formalizable and universalizable, over a postmodern view of justice as radically individual yet commanding. Notice that I am not now claiming that Mitty's character is *identical* to Atticus Finch's. Rather, I am claiming that Mitty, like Rorty, adheres to a universalizable view of justice in public, while acting as a postmodern in private. And, to repeat once more, this is Rorty's understanding of the ideal character type for a political utopia. Again, it is all a question of risk *and doubt*.

As I have described him, Rorty seems to believe that because we have *no* doubt that Mitty will follow the letter of the liberal law—while, on the other hand, we surely have significant doubts about what Julius will do—we therefore face a greater risk that things will go badly in a society of Juliuses. This *may* be true, but Rorty has only seen half the equation. He does not seem to have an appreciation for what economists call "opportunity cost." He does not seem to see that an advantage foregone is, in some sense, a disadvantage. Granted, we have no doubt how Mitty will react in public; he will always act in accordance with the liberal law. But, a society of Mittys will be utopian *only if*: one, liberalism is able to be constituted in the written law; *and* two, liberalism is the highest form of law (the *telos* of justice). Remember, in the *public* realm, Mitty, like the character in box C, but unlike Julius, does not make theoretical judgments. He does not let his private irony affect his public actions. He, like Rorty, sees a firm split between the public and the private. In public, he simply follows the letter of the law. Only if that law can be fully understood, and only if that law cannot be theoretically improved upon, will we really risk nothing by opting for a society of Mittys.

If, on the other hand, one believes with the postmoderns that liberalism cannot be embodied in the written law, and/or that liberalism is not the telos of justice, and/or, finally, that justice has no telos at all, then one might well believe we risk a great deal unless we opt for a society in which every Julius is encouraged to affirm the unaffirmable, to describe the indescribable, *and to do so in public*. Of course, in such a society there is always the risk that a particularly pernicious Julius might bring about a system worse, not better, than the one we have now. To use Rorty's own example, this is the same risk that the French bourgeoisie faced when, in 1789, they decided to try an experiment in alternative government.[65] But, surely, such a risk exists at every moment in history — *except*, of course, at the last moment in history, at the moment when all theoretical questions have been answered, and we therefore need no more political philosophy. Can it be that Rorty thinks we have arrived at just such a moment? Can it be that Rorty thinks liberalism represents, in a theoretical sense, the End of History?

This question brings us full circle, back to the Introduction of this book, and to the congruence (of sorts) that I spoke of between Richard Rorty and Francis Fukuyama. To be sure, Rorty would emphatically object to the thought that such a congruence exists. Yet as I have tried to show, on some level, this congruence is inescapable. Notice that Rorty insists we should *always* prefer a society of Mittys to a society of Juliuses. He insists, in other words, that we should *always* maintain a split between the public and the private. My contention is that Rorty could only speak in such absolutes if he were convinced that we have reached the end of political theory. But on what *basis* does he believe this? Again,

65. See Richard Rorty, "Unger, Castoriadis, and the Romance of a National Future," in *Essays on Heidegger and Others: Philosophical Papers, Volume II* (Cambridge: University Press, 1991), especially p. 192.

it is fruitless to ask such a question since Rorty does not attempt to provide any kind of a theoretically informed answer. Instead, he merely tells
us that he has a "hunch" that bourgeois liberalism is, finally, all we need
to solve our problems. Perhaps, then, the final question is: Where does
this "hunch" come from?

To answer this question, let us imagine a liberal intellectual in an
act of self-creation in the private realm. Such an act might take the form
of musing about, possibly designing, a political utopia. Notice that there
is no reason to see the act of designing political utopias as being at odds
with the goal of self-creation. Perhaps this kind of activity (designing
political utopias) was not the kind of exercise that appealed to Proust; but
it surely was the kind that appealed to Plato. The only requirement is that
our ironist keep this utopia to himself or herself. Now, for an intellectual
who is also a *liberal*, such a political utopia might very well take the *general* form of a society in which each individual is in turn free to engage
in his or her own acts of self-creation, as long as he or she does not prevent others from doing so. But since our liberal intellectual is sophisticated about the economics of interdependence, he or she will want to
specify that this political utopia must also provide (or guarantee one the
opportunity to secure for himself or herself) the minimum amount of
resources needed to engage in self-creation, while preventing any one
individual from using more than he or she needs. In the end, our liberal
intellectual's utopia might look like what Fukuyama described as "liberal
democracy in the political sphere combined with easy access to VCRs
and stereos [and, I would add, books and computers for the intellectuals]
in the economic."[66]

Now let me drop the pretense here and simply assert that Rorty has
engaged in such an act of self-creation. Is there a chance that he has
turned this act toward the public realm? Is there evidence that he has
done the kind of thing he suggested we need to watch out for in ironist
theorists like Derrida and Foucault? Has Rorty become an Uncle Julius?
I believe so, and I believe that he gives the game away (so to speak) when
he reveals his "hunch" that bourgeoisie liberalism is the last conceptual
(read: *theoretical*) revolution humankind needs. This hunch turns out to
be an absolutely critical part of Rorty's entire project, and it is difficult to
make too much of it. After articulating this hunch in *Contingency, Irony,
and Solidarity*, Rorty seems emphatically to defend this position in a

---

66. Francis Fukuyama, "The End of History?" *The National Interest* (summer 1989): 8.

debate with McCarthy. I quote at length from what is essentially the per-
oration of Rorty's 1990 article, "Truth and Freedom: A Reply to Thomas
McCarthy." Rorty says

> There is nothing in my view [of the uselessness of contempo-
> rary social theory] that hinders our noticing the misery and
> hopelessness of inner-city American blacks or Latin American
> slum-dwellers or Cambodian peasants. Nor is there anything
> that suggests such misery and hopelessness is irremediable.
> There is only the suggestion that we already have as much the-
> ory as we need, and that what we need now are concrete
> utopias, and concrete proposals about how to get to those
> utopias from where we are now.
>
> That the middle class of the United States, as of South
> Africa, is unwilling to pay the taxes necessary to give poor
> blacks a decent education and a chance in life seems to me a
> fact we need no fancier theoretical notions than 'greed,' 'self-
> ishness,' and 'racial prejudice' to explain. That successive
> American presidents have ordered or allowed the CIA to
> make it as difficult as possible to depose Latin American oli-
> garchies seems another such well-known fact, whose explana-
> tion is to be found on the level of details about the activities
> of, for example, the United Fruit Company and Anaconda
> Copper in Washington's corridors of power. When I am told
> that to appreciate the significance of these facts I need a
> deeper understanding of, for example, the discourses of power
> characteristic of late capitalism, I am incredulous.
>
> Maybe I have not been reading the right theorists, but I
> really have no clear idea what it means to say that 'the basic
> structures of society' (capitalist society, presumably) are
> responsible for these facts, any more than to say that other
> 'basic structures' (those of noncapitalist societies) are respon-
> sible for the plight of the Romanians or the Tibetans. I am not
> sure what a 'theoretically informed way' to think about these
> matters would be, as opposed to a historically and journalisti-
> cally informed way. I can happily agree that philosophers and
> social theorists have, *in the past*, done a lot of good by giving
> us ways to put in words our vague sense that something has
> gone terribly wrong. Notions like 'the rights of man,' 'surplus

values,' 'the new class,' and the like have been indispensable for moral and political progress. But I am not convinced that we are currently in need of new notions of this sort.[67]

Notice that Rorty does in fact concede that social theory was at one time "indispensable" for progress. Presumably, this means, for example, that during the eighteenth century (i.e., during the time at which the concept of the "rights of man" was being theoretically formulated) society could not have replaced that theoretical concept with a simple "historically and journalistically informed way" of talking about what was terribly wrong with some of its practices. Or, to put this point another way: during the eighteenth century journalistic accounts of human "misery and hopelessness" could not have worked without being *coupled* with the theoretical concept of "the rights of man." Simple journalistic accounts could not have worked precisely because, as Rorty notes, although eighteenth-century society had a "vague sense" of this misery and hopelessness, it could not "put in words" what it was sensing. The "words" are, of course, exactly what social and political *theories* give us. So in the end it seems that Rorty is *not* saying (as a good pragmatist, or a standard "end of ideologist" might) that social theory is—and has always been—useless, and that all we ever needed were concrete utopias and concrete proposals about how to get to those utopias. Rather, he is saying that theorizing in the social realm *has been* indispensable, but that such theorizing has now reached a conclusion. We have, in other words, *progressed* to the end of theory.

Surely, Rorty the *ironist* could never make such a claim. It would amount to the claim that there is a last word, a final argument, a beginning *and an end* to theory. Rorty could never make this claim, that is, *unless* this very claim itself stood outside of the domain of *theoretical* speculation. And that, finally, is precisely where it does stand. Rorty shrewdly offers us . . . a "hunch." This "hunch" that Western social and political thought has had the last conception revolution it needs sounds strangely like what I called (in chapter 3) a "faith" in the Enlightenment era vocabulary of liberal democracy. A "hunch" or a "faith." Perhaps it does not matter what we call it. By any name, it is that which liberalism cannot do without.

---

67. Rorty, "Truth and Freedom: A Reply to Thomas McCarthy," 644, emphasis added.

Index

Action: allowable, 69; causes of, 121; choice of, 12; collective, 14; consciousness of, 130; cruel, 69, 70, 72; determining, 69; educational, 81; effects of, 14; empowering, 81; excusing, 126; forms of, 121; freedom of, 12; humiliation producing, 80, 111; individual, 14; inducements to, 121, 125–126; intentional, 69, 70, 72, 81; interference with, 12; motivation for, 130; prevention of, 72; private, 70; public, 70, 94; and reason, 130; reduced to motion, 125; regulation of, 121–122; responsibility for, 128; shared habits of, 116n1; and speech, 122, 123; symbolic, 121
Adorno, Theodore W., 141
Agon, 61
Areopagitica (Milton), 13, 120, 135
Argument, 40; noncircular, 39; vocabulary of, 39
Argumentation, 26
Aristotle, 46, 48, 79, 134, 134n30, 155
Art as Experience (Dewey), 10
Artificial intelligence, 152
The Art of the Novel (Kundera), 172–173
Asimov, Isaac, 157–160
Atlas, James, 2

Augustine, 106
Aune, James, 7, 61, 156
Axioms, 30, 31; acceptance of, 32

Baker, Lynn, 92, 139
Beiner, Ronald, 11
Being and Time (Heidegger), 172–173
Beliefs: ability to hold, 107; on ability to reason, 116–117, 118–146; accomodation of, 83, 83n21; central, 37–38; changes in, 107, 109, 110; contingency of, 37–38; denial of, 112; moral, 68; most important, 38; need for, 116; new, 83, 83n21; non-offensive, 83; objection to, 30; prior, 164–165; private, 94; public practice, 94; rational, 164–165; systems, 107
Benjamin, Walter, 221
Berlin, Isaiah, 77
Bernal, Martin, 148
Bernstein, Richard, 5
Bill for Establishing Religious Freedom (Jefferson), 132, 132n27, 135, 146
Billy Budd (Melville), 133–134
Bloom, Allan, 8
Bloom, Harold, ix, 10, 47n35, 48, 57, 58, 61, 181
Bolt, Robert, 51, 186–189, 191–193

227